AMBIVALENT ACTIVISM

Working with Contradiction,
Hesitation and Doubt for Social Change

Edited by
Akwugo Emejulu,
Marlies Kustatscher and Callum McGregor

First published in Great Britain in 2025 by

Bristol University Press
University of Bristol
1–9 Old Park Hill
Bristol
BS2 8BB
UK
t: +44 (0)117 374 6645
e: bup-info@bristol.ac.uk

Details of international sales and distribution partners are available at bristoluniversitypress.co.uk

© Bristol University Press 2025 excluding Chapter 2 © Bristol University Press 2019

British Library Cataloguing in Publication Data
A catalogue record for this book is available from the British Library

ISBN 978-1-5292-3972-0 hardcover
ISBN 978-1-5292-3973-7 paperback
ISBN 978-1-5292-3974-4 ePub
ISBN 978-1-5292-3975-1 ePdf

The right of Akwugo Emejulu, Marlies Kustatscher and Callum McGregor to be identified as editors of this work has been asserted by them in accordance with the Copyright, Designs and Patents Act 1988.

All rights reserved: no part of this publication may be reproduced, stored in a retrieval system, or transmitted in any form or by any means, electronic, mechanical, photocopying, recording, or otherwise without the prior permission of Bristol University Press.

Every reasonable effort has been made to obtain permission to reproduce copyrighted material. If, however, anyone knows of an oversight, please contact the publisher.

The statements and opinions contained within this publication are solely those of the editors and contributors and not of the University of Bristol or Bristol University Press. The University of Bristol and Bristol University Press disclaim responsibility for any injury to persons or property resulting from any material published in this publication.

Bristol University Press works to counter discrimination on grounds of gender, race, disability, age and sexuality.

Cover design: Qube Design
Front cover image: Stocksy/Julia Potato

Contents

Notes on Contributors   v
Acknowledgements   xi

Introduction: Working with Contradiction, Hesitation   1
and Doubt
Akwugo Emejulu, Marlies Kustatscher and Callum McGregor

PART I   Theorizing Ambivalence

1. Ambivalence as Misfeeling, Ambivalence as Refusal   13
   Akwugo Emejulu
2. On (Not) Knowing What Is to Be Done   20
   (in 17 Affective Registers)
   Deborah Gould
3. Facing Defeat: Rosa Luxemburg in Dialogue with   50
   Prefigurative Politics
   Maša Mrovlje
4. Orchestrating the Furies: Anzaldúa's Evolving   63
   Conception of Ambivalent Political Struggle
   Alyson Cole

PART II   Activism as Ambivalent Praxis

5. An Activism of the In-between   77
   Melody Howse
6. Resisting with People I Do Not Like: Exploring   87
   the Internal Tensions Among Queer Activists in
   Lagos, Nigeria
   Adebayo Quadry-Adekanbi
7. Ambivalent Activism: Recontextualizing Mental   103
   Health Politics
   Hel Spandler, Dina Poursanidou and Sonia Soans
8. Ambivalence and Veganism: Rethinking Sentiment   120
   in Moral Choices
   Jordan McKenzie and Zoei Sutton

9	The Embroidery Collective: Embroidering and Reimagining Community in Times of Struggle *Cristina Florescu*	133
10	Ambivalent Emotions Empowering Activism: Learning from Youth Activists in Aotearoa *Carisa R. Showden and Karen Nairn*	143

PART III Activism and the Ambivalent Academy

11	Working with Discomfort: Contesting Ambivalence through Care and Accountability in the University of Edinburgh's 'Skull Room' *Nicole Anderson*	159
12	The Poetry of Ambivalence: A Nudge toward Tending *Roxani Krystalli*	172
13	The Role of 'Stuckedness': Ambivalence in Scholar-Activism *Aylwyn Walsh and Paul Routledge*	178

Conclusion: Thinking with Pessimism   190
Akwugo Emejulu, Marlies Kustatscher and Callum McGregor

Index   195

Notes on Contributors

Nicole Anderson (she/her) is an ethnographer, provenance researcher and doctoral candidate in Social Anthropology at the University of Edinburgh whose research investigates what justice may look like for First Nations and Inuit ancestors in the University of Edinburgh's Anatomical Museum. She is also Curator of the Americas at National Museums Scotland. She has a Masters in Social Justice Education from the University of Toronto and continues to explore the value of anti-colonial pedagogies in heritage spaces. She has been published in the *Journal of Museum Ethnography* and *Unfamiliar*, and has an upcoming chapter on the role of transnational knowledge production in the repatriation of cultural heritage.

Alyson Cole is Professor of Political Science, Women's & Gender Studies, American Studies, and Liberal Studies at Queens College and The Graduate Center of the City University of New York. Cole's work focuses on gender, race, sexuality and disability, linking central questions of political thought – formulations of injustice, the nature of victimization, vulnerability and precarity – with an examination of rhetoric, law and forms of political resistance (including digital activism). Her scholarship has been translated into French, Japanese, Spanish, Swedish and Turkish. Cole's books include: *The Cult of True Victimhood: From the war on welfare to the war on terror* (Stanford University Press, 2006), *Derangement and Liberalism* (Routledge Press, 2019), and *How Capitalism Forms Our Lives* (Routledge Press, 2019). Her articles have appeared in journals such as *Signs, The European Journal of Cultural Studies, Critical Horizons, American Studies, Theory & Event* and *Women's Studies in Communication*. Alyson serves as co-editor-in-chief of two academic journals: *Polity* and *philoSOPHIA: A Journal of transContinental Feminism*.

Akwugo Emejulu is Chair in Sociological Studies at the University of Sheffield. Her research interests include the political sociology of race, class and gender, and grassroots activism by women of colour in Europe and the United States. She is the author of several books including *Precarious Solidarity* (forthcoming, Manchester University Press), *Fugitive Feminism* (Silver Press, 2022) and *Minority Women and Austerity: Survival and resistance in France and*

Britain (Policy Press, 2017). She is co-editor of *To Exist Is to Resist: Black feminism in Europe* (Pluto Press, 2019).

Cristina Florescu is a community organizer currently based in Spain. While living in Ireland, she was heavily involved with MERJ (Migrants and Ethnic Minorities for Reproductive Justice), where she was active during the abortion referendum in 2018. She believes all struggles are interconnected and should go hand in hand in political organizing. For this reason, she has also worked more widely on reproductive justice, housing, anti-racism and queer solidarity. Cristina's politics are anti-capitalist, anti-imperialist and anti-racist. She believes in the power of horizontal organizing, and is a strong proponent of empowering experts-by-experience of oppression to speak about their own lives. Her experience living in five different countries has informed her exploration of what creating community and setting roots means while on the move. Her current areas of interest include generative work such as the exploration of identity in a fluid, globalized world, and reimagining society and community under late-stage capitalism.

Deborah Gould is Professor of Sociology at the University of California, Santa Cruz (and Affiliated Faculty in the Departments of Feminist Studies, History of Consciousness, and Politics). They received their PhD in Political Science from the University of Chicago (2000) where they also were a post-doctoral Harper-Schmidt Fellow in the Society of Fellows in the Liberal Arts (2000–04). Their book *Moving Politics: Emotion and ACT UP's fight against AIDS* (University of Chicago Press, 2009) won the Distinguished Contribution to Scholarship Best Book Award (American Sociological Association's Political Sociology Section, 2010) and the Ruth Benedict Book Prize (American Anthropological Association, 2010). They are currently working on another book about political emotion, *The Not-Yet of Politics*. Gould was involved in ACT UP/Chicago and Queer to the Left and was a founding member of the research/art/activism collaborative, Feel Tank Chicago, most famous for its 'International Parades of the Politically Depressed'.

Melody Howse is an interdisciplinary researcher and filmmaker from Belize and the UK. She is currently a research fellow in Germany and holds a Master's in Visual and Media Anthropology from the Freie Universität and PhD in Social and Cultural Anthropology from the University of Leipzig, where her doctoral thesis 'Black Formations and the Politics of Space' focused on the sensory and spatial dimensions of racial encounters. Her current work continues to be concerned with Black experience, race and representation, further exploring practices of refusal within Black diasporic art forms.

Alongside work within the academy as a researcher and educator, Melody works as a community researcher, using her skills in research, writing and video production in service of Black-led organizations in Berlin.

Roxani Krystalli is a senior lecturer (associate professor) at the University of St Andrews. Her interdisciplinary research and teaching focus on feminist peace and conflict studies, as well as on the politics of nature and place. She is currently the co-principal investigator of a research project on the politics of love and care in the wake of violence, ecological loss and mass grief. The project is funded by the Arts and Humanities Research Council and German Research Foundation, and unfolds in collaboration with Dr Philipp Schulz. Roxani's first book, *Good Victims: The political as a feminist question* was published by Oxford University Press in 2024.

Marlies Kustatscher is Senior Lecturer in Childhood Studies at the University of Edinburgh. She is a member of the Childhood and Youth Studies research group and the Race and Inclusivity in Global Education Network (RIGEN). Marlies' research interests include childhood and intersectionality, children's human rights and participation, and emotions. Her work draws on interdisciplinary, arts-based approaches to activism and social change with children and young people. She currently works on projects on these themes with colleagues in Brazil, Colombia, Eswatini, Palestine, Scotland and South Africa.

Callum McGregor is Senior Lecturer in Education at the University of Edinburgh, where he teaches on the MSc Social Justice and Community Action and the MA Learning in Communities. His research addresses the relationship between education and democratic citizenship across a range of contexts but with particular interests in education and action for climate justice and the challenges of populist politics. His research is influenced by the Essex School of discourse analysis and he draws on agonistic and psychoanalytic political theories to understand the affective dimensions of critical and activist pedagogies.

Jordan McKenzie completed his PhD at Flinders University and is now Associate Professor in Sociology at the University of Wollongong. His research is largely informed by European social and critical theory, and these perspectives contribute to his current research into the sociology of emotion. In particular, Jordan's work critically engages with the current cultural fascination with happiness and the good life in order to better understand how emotional experience reflects modernization and social change. More recently, his work has focused on future-oriented emotions in perceptions of environmental disaster and apocalypse scenarios. His most recent book is *Dystopian Emotions* (Bristol University Press, 2021).

Maša Mrovlje is Associate Professor of Political Theory at the University of Leeds. Her research interests are located within contemporary political theory, with a focus on existential, decolonial and feminist theory. Within this focus, she has contributed to pressing issues of political judgement, memory politics, transitional justice, political violence and, most recently, resistance. She is author of *Rethinking Political Judgement: Arendt and existentialism* (Edinburgh University Press, 2019). Her articles have appeared in leading international peer-reviewed journals, including *Political Theory*, *Philosophy & Social Criticism*, *Millennium* and *The Journal of Politics*. She is currently working on a project entitled Disappointment: Reclaiming the Unfulfilled Promise of Resistance, which explores the political potential of disappointment within the modern revolutionary tradition. In addition, she has been researching women's embodied resistance experience, neglected within dominant masculine understandings of resistance.

Karen Nairn's research is youth-focused and multidisciplinary. She works at the intersections of geography, education and sociology. Her current research, published in the book *Fierce Hope: Youth activism in Aotearoa* (Bridget William Books, 2022) is about what inspires young people to join others to create social change. This project builds on her earlier book *Children of Rogernomics: A neoliberal generation leaves school* (Otago University Press, 2012) about young people who grew up during New Zealand's neoliberal reforms. She is particularly interested in the role of hope for inspiring and sustaining young people's engagement in social justice movements, how place matters in understanding the influence of decolonial politics on these movements, and how social justice groups prefigure the practices they advocate for wider society. She has been employed at the University of Otago for the past 23 years and is currently a professor based at the University of Otago College of Education.

Dina (Konstantina) Poursanidou is a service user researcher in mental health. She started using mental health services in 1991. Her doctoral and post-doctoral research has spanned a range of fields including mental health, education, child health, youth justice and social policy/social welfare. Originally from Greece, she has worked in several English universities as a service user researcher, including the Service User Research Enterprise in the Institute of Psychiatry, Psychology and Neuroscience, King's College London. Her latest project, while based at the University of Central Lancashire, was concerned with the physical health needs of people with severe mental health conditions in forensic/secure settings. She is a member of the editorial group on *Asylum: the radical mental health magazine*.

Adebayo Quadry-Adekanbi (he/him) is a Sociology PhD candidate at the University of Warwick, funded by the Economic and Social Research

Council. His research focuses on the intersectional politics of queer activism and feminism in Nigeria, utilizing postcolonial and Black queer feminist theory. A recipient of the 2024/25 Camargo Fellowship, he has received international educational training at institutions such as Yale University, USA, and the University of Fort Hare, South Africa. Adebayo analyses the cultural and sociopolitical dimensions of various subjects, including mainstream pop culture, politics, art and academic debates. He serves as an editor at Shado Mag, a UK-based multimedia platform exploring the intersection of arts, activism and academia. Additionally, he is Gender and Sexuality Editor at *The Republic*, a platform that delves into culture, politics and art from a Nigerian and African perspective.

Paul Routledge is Emeritus Professor in Contentious Politics and Social Change, at the School of Geography, University of Leeds. His research interests include critical geopolitics, climate justice and the spatiality of social movements. He has been a scholar activist for over 30 years, working in alliance with movements in South Asia and Southeast Asia, and in the Minority World. He is author of *Space Invaders: Radical geographies of protest* (Pluto Press, 2017) and co-author (with A. Walsh and A. Sutherland) of *Arts Activism Toolkit* (Tshisimani Centre for Activist Education, 2022).

Carisa R. Showden teaches and researches in the School of Social Sciences at the University of Auckland, New Zealand. Her work draws on and contributes to debates in feminist political theory, law and society, social movements, queer theory, and gender and politics scholarship. Her books include *Choices Women Make: Agency in domestic violence, assisted reproduction, and sex work* (University of Minnesota Press, 2011); *Youth Who Trade Sex in the U.S.: Intersectionality, agency, and vulnerability* (with Samantha Majic; Temple University Press, 2018)); *Fierce Hope: Youth activism in Aotearoa* (with Karen Nairn, Judith Sligo, Kyle Matthews, and Joanna Kidman; Bridget William Books, 2022), and the edited volume *Negotiating Sex Work: Unintended consequences of policy and activism* (with Samantha Majic; University of Minnesota Press, 2014). She is particularly interested in the evolution of social movements over time, the relationship between movements and groups, and the ways that gender and sexuality structure movement spaces, activist identities and imagined possibilities for change.

Sonia Soans is a critical psychologist and the founder of the Afro-Asian Critical Psychology Forum. This is a space for activists and scholars who have an interest in critical psychology and work in the Majority World. She is an intersectional feminist whose research interests are in gender, mental illness, nationalism and cinema. Fascinated by history, she is keen on learning about the history of psychology from around the world and the context in which the discipline developed. She is on the editorial collective of *Asylum: The radical mental health magazine.*

Hel Spandler is Professor of Mental Health Studies at the University of Central Lancashire, Preston, UK. They are Managing Editor of *Asylum: the radical mental health magazine*, and one of the lead editors of the *International Journal of Mad Studies*. They have undertaken several national studies in the field of mental health and have published widely on the history, practice and politics of mental health care in the UK. Most recently, they held a Wellcome Trust Investigator Award to research radical mental health zines (or Madzines).

Zoei Sutton is Senior Lecturer in Sociology who lives, learns and works on unceded Kaurna country (Adelaide, South Australia). She co-founded and co-facilitates the International Association of Vegan Sociologists with Corey Wrenn and currently serves as the Deputy Chair of the Australian Animal Studies Association. She pursues critical, nonhuman animal-centric scholarship that meaningfully considers the experiences of other animals and their entanglement with humans in our shared social world, and has published on myriad animal–human entanglements including petkeeping, construction of 'pest' narratives, multispecies research methods and nonhuman animals in disaster preparation. This research is further bolstered by her extensive research experience in qualitative policy and programme evaluation through which she has developed a nuanced understanding of the complexities of human marginalization and the intersecting structures of domination that shape both human and nonhuman animal navigations of life in Australian society.

Aylwyn Walsh is Professor of Performance and Social Change in the School of Performance and Cultural Industries at the University of Leeds. She has worked on arts and mental health, arts in criminal justice and abolitionist organizing as well as in community settings in South Africa, Greece and the UK. Her books are *Prison Cultures: Performance, resistance, desire* (Intellect, 2019) and *Remapping Crisis: A guide to Athens* (Zero Books, 2014).

Acknowledgements

We are grateful to all the contributors who have shared their experiences and insights, challenges and resistances, and their own and others' ambivalent emotions to bring this book out into the world.

This book originates from a series of webinars on 'Ambivalent Activism' that we organized in 2022. We would like to thank all contributors to the series for collectively exploring the contradictory emotional terrain by which activism might be organized, including: Nicole Anderson, Jacob Breslow, Cristina Florescu, Maša Mrovlje, Karen Nairn, Konstantina (Dina) Poursanidou, El Reid-Buckley, Louise Ryan, Carisa R. Showden, Sonia Soans, Hel Spandler and Andy West.

We are thankful to the activists who have inspired this book. In our own work, we were struck by young people's critical (not naive) hope in the face of climate destruction, and how children are often upheld as the future solution to global problems, while their agency can go unrecognized or be oppressed when it does not suit mainstream politics.

Perhaps one of our first and most profound encounters with an idea of ambivalent activism was through the late Bernice Johnson Reagon's classic text from 1983 called *Coalition Politics: Turning the century*. We acknowledge her tireless work and dedication to justice.

Introduction: Working with Contradiction, Hesitation and Doubt

Akwugo Emejulu, Marlies Kustatscher and Callum McGregor

In recent years, we have seen an increased interest in the emotional relations of activism, with scholars approaching emotions as sociopolitical relations that influence our identities and behaviours in public and private spaces. The polyphony of emotions that shape activism and circulate within activist collectives – for example, anger, disgust, love, fear, anxiety and grief – can be conceived as 'political emotions' in the sense that they are directed toward political objects and thus tied up in power relations and socially contested ideas about equality and justice (Nussbaum, 2013). Although ambivalence, as an emotion, functions in this way as well, to be ambivalent is to experience a contradictory set of emotions simultaneously. Although this experience gives rise to a constellation of responses, some of those, such as hesitation and vacillation are not intuitively associated with activism. Perhaps for this reason, there remains much to learn about the challenges and role of ambivalence in the emotional relations of activism. In this edited collection, we examine the different manifestations of ambivalence in activist spaces, and what impact ambivalence has on different kinds of activists.

Despite being a common emotional experience for activists, there has been little substantive discussion about how ambivalence is articulated, experienced, negotiated or potentially used as a resource in activists' work (Emejulu, 2022; Jacobsen, 2023). A useful starting point is Rothman et al's definition of ambivalence as the 'simultaneous experience of positive and negative emotional or cognitive orientations toward a person, situation, object, task, goal, or idea and the feelings of tension and conflict that result' (Rothman et al, 2017: 33). Thus, one way to understand ambivalence is as a particular kind of 'epistemic feeling', other examples of which might include certainty, hunch or inspiration. Epistemic feelings guide intellectual activity and inform the confidence with which knowledge is held (Terpe, 2016). As political emotions, then, epistemic feelings help us better understand what we do and do not know about struggles for social change. Ambivalence, as an epistemic feeling of paradox which in turn sparks self-doubt and hesitation in thought and action, is an important but difficult political emotion to hold.

Because ambivalence is a difficult emotion to hold, within the constellation of available responses lie various defences, including disavowal and the 'splitting' of political objects into 'good' and 'bad' that results in moral idealism and Manichean politics rooted in a desire to restitute threatened identities by demonizing an 'other' as the enemy of the ideality that we fear the loss of (Allen and Ruti, 2019). Arguably, the contemporary political landscape is replete with the morbid symptoms of an inability to hold ambivalence and work through it as political praxis. In contrast, a reparative orientation toward justice is intrinsically connected to the ability to tolerate ambivalence and, by association, imperfection and loss. McAfee (2019) goes so far as to suggest that political deliberation itself, which has been radically misconstrued as 'rational' consensus-seeking dialogue, can be conceived more fully as a process of working through ambivalence by 'mourning' the necessity of loss in the presence of political disagreement and uncertainty. Following this line of thought opens up the possibility of thinking about ambivalent activism as a hallmark of political maturity, as opposed to 'heroic' forms of activism that offer facile and unambiguous solutions to complex political dilemmas, as well as melancholic modes of politics often based on problematic fantasies of restoring wholeness to the objects of our cathexis.

Accordingly, this book takes an expansive view of activism and defines it as a collective process of individuals coming together to make change in public space. As Mai (2022: 183) states, 'a social movement is not simply a protest, nor is an activist a protestor'. Activism can be understood as encompassing a range of discrete and oftentimes mundane activities which include actions such as demonstrations, pickets and boycotts but also the thankless and unglamourous work such as mutual aid, peer learning and event planning. Understanding the different permutations of activism is important to clarify as it informs the focus, selection and breadth of chapters in this edited volume. Our capacious definition of activism allows us to expand our lens to focus on quotidian forms of collective action sometimes rendered invisible through a disproportionate focus on more 'heroic' forms of direct action. The important point being that the tendency to conflate social movements with hypervisible protest too often erases the forms of social reproductive and emotional work that sustain activist communities and is, not incidentally, often undertaken by women and femmes. Therefore, our approach foregrounds the unceasing and exhausting collective 'emotion work' (Hochschild, 1979) taking place 'backstage' that, despite being devalued and dismissed, is where ambivalent activism is often to be found (Mai, 2022; Kavada, 2023; Roth and Saunders, 2024).

Contributions in this book explore how ambivalence is embodied and conveyed between different people, and how it can be a rich if murky terrain by which activism might be organized. Inevitably, the forms of activism included in this book are not exhaustive, but we ask readers to consider how the analysis and discussion in these different activist contexts might illuminate and inspire work elsewhere. Since activists undertake the work they do because they passionately believe in their cause, it is easy to assume that activism is hostile to ambivalence. In this volume, we question this assumption by asking what can be learned by centring activists' experiences of what Ngai (2004) calls 'ugly feelings' or non-heroic, unflattering emotions. Considering the multipolar character of collective action (Melucci, 1996), we investigate and explore the ways in which ambivalence might foster or foreclose solidarity via diverse analyses of how activists negotiate and make sense of their epistemic feelings about themselves, their comrades and their activist work. Among the relatively few scholars operating in this space, Gould's (2019: 16) commitment to understanding how 'activists inhabit uncertainty and figure out what to do even so', is both exemplary and instructive. Thus, one question that this book explores is whether some types of activism are ambivalent, or if all activism is ambivalent to some degree. After all, when activists challenge the rationality of hegemonic social arrangements, they simultaneously prise open spaces of alterity, undecidability and, thus, ambivalence (see, for example, Svirsky, 2010; Gould, 2019; Linz and Secor, 2021). The question then becomes, how do activist communities make sense of and negotiate diverse experiences of ambivalence?

When the blueprint of the status quo is questioned, ambivalence may be registered or ignored, fostered or strategically suppressed. The fact that ambivalence can be either disavowed or harnessed suggests that the consequences of ambivalence in and for activism are, themselves, ambivalent. As discussed above, the disavowal of ambivalence can lead to facile forms of moral idealism, as well as problematic Manichean forms of politics. However, it can also lead to derisory forms of 'knowingness' that undermine activist efforts, as well as situations where cultivated 'apathy' acts as a defence mechanism for those who perceive that there is no space to work through the surplus of feeling, the ambivalence, that they hold. However, if 'ambivalence is described, not as the lack of interest, but as a surplus of interest and/or knowledge' (McKenzie, 2018: 38) that arises from and informs political praxis, then we need to recognize that it is vital for activism.

On the other hand, detached equivocation is often, with good reason, regarded with suspicion by those on the sharp end of particular injustices as bad faith indifference. Worse still, like any political emotion, ambivalence can be weaponized by bad faith actors through pseudo-sceptical tactics such as 'Just Asking Questions' where the barely concealed aim is to normalize egregious political claims and wear down one's opposition. Moreover, the sense of vulnerability that comes with addressing ambivalence may often be suppressed in order to demonstrate strength and resolve in the face of powerful opposition. Thus, even if a reparative orientation toward justice requires the capacity to work through ambivalence, there are good reasons to be ambivalent about ambivalence.

However, rather than ensnaring ourselves in vacillation about the merits or demerits of ambivalence in activist spaces, the diverse chapters in this book perhaps suggest that it is more productive to understand ambivalence in thoroughly relational terms. In other words, the significance of ambivalence is contingent on activists' positionalities within various social matrices of power. For example, in some circumstances activists with lived experience of injustice might regard the ambivalence of allies as a privilege or luxury that they cannot afford. In other contexts, the same activists may, themselves, experience ambivalence as the uncomfortable cost of coalition work in contexts where they do not occupy a mainstream or normative position within a wider campaign (Reagon, 1983).

Theorizing ambivalence

Part I of this book opens a space for theoretical discussions around ambivalence. In the opening chapter, Akwugo Emejulu explores how ambivalence can operate as an oppositional politics for women of colour activists in Europe. She argues that ambivalence is often considered a problem, an emotional conflict that we should try to resolve quickly or seek to avoid altogether. However, ambivalence can be a crucial emotional process by which solidarity can be built and sustained. Ambivalence is an opportunity for contemplation, recuperation and critical self-reflection – a pause, a hesitation – before meaningful action takes place. Ambivalence can also be seen as emotional repair and the reconciliation of different ways of feeling.

Deborah Gould's (2019) article, reprinted as a chapter in this volume, discusses how knowingness – encapsulated in the Thatcherian mantra 'there is no alternative' (to capitalism) – is enacted through epistemic feelings of certainty and emotional registers of scold, contempt or mockery on the part of both political and economic elites as well as by liberal and left actors and 'armchair' activists. This knowingness dismisses and ridicules activist efforts, and can prevent others from joining activist causes. Many activists, on the other hand, embrace the unknowingness as an essential element of activism: activism inevitably unfolds on uncertain terrains with no way of knowing where it will lead. Knowingness can disallow fear and doubt – but unknowingness holds potential and possibilities for social transformation, and its value can therefore not be overestimated.

Building on the analysis of ambivalence as an opportunity for recuperation and critical self-reflection that unfolds on uncertain terrain, Maša Mrovlje places Rosa Luxemburg in dialogue with prefigurative politics in order to theorize ambivalent activism as a process of learning from failure. While prefigurative approaches repudiate mastery through social practices that refuse instrumental distinctions between means and ends, Mrovlje argues that they nonetheless focus largely on positive examples. Here, it is argued that the Luxemburgian notion of learning collectively from experiences of failure can enrich contemporary activist struggles by enjoining us to work through our contradictory thoughts and feelings about collective action. In this way, activism is conceived as ambivalent praxis.

In Alyson Cole's intriguing chapter, she argues that ambivalence should be understood as a so-called 'outlaw emotion', an affective way of being that provides support for individuals dealing with contradictions but also inspires solidaristic actions with and for the collective. Drawing on feminist theorist Gloria Anzaldúa's characterization of three figures of ambivalence – Shiva, Mestiza and Nepantlera – she examines how we might reconstruct ambivalence as a condition of political possibility rather than a state of ambiguity and paralysis.

Activism as ambivalent praxis

Part II, the most expansive section of this book, is rightly dedicated to voices of activists and scholars who explore how ambivalence manifests itself in different activist spaces, how activists negotiate this complex emotion and how they use it as a resource for their work. Melody Howse's chapter explores the reasons and consequences of the collapse of the anti-racist activist network she was involved with in Berlin, Germany. In her clear-eyed albeit gloomy analysis, she recounts the challenging conditions in which her network operated. From the rising tide of far-right violence, to constant requests for help and support from vulnerable people, to the lack of resources, Howse's network was constantly overwhelmed and the activists exhausted and burned out. However, it was the network's dogged ideological commitment to a particular organizational form that eventually spelled its downfall. In reflecting on and drawing lessons from the aftermath, Howse argues for a more sustainable mode of engagement through the practice of an 'activism of the in-between' as an alternative that considers and purposefully avoids burn-out as an inevitability.

Adebayo Quadry-Adekanbi's insightful and self-reflective chapter explores ambivalent queer activism in Lagos, Nigeria. He argues that queer activists must, alongside their activist work, negotiate both state-sponsored violence against queer people and the interpersonal conflict that these insecurities sparks among fellow activists. The social and economic precarity that shape many queer people's lives lead many activists to prioritize individual security and prosperity over solidarity and collective justice. Drawing on Lauren Berlant's (2022) conceptualization of inconvenience as an affective sense of relational friction, Quadry-Adekanbi considers how ambivalence might be the salve to resolve the problems of working with people whom one may not like or respect.

Hel Spandler, Dina Poursanidou and Sonia Soans explore the importance of creating and sustaining spaces of ambivalent mental health activism in the face of acutely polarized debates that often shape the discourse of mental health politics. They approach this by discussing their involvement with *Asylum Magazine*, describing it as a 'third space' that actively fosters the concurrent expression and publication of contradictory and opposing positions. Their incisive analysis of ambivalent mental health activism through the case of *Asylum Magazine* offers a concrete example of the democratic impulse at the heart of ambivalence.

Jordan McKenzie and Zoei Sutton critically assess the function of ambivalence in vegan activism, drawing on a case study of non-violent direct action in Sydney, Australia. McKenzie and Sutton consider the limits of activism designed to elicit 'sentiment-based' responses to animal cruelty, arguing that a measure of ambivalence is actually essential for sustaining alternative moral practices in societies where cruelty to animals is commonplace. Crucially, the authors paint a picture of ambivalence as a dynamic, rather than static, phenomenon. In doing so, they make an important distinction between ambivalence as a way to avoid or disavow troubling knowledge and ambivalence as a process of working through overwhelming and complex issues.

Cristina Florescu reflects on her experience of being part of The Embroidery Collective, a group of activists from migrant backgrounds and minoritized genders and ethnicities in Ireland who gathered online during the COVID-19 pandemic to create a space for mutual care, community and critical reflection. Describing the experience of engaging in embroidery together, Florescu questions what it means *to be political* in an increasingly tumultuous political environment. The chapter draws parallels between the cultural practice of embroidery, often associated with femininity, and broader ideas around gendered politics, non-hierarchical organizing and the often invisibilized yet crucial care work required to enable collective action. Echoing Audre Lorde's (2017: 95) ideas on self-care as 'an act of political warfare', the chapter resists neoliberal discourses of productivity that can creep into activist spaces. Florescu's chapter leaves an ambivalent taste with the reader, as she invites us to ponder the after-effects of the COVID-19 pandemic for social justice struggles and activist spaces.

Finally, Carisa R. Showden and Karen Nairn write about the experiences of young social justice activists organizing on issues such as climate change,

LGBT+ rights, housing and land ownership, and gender-based violence in Aotearoa New Zealand. The complexity of the activist causes that the young people are dedicated to calls for acknowledging that no singular emotional register can be their driving force. Drawing on Hochschild (1979) and Emejulu (2022), the authors illustrate how holding space for ambivalence in activism constitutes emotion work for these young people. At the same time, the pause and 'unknowingness' generated by ambivalence enable the activists to reflect on their remit and purpose, their obligations and leadership, and their individual and collective motivations and goals – and thus ultimately contribute to their activist journeys.

Activism and the ambivalent academy

Part III of the book turns to academic institutions and their ambivalent role in supporting or impeding activist causes. Nicole Anderson reflects on personal and institutional ambivalence in the context of the University of Edinburgh's 'Skull Room', a craniological collection looted from graves and battlefields by anatomists and naturalists in the 19th century. The chapter examines the discomfort and uncertainty generated in asking what restorative justice may look like for First Nations and Inuit ancestral remains, and suggests that confronting uncomfortable and unsettling conversations is required as part of individuals' (and institutions') anti-colonial commitment in order to challenge historical and contemporary complicity. The chapter proposes that working with ambivalence has the potential to create pedagogical openings for seeking redress and reparation for First Nations and Inuit ancestors and their descendants.

Roxani Krystalli shares her thoughts on how she uses poetry to invite hesitation, multiplicity, doubt and generosity in what she considers to be her 'domain of action' – academic teaching. She invites the reader to consider how individual and collective imagination can support us to envisage flourishing in the face of so much hurt and adversity in the world. Activism is about imagining and building new worlds, and poems can help us to tune into the embodied, sensory and relational experiences of ambivalence which accompany the uncertainty of what just worlds may look like.

Finally, Aylwyn Walsh and Paul Routledge offer a critical and reflexive analysis of their own positionalities in processes of scholar-activism, by working through the idea of ambivalence as 'stuckedness' (Hage, 2009, 2015). Drawing on several diverse examples, including arts activism in climate justice (Leeds), youth arts activism (South Africa), Climate Change, Gender and Food Sovereignty Caravan (Bangladesh), and People's Global Action (pan-Asian), they advance a model of three mutually constitutive registers of ambivalent scholar-activism focused on themes of radical vulnerability, language in common and dissonant intimacy. They demonstrate that together, these registers create the conditions for 'stuckedness' to emerge from the power dynamics in specific movements.

Conclusion: Living with ambivalence

The wide range of ambivalent emotions described by the contributors in this book – from joy and flourishing to struggles and despair – go some way toward capturing the complexity of activism. Ambivalence is experienced in affective, embodied and intellectual ways, and often located in the tension between individual and collective imaginations. Yet at the same time, ambivalence helps us to pause, ponder, reflect, imagine and connect. Some circumstances might require the suppression of ambivalence in order to present a united front to advance a shared goal. In other circumstances, collectives might allow their members to 'share' ambivalence, 'to let someone else hold the love for a minute, while we hold the hate, and vice versa' (Dango and Post, 2022: np).

We hope that this book provides some resonance and affirmation for readers engaged in and interested in activism and its ambivalent dimensions. While perhaps tempting, we do not aim to provide firm conclusions on how to navigate the murky terrain of ambivalent activism, or advance an understanding of ambivalence as a means to better, more effective or more sustainable activism. In fact, resisting such instrumental narratives about productivity and improvement when imagining alternative world-building is part of many activists' experiences of ambivalence. Ambivalence itself can be a form of resistance in the face of the state's ambitions to impose a spurious order and rationality on its citizens (Bauman, 1991), as well as powerholders' attempts to hegemonize the social space, more generally (Laclau and Mouffe, 1985).

While many of the contributions in this book value ambivalence for its inherent potential, it remains, well, ambivalent. There might be a resolution to some ambivalent emotions and dilemmas, but for others, ambivalence will remain as a constant, if dynamic, phenomenon in their activism. It is important because it holds us 'in intimate relation' (Linz and Secor, 2021: 110) to the problems around which collectives organize and mobilize as well as the problems of organizing and mobilizing. Earlier in this chapter, we have defined activism as the collective process of individuals coming together to make change in public space. While ambivalent emotions and beliefs can drive people apart, they can also be the glue that enables people to come together, to recognize each other in their humanity, and to travel together on their uncertain journeys toward new worlds.

References

Allen, A. and Ruti, M. (2019) *Critical Theory Between Klein and Lacan: A dialogue*, Bloomsbury.

Bauman, Z. (1991) *Modernity and Ambivalence*, Polity Press.

Berlant, L. (2022) *On the Inconvenience of Other People* (1st edition), Duke University Press.

Dango, M. and Post, T. (2022) 'An Introduction to Ambivalent Criticism', *Post45*. Available at: https://post45.org/2022/10/introduction-to-ambivalent-criticism/ (accessed 29 August 2024).

Emejulu, A. (2022) 'Ambivalence as Misfeeling, Ambivalence as Refusal', *Post45*. Available at: https://post45.org/2022/10/ambivalence-as-misfeeling-ambivalence-as-refusal/ (accessed 27 April 2023).

Gould, D. (2019) 'On (not) knowing what is to be done (in 17 affective registers)', *Emotions and Society*, 1(1): 15–43.

Hage, G. (2009) 'Waiting out the crisis: on stuckedness and governmentality'. In G. Hage (ed) *Waiting*, Melbourne University Press, pp 97–106.

Hage, G. (2015) *Alter-politics: Critical anthropology and the radical imagination*, Melbourne University Press.

Hochschild, A.R. (1979) 'Emotion work, feeling rules and social structure', *American Journal of Sociology*, 85(3): 551–575.

Jacobsen, M.H. (2023) 'Ambivalence: exploring a mixed emotion'. In M.H. Jacobsen (ed) *Emotions in Culture and Everyday Life*, Routledge, pp 233–252.

Kavada, A. (2023) 'Project Democracy in Protest Camps: Caring, the commons and feminist democratic theory'. In C. Eschle and A. Bartlett (eds) *Feminism and Protest Camps*, Bristol University Press, pp 176–194.

Laclau, E. and Mouffe, C. (1985) *Hegemony and Socialist Strategy*, Verso.

Linz, J. and Secor, A.J. (2021) 'Undoing mastery: with ambivalence? *Dialogues in Human Geography*, 11(1): 108–111.

Lorde, A. (2017) *A Burst of Light and Other Essays*, Ixia Press.

Mai, Y. (2022) 'What happens on the backstage? Emotion work and LGBTQ activism in a collectivist culture', *Emotions and Society*, 4(2): 181–198.

McAfee, N. (2019) *Fear of Breakdown: Politics and psychoanalysis*, Columbia University Press.

McKenzie, J. (2018) 'Political ambivalence as praxis: the limits of consensus in Habermas's Theory of the Public Sphere', *Critical Horizons*, 19(1): 35–48.

Melucci, A. (1996) *Challenging Codes: Collective action in the information age*, Cambridge University Press.

Ngai, S. (2004) *Ugly Feelings*, Harvard University Press.

Nussbaum, M.C. (2013) *Political Emotions: Why love matters for justice*, Belknap Press.

Reagon, B.J. (1983) 'Coalition Politics: Turning the century'. In B. Smith (ed) *Home Girls: A Black feminist anthology*, Kitchen Table – Women of Color Press, pp 356–368.

Roth, S. and Saunders, C. (2024) *Organising for Change: Social change makers and social change organisations*, Bristol University Press.

Rothman, N.B., Pratt, M.G., Rees, L. and Vogus, T.J. (2017) 'Understanding the dual nature of ambivalence: why and when ambivalence leads to good and bad outcomes', *Academy of Management Annals*, 11(1): 33–72.

Svirsky, M.G. (2010) 'Defining activism', *Deleuze Studies*, 4(Suppl. 1): 163–182.

Terpe, S. (2016) 'Epistemic feelings in moral experiences and moral dynamics in everyday life', *Digithum: A Relational Perspective on Culture in Late Modernity*, 18: 5–12.

PART I

Theorizing Ambivalence

1

Ambivalence as Misfeeling, Ambivalence as Refusal

Akwugo Emejulu

Introduction

How can ambivalence operate as oppositional emotion work for women of colour activists in Europe?[1] As the 'simultaneous experience of positive and negative emotional or cognitive orientations toward a person, situation, object, task, goal, or idea and the feelings of tension and conflict that result', ambivalence ushers us into a state of liminality – of being on a threshold, being neither here nor there but precariously balanced between competing ways of feeling (Rothman et al, 2017; 33). Ambivalence is often considered a problem, an emotional conflict that can be confusing, paralysing and debilitating. Ambivalence is presented as something we should try to resolve quickly or seek to avoid altogether. Since activists are constituted by their labour, ambivalence seems to be an emotion to eschew since it poses a threat to individual and collective action.

Arlie Hochschild argues that emotions are 'governed by social rules' that dictate which feelings are (un)acceptable in particular social situations. These so-called 'feeling rules' demand from us 'emotion work' through which we try to reconcile our discrete reactions to certain events to expected and hegemonic emotional gestures (Hochschild, 1979). Through our struggles to conform to emotional norms, dominant ideologies are encoded onto our minds and bodies. Adia Wingfield demonstrates how racialized and gendered feeling rules in the workplace suppress Black workers' emotional expressions and reinforce white supremacy and patriarchy through emotional domination (Wingfield, 2010). Feeling rules, however, are not totalizing. There is always an exit, a space for refusing this emotional violence – if one is willing to pay the high social costs of resisting. Defying feeling rules is possible through oppositional emotion work in which misfeeling – a refusal to 'perform certain kinds of emotional management necessary to feel' – becomes a practice of resistance (Hochschild, 1979: 567). To misfeel is to purposefully turn away from emotional social conventions. Note, however, that misfeeling is still emotion work, although this is work that can perhaps lead to different kinds of becoming and new forms of solidarity.

Experiencing ambivalence can be a way to misfeel and an emotional process by which solidarity can be built and sustained. There can be deep satisfaction and pleasure in ambivalence, as this emotion need not always be understood as a mode of internal conflict. Rather, ambivalence can be understood as a moment of contemplation, of recuperation, a state of critical self-reflection – a pause, a hesitation – before meaningful action can take place. Thus, the feeling of ambivalence can also be seen as emotional repair and the reconciliation of different ways of feeling. For women of colour activists, ambivalence can be a process by which to recover themselves, to recuperate from the gross everyday and institutionalized inequalities and violence they experience as they collectively insist on moments of care, joy and pleasure in their activism. Ambivalence, then, is that precarious balance between understanding the forces arrayed against you that cause deep harm and the possibilities, the longings for self-tending and pleasure in community with like-minded others.

Ambivalence as recuperation

It is not totally clear whether ambivalence is a discrete emotion – a discomfort that arises when different emotions cannot be reconciled – or whether ambivalence *is* that messy and confusing conflict between opposing emotions. Maybe it is not a single emotion, per se, but a combination of contradictory feelings. In any event, ambivalence is felt when a range of opposite emotions about a person or situation comingle. Ambivalence calls us into a different state of being, one in which, at least in the Global North, we seek to avoid at all costs: uneasiness. We are uncertain and unsure because we do not know how to feel; the social rules that govern our emotions have broken down and we are set adrift, alone, seeking the firm ground of certainty and clear sightedness. Ambivalence is the process of being unmoored from emotional conventions. Ambivalence contains within it a possibility of being free from emotional domination – that power relation in which our feelings are dictated by others and we are forced to suppress other emotional possibilities. Ambivalence might be a teacher through which we learn other ways to feel and, perhaps, we can feel our way to other kinds of social relations and modes of being. Maybe we can feel ourselves to liberation.

Ambivalence is a kind of temporal politics in which, if attuned to it, we are forced to slow down, to wait, to pause, to hesitate. Ambivalence makes us uneasy because we are forced to confront ourselves, to spend time with ourselves and to be self-reflective, if only simply to try to reconcile and resolve our oppositional feelings. In this current political moment, in which we are encouraged to always be hustling in service to capitalism, ambivalence becomes an emotional space of refusal, a retreat from the prevailing winds that push us to consume, to compete and to work until we drop. Ambivalence, in a sense, is an anti-capitalist emotion because it is 'unproductive' and forces us to forestall and postpone.

Ambivalence can be where an oppositional heart is nurtured. As a practice of misfeeling, ambivalence is a dissenting emotional practice.[2] Ambivalence can be recruited as a way to refuse the emotional domination of white supremacy, capitalism and patriarchy. Because ambivalence ushers us into a state of liminality, of being in an in-between state, ambivalence contains within it the possibility for acting *and feeling* otherwise. White supremacy manifests itself in emotions in two important ways (Mirchandani, 2003).[3] First, people of colour, and Black people in particular, face serious social sanctions and real physical harms if we publicly emote in ways that violate dominant feeling rules. Hence, Black people struggle against being seen as angry or frustrated in public, as this will reinforce negative stereotypes about the 'angry Black man/woman' and can also invite violence from white people and other non-Black people of colour to try to control and police us (Bonilla-Silva, 2019). Second, white supremacy manifests in emotions by imposing white ideals of propriety onto people of colour. Here, it is important to see how white supremacy and capitalism interact in the regulation of public emotions. A white bourgeois sense of decorum – to be seen as affable, to be seen as non-threatening, to be seen as even-tempered – is how conformity is felt and how people of colour are disciplined into feeling in order to stay safe (Wingfield, 2021). Further still, capitalism imposes its own discrete feeling rules: most notably for our purposes here, those of consumption, competition and social comparison. Capitalism engenders feelings of perpetual inadequacy, dissatisfaction and deficiency in order to keep us shopping, to keep us lonely and divided from each other through petty jealousies and meaningless rivalries. Finally, patriarchy imposes all the privations of performing hegemonic femininity and masculinity, which generates dislocation and alienation from who we might be if we were not so busy trying to look and feel like 'real' women and men.

Given this complex terrain of emotions and how emotions intersect with and generate particular kinds of politics and political forms, ambivalence can be seen, or better yet, felt as respite. No feeling rules are all-encompassing. As arbitrary constructions, they might be difficult to understand, and they might be almost impossible to escape, but they can always be refused. What that refusal, that misfeeling, looks like will differ across space and time. However, I am interested in how we can find opposition in unlikely places, in ugly or non-heroic feelings that we would normally disavow or dismiss. Sianne Ngai theorizes the aesthetic, political and affective dimensions and possibilities (negative, nonproductive and otherwise) of ugly feelings, suggesting their ability to refuse the dictates of consumption (Ngai, 2007). For me, this is the promise of ambivalence. Because ambivalence is not a celebratory or triumphant emotion, because it is not an obvious way of feeling oneself to liberation, it has the potential to support us in surprising ways to divest from how structures of inequality encode themselves on our bodies and minds.

Because ambivalence forces us to pause – ambivalence is perhaps the pause in the first place – it makes us stop and consider what our true feelings about something or someone might be at that moment. This is an opportunity to camp out, temporarily, in this liminal space of hesitation. Here, in this in-between space we might take shelter from the feeling rules imposed by capitalism, patriarchy and white supremacy. Ambivalence becomes a gateway to misfeeling because it interrupts our taken-for-granted emotion work. Ambivalence is a possibility to feel otherwise about ourselves and the social world. This does mean, however, that ambivalence must be resolved before action can take place. Rather, ambivalence is the opportunity to pluck us out of these linear modes of thinking and resolution to consider what we might or might not do instead, how we might or might not act otherwise, through the timeshift that this non-heroic feeling affords us.

What I want to do now is shift to consider how ambivalence operates in women of colour activist spaces – and how that offers us an intriguing model for emotional defiance.

The space between exhaustion and joy

I have been mapping women of colour's activism in Europe over the last 15 years and have been particularly struck by how an expanded emotional lexicon has been adopted by activists across the continent. By 'women of colour activists' I mean cis and trans women and non-binary femmes who experience processes of racialization, minoritization and gender hierarchies, and who organize and mobilize in public space to advance their interests (Bassel and Emejulu, 2017). As public discussions about mental health are slowly being destigmatized, this has also created a space to speak more frankly about emotions and how they are experienced individually and collectively. Activists, of course, discuss and deploy emotions all the time in their work – fear, anger and hope are commonly used to mobilize comrades and to persuade the wider public to their cause. However, these rather commonplace emotions in activist spaces have also been supplemented by discussion of exhaustion, trauma, joy, pleasure and the burden of managing others' emotions – oftentimes mislabelled as 'emotional labour' (Emejulu and Bassel, 2021). The presence of these emotions and their articulations is not the focus of my concern here; rather, I am interested in the implications of the comingling of this range of emotions and how the process by which activists might reconcile themselves to oppositional emotions creates new possibilities, new emotional expressions that have material consequences.

Two key emotions have come to prominence over the last five years or so in activist spaces: exhaustion and joy. I have written about how these emotions operate in women of colour activist spaces elsewhere and will not repeat my arguments here (Emejulu and Bassel, 2021). However, I want to make a firmer connection between these emotional trends and consider their meaning in relation to misfeeling. It is no coincidence that we see exhaustion and joy explicitly discussed by activists in this unstable political moment. We are still living with the consequences of the 2008 economic crisis – the household wealth that was wiped out, the eliminations and privatizations of public services, increases in poverty – this precarity which always existed but which was worsened by the crisis and subsequent austerity measures has never been seriously addressed. And now, almost 15 years after the crisis, it seems clear, as was the case with previous crises, that it will never be a policy priority. Precarity is a way of life, especially for the most marginalized groups, women of colour. Added to this institutionalized precarity is the mainstreaming of far-right groups, parties and rhetoric. The successful colonization of far-right ideology on both the mainstream left and right – whether that be in the form of virulent xenophobia and Islamophobia, biological essentialism masquerading as 'women's rights' or blanket denials of the existence of institutionalized racism – we are in a harrowing moment of revanchist politics.

Given these dynamics, women of colour activists are exhausted. These are exhausting economic and political circumstances which are further exacerbated by the on-going conflicts within multi-racial, multi-ethnic and multi-class activist spaces in which racism, sexism, homophobia, transphobia and classism are also reproduced. Seemingly there is nowhere to turn, no safe space for retreat and recovery. In response, activists declare themselves exhausted and burned out. And who can blame them? And yet, simultaneously, we also see activists insisting on creating moments of pleasure and joy amid the sorrow, pain and frustration. Joy, the activists declare, like Toi Derricote's poetry declares, is an act of resistance (Dericotte, 2008). And they are absolutely right. To refuse to be demoralized and disillusioned is a powerful dissenting act. To join together with like-minded others for play, for pleasure, for fleeting moments of happiness is what binds activists together. Joy sustains solidarity and makes it possible to go out again into the unkind world that wants to destroy you. In my research with activists, they have discussed how organizing parties for trans migrant women with all the profits from the entry fees and bar sales going directly to their pockets is resistance politics. They say how cooking together and sharing meals, just being in community together, is a recuperative act of defiance. Building and sustaining a beloved community, to borrow the old phrase from the American Civil Rights Movement, is a radical act.

The exhaustion of precarity and the far-right backlash. The longing for pleasure and joy. These emotions are co-constitutive in their opposition to each other. Feeling precarious and yearning for happiness cannot be understood outside of one another and the broader sociopolitical context which sets the terms of feeling in this moment. The fact that activists are feeling exhaustion and joy simultaneously marks a moment of ambivalence that creates new possibilities for being and becoming. These lines of desire, of wanting to feel individual and collective joy are stained by the pain of precarity, exhaustion and disappointment. The joy that is possible is somehow limited – but then so is the pain. This is the terrain of ambivalence. We can see here how misfeeling is generated by these oppositional emotions. One can learn from the feeling of ambivalence. Activists understand that the joy they experience is contained and reduced by the violence of precarity. They also learn that the exhaustion and disillusionment they feel has a boundary, that it can repelled, but not resolved, through collective pleasure. This is joyful pain in which one learns about structural harms from the joys one pursues, and one learns the limits of happiness from the harms that cannot be avoided. The ambivalence generated from these harms experienced while being joyful helps build a politics desirous of something else, of something better: another world in which joy exceeds misery, in which misery need not be the political project of the state. It is in the comingling of these oppositional emotions – exhaustion and joy, pleasure and precarity – that ambivalence can be harnessed as a defiant feeling, allowing activists to dissent and refuse the world as it is and help feel themselves toward building the world anew.

Conclusions

Thinking about ambivalence as a misfeeling allows us to consider how the violence that women of colour face in this unstable political moment of ruinous austerity measures and a deadly far-right backlash can be combatted and refused through different modes and registers. Considering the emotion work – the misfeeling, the refusal – to be disillusioned and disheartened when the circumstances demand such emotions from activists is radical. Focusing on joy does not mean that fear, exhaustion, sadness and anger are not also present in women of colour's activism, but rather that joy functions as defiance in the face of relentless harm and contains the possibilities of building alternative feeling rules for women of colour. Precarity and exhaustion are an emotional fact of life for activists, but contained within these negative emotions is an education in desire, an emotional transgression against the dominant feeling rules that demand misery and alienation. Holding onto exhaustion and joy simultaneously creates an ambivalent subject yearning to feel otherwise. Deciding what to feel, how to feel, when the world is so dark, is the urgent task of this moment. The lesson here is that we do not have to make this decision by ourselves – we can talk, think and feel together. These collective acts might not resolve our ambivalence, but they create a possibility of breaking out of the dislocation and loneliness of this time, to join with others in our respective ambivalences and consider who we might be, what we might do, and how we might feel in order to bring some beauty to this ugly world.

Notes

[1] This chapter was originally published by Post45 on 27 October 2022: https://post45.org/2022/10/ambivalence-as-misfeeling-ambivalence-as-refusal/

[2] In making this claim, I draw from and build on Hochschild, who, as I point out above, suggests that in certain settings, misfeeling can be a refusal to abide by and resistance to feeling rules.

[3] In this article, Mirchandani offers one of the first conceptual breaks from 'white feelings' as a framing orientation.

References

Bassel, L. and Emejulu, A. (2017) *Minority Women and Austerity: Survival and Resistance in France and Britain*, Policy Press.

Bonilla-Silva, E. (2019) 'Feeling race: theorizing the racial economy of emotions', *American Sociological Review*, 84(1): 1–25.

Dericotte, T. (2008) 'Joy is an act of resistance, and: Special ears, and: Another poem of a small grieving for my fish Telly, and: On the reasons I loved Telly the fish', *Prairie Schooner*, 82(3): 22–27.

Emejulu, A. and Bassel, L. (2021) *Women of Colour Resist: Exploring Women of Colour's Activism in Europe*, University of Warwick Press.

Hochschild, A. (1979) 'Emotion work, feeling rules, and social structure', *American Journal of Sociology*, 85(3): 551–575.

Mirchandani, K. (2003) 'Challenging racial silences in studies of emotion work: contributions from anti-racist feminist theory', *Organization Studies*, 24(5): 721–742.

Ngai, S. (2007) *Ugly Feelings*, Harvard University Press.

Rothman, N.B., Pratt, M.G., Rees, L. and Vogus T.J. (2017) 'Understanding the dual nature of ambivalence: why and when ambivalence leads to good and bad outcomes', *Academy of Management Annals*, 11(1): 33–72.

Wingfield, A. (2010) 'Are some emotions marked "whites only"? Racialized feeling rules in professional workplaces', *Social Problems*, 57(2): 251–268.

Wingfield, A. (2021) 'The (un) managed heart: racial contours of emotion work in gendered occupations', *Annual Review of Sociology*, 47: 197–212.

2

On (Not) Knowing What Is to Be Done (in 17 Affective Registers)

Deborah Gould

This chapter[1] plumbs the sounds of knowing, and not knowing, what is to be done. I search out these sounds as they percolate through various US political discourses, paying particular attention to the affective charge that attaches to knowing what is to be done, or not, that is, to the affects that are produced in, through and around knowingness and unknowingness.[2] In the shadow of pronouncements by all manner of those who know what is to be done – from conservative, moderate and liberal establishmentarians invested in existing power relations to armchair activists and progressive or leftist scolds – I am especially interested in how progressive and left activists navigate knowing and not knowing, certainty and its absence. In a world that has passed from 'actually existing socialism' to 'the end of history' to the Great Recession to the global rise of authoritarianism and xenophobia, and in the face of amplifying ecological catastrophe, ongoing white and male supremacy and vast and growing economic inequality, how do activists inhabit uncertainty and figure out what to do even so? What is opened, and foreclosed, with the genre of the blueprint as compared with the genre of the brainstorm? Along with their sounds and affects, I am interested as well in the consequences of expressions of knowingness and uncertainty, especially on the formation of activist publics and their collective doings.

The coming together of a political collectivity is both ordinary and not. It happens all the time but is never natural or inevitable. Which is to say that 'composition' – whether class-based or one that revolves around other dimension(s) of being and desiring – is a question rather than a given, always. And all sorts of things can get in the way. Although no one can simply will a collectivity into being, attuning to what blocks or undoes those collectivizing processes, and how, might help people to navigate such barriers and decompositions. My sense is that different modes of knowing what is to be done – from the right, centre and left – get in the way of people coming together to engage in progressive and left activism. We thus need to explore knowingness and its effects, and consider as well the generative potential of *not* knowing what is to be done.

My particular curiosity is in how progressive and left activist collectivities figure out what to do amid unknowingness, but because not knowing what is to be done is in relation to knowing what is to be done, I begin there, with knowing. And although my main focus is on activist knowingness and unknowingness, I want to begin with knowing what is to be done from the perspective and attitude of the status quo.

The big knowing what is to be done

The economic and political elite's attitude of knowing what is to be done is encapsulated by, and follows from, British Prime Minister Margaret Thatcher's famous assertion that 'there is no alternative' to capitalism. There is no alternative, or in shorthand, TINA, which is to say, there is nothing to be done. Indeed, Lenin's famous question – what is to be done? – simply makes no sense when it is self-evidently true that there is no alternative to the status quo and when there need not be an alternative because there is no serious critique to be made, no fundamental transformation necessary to undertake, no reason even to imagine something other than, something beyond, capitalism. In a 1979 appearance on *The Phil Donahue Show*, economist Milton Friedman put it this way: '[T]he record of history is absolutely crystal clear. That there is no alternative way, so far discovered, of improving the lot of the ordinary people that can hold a candle to the productive activities that are unleashed by a free enterprise system' (Friedman, 1979).

In addition to crossing the Atlantic Ocean and national boundaries, TINA spans US political party boundaries and continues to have force in the contemporary moment. For example, during a January 2017 CNN-moderated town hall to discuss Democratic Party strategy in the Trump era, House Minority Leader Nancy Pelosi exasperatedly echoed Thatcher's and Friedman's assertion that there is no alternative to capitalism in response to a college student's question (Marans, 2017). Here is the student, Trevor Hill, asking his question, and Pelosi's response:

Trevor Hill: What I've seen on NYU's campus and what I've seen in polls all over, in CNN even, a Harvard University poll last May showed that people between the ages of 18 and 29 – not just Democrats, not just leftists – 51 per cent of people between 18 and 29 no longer support the system of capitalism.

Nancy Pelosi: [raising her eyebrows, turning her head away from the questioner and towards actual or imagined coconspirators, mouths]
Oh, capitalism.

Trevor Hill: That's not me asking you to make a radical statement about capitalism but I'm just telling you that my experience is the younger generation is moving left on economic issues. ... I wonder if there's anywhere you feel the Democrats could move farther left to a more populist message, the way the alt-right has sort of captured this populist strain on the right wing – if you think we could make a more stark contrast to right-wing economics?

Nancy Pelosi: [smiling] I thank you for your question [standing up, with a matter-of-fact hand gesture, head nodding up and down and eyes opening wider], but I have to say, we're capitalist, [and then, with a chuckle] and that's just the way it is.

We're capitalist, that's just the way it is, which is to say, there is no alternative.

Irrespective of who is channelling TINA, its tone is authoritative, all-knowing and irrefutable, matter-of-fact and pragmatic, delineating what is and is not open for discussion, what can be questioned and what is simply indisputable. Its tone and accompanying facial and bodily gestures police thought by dismissing any other understanding of *what is* and *what else might be*, construing those who would persist with their inclination toward something against and beyond capitalism as naive, unreasonable, irrational, idiotic.

TINA is what I call the big knowing what is to be done – the big, authoritative, father-figure elite knowing – and what is to be done is nothing. By rendering the status quo as inevitable, by naturalizing and indeed valorizing *what is*, the 'what is to be done' question cannot, need not, even be asked. Seemingly an effort by those in power to create feelings of powerlessness and individualized, resigned and thus compliant subjects, TINA is a class war manoeuvre, the efficacy of which is not guaranteed, to be sure, but its potential rides on its affective charge. And this big knowingness is saturated with affect, in the sense that affect courses through and around TINA's eternalization of capitalism and is generated from it as well. Regardless of who articulates it, this discourse always is suffused with an aggressive and smug authoritativeness, with self-satisfaction and self-confidence, a sense of surety that comes from upholding a no-nonsense, hardheaded, realist position. It also exudes scorn, disdain and condescension toward anyone who naively thinks otherwise. Power here, rather than performing a cool rationality as presumed, is drenched with feelings in service to the status quo. Importantly, those feelings potentially reverberate, spurring other feelings with a similar goal. That is to say, power works in part through eliciting feelings, and in this case, for listeners all too familiar with daily life under capitalism, expressions of that big TINA knowingness can stir up defeatism, despondency, cynicism, resignation and withdrawal.

Conservative-to-moderate-to-liberal establishment knowingness

That big knowing what is to be done provides the foundation for a refrain across the political-economic establishmentarian spectrum in the US, from conservatives to moderates to liberals, all of whom similarly know that nothing, or at most not much, is to be done. From the conservative side, the knowingness takes the form of disparagement of progressive or left activist doings, sometimes by trivializing, sometimes by demonizing, and sometimes by simultaneously trivializing and, rather contradictorily, portraying as a dangerous threat as well.

Examples are plentiful. The *Wall Street Journal* editorial page derisively described Occupy protesters as 'a collection of ne'er-do-wells raging against Wall Street, or something'. The editor's advice for what Occupy protesters should do if they 'want something better' with regard to the economy: 'try joining the tea party' (*Wall Street Journal*, 2011). Conservative columnist Charles Krauthammer similarly contrasted Occupy with the Tea Party, the latter of which evidently knew what was to be done: 'less government, less regulation, less taxation, less debt'. 'What's the Occupy Wall Street program?' Krauthammer asked and then answered, dismissively, 'Eat the rich' (Krauthammer, 2011). Precisely what is not to be done, Krauthammer suggested. Former Speaker of the House and then-Republican presidential candidate Newt Gingrich knew what Occupy Wall Street participants should do rather than occupy: 'go get a job right after you take a bath' (Volsky, 2011). Former New York City mayor Rudy Giuliani similarly disparaged Occupiers and told them what they should do: 'How about trying something different to help our economy instead of occupying Wall Street, and occupying Boston and occupying Oakland? How about you occupy a *job*? How about *working*?! Working! Woohoo, working' (Yakas, 2011).

In a similar vein, a *New York Post* editorial belittled Black Lives Matter in a headline that construed participants as immature children while pronouncing what they should do: 'It's time for "Black Lives Matter" to grow up' (*New York Post*, 2016). The content of the editorial followed the more typical conservative characterization of Black Lives Matter – and of black youth in general – as a menacing threat to social order: 'For three years, the rhetoric of the Black Lives Matter movement has grown more strident – and more life-threatening to police officers.'[3]

Conservative pundits and theorists criticized the high school students who organized the March For Our Lives (about gun violence) in March 2018, again knowing better than activists what should be done. Former Republican senator and presidential candidate Rick Santorum proclaimed that students should learn CPR (cardiopulmonary resuscitation) rather than ask legislators to pass gun control laws (*TIME*, 2018). On the heels of the march, senior editor at *The Federalist*, David Harsanyi, criticized the very idea of protesting to voice grievances, proclaiming that marching in the streets is 'not an American virtue' (Harsanyi, 2018).

Conservative knowingness typically ridicules and demonizes, portraying progressive and left activism as unnecessary and either silly, threatening, or both. Their knowingness is in the service of conserving the social order.

Expressions of knowing what is and is not to be done from the more moderate-to-liberal establishment tend to be less inflammatory and more subtle, but they similarly inhabit a certitude that not much is to be done and, if anything, certainly not what progressive or left activists are doing. A famous example is the letter written in April 1963 by white clergymen in Alabama, directed at the Civil Rights Movement and Martin Luther King Jr.

> [W]e are now confronted by a series of demonstrations by some of our Negro citizens, directed and led in part by outsiders. We recognize the natural impatience of people who feel that their hopes are slow in being realized. But we are convinced that these demonstrations are unwise and untimely.

Their criticism was as follows: '[S]uch actions as incite to hatred and violence, however technically peaceful those actions may be, have not contributed to the resolution of our local problems.'

What, in their view, should local Negroes do?

> We ... strongly urge our own Negro community to withdraw support from these demonstrations, and to unite locally in working peacefully for a better Birmingham. When rights are consistently denied, a cause should be pressed in the courts and in negotiations among local leaders, and not in the streets.

They concluded: 'We appeal to both our white and Negro citizenry to observe the principles of law and order and common sense' (*Birmingham News*, 1963).

What is to be done in the face of denial of equal rights? Wait for others – courts or local leaders – to bring change, and certainly do not engage in non-violent civil disobedience.

Martin Luther King Jr's response, his renowned 'Letter from a Birmingham jail', contrasted their abstract knowingness with the knowledge gained through the lived experience of oppression: 'We know through painful experience that freedom is never voluntarily given by the oppressor; it must be demanded by the oppressed.' He exposed their proposal for what the Civil Rights Movement should be doing as effectively a means to secure the status quo, writing, 'For years now I have heard the word "Wait!" ... This "Wait" has almost always meant "Never"' (King, Jr, 1963). King, like other activists, was well aware that the struggle for social justice requires wrestling with competing knowledges about what is to be done.

The corporate media know this as well and frequently join other establishment voices in expressing what in their view is to be done. *Life* magazine slammed King after his April 1967 Riverside Church speech where he condemned the US war in Vietnam. Describing the speech as a 'demagogic slander that sounded like a script for Radio Hanoi', *Life*'s editors wrote that if, in the wake of his speech linking the civil rights and anti-war movements, progress on the civil rights front were now to stall, 'Dr. King and his tactics must share the blame' (*Life*, 1967).

The editors of the *New York Times* similarly proclaimed their superior tactical smarts, criticizing King for drawing these two movements together: 'The political strategy of uniting the peace movement and the civil rights movement could very well be disastrous for both causes', leading, they cautioned, 'not to solutions but to deeper confusion'. Knowing better than King, they proclaimed that diverting 'the energies of the civil rights movement to the Vietnam issue' was 'both wasteful and self-defeating' (*New York Times*, 1967).

The *New York Times* frequently shows itself to be one of the key mouthpieces of the establishment, always knowing better than progressive and left activists what is to be done. The editors, for example, reprimanded AIDS activists who disrupted a speech by George H.W. Bush's Health and Human Services Secretary at the 1990 International AIDS Conference in San Francisco, instructing activists what to do instead (*New York Times*, 1990). Stating that no one could hear the Secretary's speech due to ACT UP's disruption, the editors proclaimed: 'It's hard to think of a surer way for people with AIDS to alienate their best supporters.' They wondered, 'What could have caused such a pointless breakdown in sense and civility', asserting: 'It's not as if society has turned its back on AIDS and those whom it strikes.' Here the editors elided even recent history, failing to mention, for example, that on the eve of the International AIDS Conference, President Bush had indeed turned his back on people with AIDS by announcing his opposition to a large federal AIDS disaster relief bill that had passed through Congress, and by shunning the conference to attend a fund-raiser for arch-homophobe Senator Jesse Helms. Even as the editors acknowledged that ACT UP members had reason to feel rage and despair, they cautioned against excessive emotionality, offering calm reason as the more effective route for ACT UP to take: 'But for all their righteous rage, it's important for them to see that shouting down Dr. Sullivan is counterproductive.' Indeed, 'there is little value in ACT UP's disruptions', the editors knowingly proclaimed, continuing: 'If ACT UP's members would only keep their faith in education and hard lobbying and put down their bullhorns, they might find their rage surprisingly well understood, and effective when focused in the right way on the right targets.' The *New York Times* editors ignored ACT UP's by-then obvious effectiveness, not to mention the government's negligence, and thus complicity, in the tens of thousands of AIDS deaths that had already occurred. And importantly, the editors' knowledge of what was to be done to fight AIDS – losing the bullhorns and instead putting faith in 'hard lobbying', whatever that might mean – made ACT UP's militant direct action activism utterly incomprehensible. The power that operates through knowingness delimits proper behaviour in the political realm, thereby producing those who veer from that track as extreme, unreasonable and, indeed, unintelligible.

With regard to Occupy Wall Street, the sound of the moderate-to-liberal establishment knowing better what is to be done began with silence. National Public Radio (NPR) did not air a story about Occupy until 11 days into protesters' occupation of Zuccotti Park, and then only after letters of complaint prompted the NPR ombudsman to ask the newsroom to explain their editorial decision (Goodman, 2011). The explanation: 'The recent protests on Wall Street did not involve large numbers of people, prominent people, a great disruption or an especially clear objective' (Schumacher-Matos, 2011).[4] They deemed a continuous protest occupation, ongoing for 11 days by that point, with daily protest actions, arrests and incidents of police pepper-spraying 'kettled' protesters, not newsworthy. NPR's silence spoke volumes about the establishment's attitude about these protesters' grievances and actions: what they were doing was so obviously not what was to be done that it need not even be mentioned.

Other moderate-to-liberal establishmentarians similarly initially ignored Occupy, after which they elevated their own expertise by belittling and trivializing the movement, repeatedly intimating that participants did not know what they were doing.[5] Initially sparse, coverage in the *New York Times* quickly voiced the critique that Occupy protesters lacked clarity and focus. Its first real coverage appeared one week into Occupy Wall Street with a column by Ginia Bellafante. She began mockingly, describing a woman — blonde, dancing, half-naked and with a 'wish to burrow through the space-time continuum and hunker down in 1968' — as Occupy's 'default ambassador' (Bellafante, 2011). 'Tourists stopped to take pictures' of her, 'cops smiled' and 'the insidiously favorable tax treatment of private equity and hedge-fund managers was looking as though it would endure.' The reader is asked to believe that Bellafante shared the protesters' critique of the 'nasty byproducts of wayward capitalism' and, in fact, would have joined their occupation of Wall Street, if only the movement were not so 'airy', if only it were not 'diffuse and leaderless', if only it were not 'air[ing] societal grievances as carnival', if only it was more than 'street theater'.

In a similar vein, *New York Times* financial columnist Andrew Ross Sorkin seemed simultaneously quasi-sympathetic toward but pointedly doubtful of Occupy. 'Some people have suggested the Occupy Wall Street protest is a mere form of street theater, that the protesters have a myriad of grievances with no particular agenda', he wrote, suggesting that he might indicate otherwise, but then proclaiming, 'All of that may be true' (Sorkin, 2011). More interested in whether Occupy posed a threat to social order than in the protesters' genuine grievances, Sorkin recounted his interviews of participants in a manner that intimated that they were ignorant and hypocritical, presenting himself as knowing things about the workings of capitalism that the protesters presumably did not: one protester wanted 'a more fair tax regime' but had not heard of Warren Buffett and the 'Buffett Rule'; another was unfazed by having flown to New York on Virgin America, a company Sorkin suggested represents the corporations protesters were fighting; two protesters were heading over to withdraw money from a Bank of America ATM. Such ignorant protesters, and complicit to boot.[6]

The Associated Press began its coverage of Occupy Wall Street with a similarly dismissive and trivializing characterization:

> The dozens of people in tie-dyed T-shirts and star-spangled underwear have been camped out in a granite plaza in lower Manhattan for more than a week — and show no signs of going away. They sleep on air mattresses, use Mac laptops and play drums. They go to the bathroom at the local McDonald's. A few times a day, they march down to Wall Street, yelling, 'This is what democracy looks like!' It all has the feel of a classic street protest with one exception: It's unclear exactly what the demonstrators want. (Long, 2011)

The *Los Angeles Times* praised Occupy's 'heart' but joined those criticizing the movement for its supposed lack of clarity and focus: 'While the grass-roots movement certainly has its heart in the right place, the so-called 99% has failed thus far to craft a clear mission' (*Los Angeles Times*, 2011b). CNN anchor Erin Burnett began a segment called 'Seriously, Protesters?!' by similarly asserting that she and others could not comprehend what Occupy was protesting (Burnett, 2011). Burnett's sneering segment continued with video shots of individual protesters which conjure colonial depictions of exotic natives, as she condescendingly suggested that protesters were naive and unserious college youth, ageing hippies and whacked-out crazies. Not only were they evidently ignorant about the corporate bailout, they were hypocritical as well, protesting capitalism even as they consumed the latest techno gadgets. Gotcha! If you are critical of capitalism, you are not allowed to buy anything.

While asserting that Occupy could be 'a positive thing', former president Bill Clinton also knew better what protesters actually should be doing: 'but they're going to have to transfer their energies at some point to making some specific suggestions or bringing in people who know more to try to put the country back to work' (Farber, 2011). 'You need to be *for* something, not just *against* something', he proclaimed, adding, 'to make the change, eventually what it is you're advocating has to be clear enough and focused enough that either there's a new political movement which embraces it or people in one of the two parties embraces it' (Hall, 2011).

Knowing better than protesters in Ferguson, the *New York Times* evoked defeat just as the Movement for Black Lives was getting started. The headline proclaimed 'Lack of leadership and a generational split hinder protests in Ferguson', and the reporter continued the diagnosis: 'Neither the peaceful protesters nor the hotheaded elements appear to have any direction or a unified leadership' (Bosman, 2014). CNN news anchor Don Lemon reprimanded Black Lives Matter activists for thinking they might be able to stop police killings of African Americans without 'being involved in the political or legislative process', presenting himself as the knowing subject with regard to the correct tactics for bringing about social change: 'It doesn't just happen from yelling' (Feldman, 2015). President Obama also knew better, similarly proclaiming action within existing political channels as the only way forward. Even as he noted that the movement had been 'effective in bringing attention to problems', he criticized it, saying activists 'should be more willing to work with political leaders to craft solutions instead of criticizing from outside the political process'. Activists, he chastised, 'have a responsibility to prepare an agenda that is achievable' (Shear and Stack, 2016). The *New York Times*' headline shows the newspaper using Obama to continue advancing its own critique of Black Lives Matter as well: 'Obama says movements like Black Lives Matter "Can't just keep on yelling."'

Even after a coalition of over 50 organizations under the banner Movement for Black Lives released a detailed platform with concrete policy demands toward the goal of 'black power, freedom and justice', CNN commentator John Blake wondered 'What does Black Lives Matter want?' The release of their platform was 'a step … in defining their movement', Blake suggested, but 'people still don't know what it [the movement] is'. Blake's conclusion indicated he knew what the Movement for Black Lives should be doing while the activists themselves were pursuing precisely the wrong course of action: 'Will a "leaderful" movement that refuses to speak white America's language adapt? Or will it squander the momentum built the last four years?' (Blake, 2016).

The examples are plentiful: whether from the right or the moderate-to-liberal centre, US American political and economic elites typically adopt a disposition of knowingness with regard to what is to be done. Sometimes they echo TINA's refrain that nothing needs to be done, or, at most, tinkering. Even those members of the elite who express some sympathy with a movement's cause always know better: that, for example, fundamental social change is both unnecessary and unrealistic; you have to work within the system; whatever is done must follow standard, routine interest group politics; disruption will not work; activist groups must have a traditional structure with recognizable leaders and demands; and so on. Theirs is the voice of the authoritative, conservative, parental disciplinarian who knows best. And the affects saturating this form of knowing what is to be done are like those coursing through the TINA narrative: certainty, smug self-satisfaction and authoritativeness, along with the perennial dismissiveness and mockery toward activists fighting for social transformation.[7]

This establishment knowingness is part of the ongoing work elites do to ratify and conserve the existing social order by circumscribing the political and pronouncing what is appropriate to that domain. Their knowingness attempts to, in Stuart Hall's (1974: 286) words, '"distance" the mass of the public from any commitment to the event', from any commitment to a given activist intervention, for example, or to an entire movement, or to the necessity and possibility of fundamental social change.

An effort to suppress insurgency and hold on to power, this elite knowingness betrays an anxiety about the efficacy of activism, and also about activism's indeterminacy, about the impossibility of knowing in advance what actually might flow from activist doings. Their knowingness seems designed to squash any emergent critique, to put the kibosh on feelings and thoughts that open out toward alternative ways of organizing society, to turn intensities and potentialities that point beyond *what is* toward a more just world into desires that are simply wrong. And again, these expressions of knowingness can generate feelings of powerlessness, despondency, cynicism, resignation to what is, and consequent political withdrawal. Such feelings certainly are not a given, but they are a possibility.

Armchair activist knowingness

I have spent some time trying to pull out the sounds and affects of this elite knowing what is (and is not) to be done because it gives a sense of the terrain on which progressive and left activism unfolds, and on which activist knowing, and not knowing, occurs. I turn now to the question of activist knowingness, first to a form that pulls liberally from this elite knowingness. This type of activist knowing takes the form of the liberal or leftist scold who, usually from a distance, in fact often sitting in an armchair, disapprovingly lectures and chastises other activists about what they have done wrong, and authoritatively tells them what is, in fact, to be done.

Examples, again, are plentiful. Gay journalist Randy Shilts repeatedly told ACT UP what was, and was not, to be done.[8] The following instance occurred in 1989 after AIDS activists disrupted the opening ceremony of the Fifth International Conference on AIDS in Montreal by taking over the stage and demanding the implementation of their parallel-track drug-testing plan to make experimental drugs available to people not able to enrol in clinical trials. In a *San Francisco Chronicle* column, Shilts (1989) argued that ACT UP's dissent had gone too far. Declaring that 'the goals of political action should not be confused with those of psychotherapy' and that 'expressing anger for the sake of expressing anger is infantile', Shilts contended that AIDS activists were becoming too 'confrontational' and did not 'know how to put their anger to the best tactical use'. ACT UP, he warned, was prompting a 'backlash', and in the end 'may ultimately be counted as among the forces of death'. What, instead, was to be done? '[E]very action of protest', Shilts proclaimed, 'must be tactically timed and strategically aimed' to hasten 'the solution to AIDS'.

Shilts presented himself as having a monopoly on knowledge, the sole knowing subject with regard to AIDS activism. His knowledge created distance between himself and ACT UP activists; they were 'obnoxious' and 'infantile', he was tactically and strategically savvy (never mind that his proposal for action – something 'tactically timed and strategically aimed'– was vague). The aggressiveness of his critique of ACT UP and of his knowingness about what was and was not to be done raises a question about Shilts' intensity. Did it derive from being caught out sitting in an armchair when others were putting their bodies on the line and risking arrest? Was his hostility driven by competition, the political version of sibling rivalry? Was the aggression toward ACT UP actually a shame-induced embrace of a politics of respectability? Was Shilts feeling despair about the possibility of defeating AIDS and angry that others somehow were able to fight on anyway? Was his fundamental orientation toward getting a seat at the table while essentially conserving existing social relations?

It is hard to say, but what is apparent is that Shilts' knowingness here, like all armchair knowing, is an a priori knowing, knowing in an abstract, deductive manner rather than knowing from experience or from a concrete analysis of the actual conditions activists are facing. Shilts here is enacting the liberal scold, and we might note how the armchair activist's scold mimics the establishment naysayers who, in their a priori knowingness, similarly construe activists as naive, infantile, self-indulgent and ineffective. Importantly, just days after ACT UP's disruption in Montreal, the US Food and Drug Administration announced that it would meet ACT UP's demand to implement a parallel-track drug-testing plan. That is to say, the disruption succeeded in altering government policy, unquestionably prolonging and saving lives and likely hastening what Shilts himself clearly wanted: 'the solution to AIDS'. Armchair activism takes no risks and secures no victories.

Another example of aggressive and authoritative armchair knowingness is leftist Todd Gitlin's critique of Occupy. Writing in May 2012 on a platform provided by the academically reputable Social Science Research Council, Gitlin reduced Occupy to apolitical psychological acting out, 'collective narcissism' in his words, pitting what he called Occupy's 'expressive impulse' against his preferred strategic politics (Gitlin, 2012). Occupy's expressive orientation, Gitlin cautioned, made it unable to secure victory 'on the field that the world recognizes as the place where politics takes place – the field of power'. Occupy, in other words, did not understand what was needed to make real change, it did not know what was to be done. 'Strategic clarity', Gitlin asserted, 'is more likely to come from ... members of unions [and] MoveOn', that is, 'people who are not especially interested in transfiguring their way of life but want reforms'.

As with Shilts, Gitlin did not provide an analysis of historical developments or of the concrete situation activists were facing which would reveal the error of Occupy's ways. Again, this is critique from an armchair and its method is assertion rather than argumentation. Lesbian feminist poet and theorist Adrienne Rich's description of why and how thinking gets shut down might help us understand these armchair activist pronouncements. 'Much of what is narrowly termed "politics",' she noted, 'seems to rest on a longing for certainty ... for an analysis which, once given, need not be reexamined' (Rich, 1979: 193).[9] Gitlin, here, seems to long for certainty, for an analysis and prescription of what is to be done that already has been decided and would never need to be reassessed. In a world that seems utterly out of control, the desire to feel mastery is understandable, but rather than insight, such performances of mastery actually may be a defence against despair, a sense that nothing progressives and leftists do will really make the change we need.[10]

Interestingly, Gitlin ended his piece saying 'it's foolhardy to demand of Occupy that it evolve ... into something other than what it is'. Instead, he suggested, insofar as he knows what is to be done and others do not, he needed to pull himself up out of his armchair and do it himself:

> Why wait for someone else to do what needs to be done? It's incumbent upon those of us who think like ... myself to formulate a reform agenda; to win support for it among groups so inclined; to splice together the coalition that can work for them beyond this election year; and not to expect anyone else to do what needs to be done. (Gitlin, 2012)

Scolding, he suggests, will only get us so far. And yet, the entire piece, launched from a dais of knowingness, is a scold.

It is instructive that unions, praised by Gitlin as activists who know what is to be done and how to do it, expressed immense admiration and 'full-throated support' for Occupy Wall Street, allowing themselves 'to be inspired (and even led) by its energy' (Lawler, 2011).[11] As one example, George Gresham, president of 1199 SEIU United Healthcare Workers East, indicated his conviction that Occupy knew exactly what was to be done and was doing it extremely well: 'To those of us in the labor movement, it's clear that Occupy Wall Street is doing what only the most tenacious organizers can: forging a way forward when progress seems impossible' (Gresham, 2011). He praised the movement's ability to open progressives' political horizons, noting as well its success in doing the difficult work of drawing disparate groups into a new collectivity: 'Like all of America's great reform movements, Occupy Wall Street is attacking problems that seemed insoluble and uniting people who never realized they had interests in common.' More than singing Occupy's praises, Gresham called into question the criticisms heaped on Occupy by other activists who thought they knew better: 'The Occupy movement might be mocked as naive for lacking a specific set of demands, but they've brilliantly identified the one fundamental problem of our time.' In putting economic inequality front and centre, Gresham wrote, 'Occupy Wall Street has reframed the national debate as quickly and dramatically as any social movement in American history', and they have successfully focused the federal government's attention on the economic precarity of the vast majority of people 'when no one else could'. He noted as well that even as Occupiers were being forced from their encampments, 'their influence on community organizations, student groups and labor unions' was 'only growing stronger'. The contrast between Gresham's appreciation of Occupy's smarts and efficacy, on the one hand, and veteran activist Gitlin's dismissive knowingness, on the other, is stark.

The Movement for Black Lives also has been subjected to armchair activists and liberal scolds. In an interview with *People* magazine, Oprah Winfrey used the film she produced, *Selma*, to draw a comparison between the Civil Rights Movement and the Movement for Black Lives then erupting around the country, implicitly chastising the latter. Winfrey began with praise: 'I think it's wonderful to march and to protest and it's wonderful to see all across the country, people doing it' (*People*, 2015). 'But,' she quickly qualified,

> what I really am looking for is some type of leadership to come out of this to say, 'This is what we want. This is what has to change, and these are the steps that we need to take to make these changes, and this is what we're willing to do to get it.'

More than lacking leadership, the problem, Winfrey suggested, was that the protests which had occurred in Ferguson and elsewhere lacked discipline and strategy, in contrast to protests during the Civil Rights Movement: 'I think that what can be gleaned from our film, *Selma*, is to really take note of the *strategic* intention required when you want real change, strategic, *peaceful* intention when you want real change.' Continuing the implicit comparison, Winfrey said the following about the demonstrations in *Selma*: 'Those marches just didn't happen, and they weren't happening haphazardly. They were happening out of an *order* and a *design* for change.' Winfrey did not say so explicitly, but her political horizon reached to the electoral sphere, no further, and that was where the current protests, she proclaimed, must aim as well.

Like all armchair activists and liberal scolds, Winfrey knew better than activists in the streets. What is to be done? Have some intention, be peaceful, be strategic, find a leader. Activists trounced Winfrey's knowingness in a tweetstorm that challenged her suggestion that the movement was leaderless and aimless (Somashekhar, 2015).[12]

Civil Rights activist and minister Al Sharpton has similarly performed the liberal scold vis-à-vis Black Lives Matter. Responding to rumours that Black Lives Matter activists feared that he wanted to take over their movement, Sharpton wondered 'What movement?' and then derisively proclaimed 'Y'all ain't got nothing to take over' (Saslow, 2015). He knew how to create a movement, he had a strategy; they did not. Similarly, knowing better than this newer generation of activists, civil rights icon and former Atlanta mayor Andrew Young accused Black Lives Matter protesters of gathering without 'a clear message' and described them as 'unlovable little brats' (Estep, 2016).

As with the big knowing what is to be done and its accompaniments from the right and from the moderate and liberal establishment, this armchair activist knowingness has a tone of omniscient authoritative righteousness, along with dismissiveness, derision and reprimand. Etymology is instructive for thinking about the affects that suffuse this version of knowingness and its possible effects. The word *authoritative* originally refers to scripture, and the armchair scold frequently does speak as if they are voicing the word of an omniscient God. The root of *dismissiveness* means to send away, and again, armchair activist knowingness effects a sort of expulsion, perhaps more like excommunication when joined with God-like authoritativeness. The root of *derision* is about laughing at and the root of *reprimand* is about holding something in check; the affects of armchair activist knowingness consort with a ridiculing contempt that effects inhibition and withdrawal. It is as if these armchair activists want to discourage insurgency and maintain the status quo.

To be sure, some armchair activist critiques might be valid and even useful, but the smug, moralistic, contemptuous tone surely makes them hard to hear. Theirs are not comradely critiques that aim at real dialogue in the interests of advancing the struggle. Their expressions of knowingness, instead, create relational distance between the speaker and those activists they are criticizing, and for the latter can generate shame and embarrassment, but also anger and reciprocal contempt.

I would venture that, at the very least, all of these forms of dismissive knowingness – from political and economic elites as well as from liberal and left armchair activist scolds – inhibit some people from turning toward activism. If authoritatively and inarguably there is no alternative, then obviously there is nothing to be done, and if those who persist with activism even so are disparaged and scorned, including by fellow liberal or left activists, political horizons may be truncated indeed. And the ruling class marches on …

Activists inhabiting uncertainty

Thus far, I have tried to plumb the sounds and affects of knowingness, asking us to consider what it is like to move in the shadow of pronouncements about what is to be done from the TINA disciplinarians, the conservative-to-moderate-to-liberal establishmentarians, and the armchair activist scolds. Here, I shift gears and explore the sounds of not knowing what is to be done.

On 17 October 2011, the one month anniversary of Occupy Wall Street, cinematographer Ed David went to Zuccotti Park to find out where the movement was headed. His resulting video begins with images from the encampment, cuts to two people talking about a feeling of excitement and the sense that people are waking up, and then with the title of the video displayed – *Where Do We Go from Here?* – you hear a woman's voice off-camera say 'I have *no* idea' (David, 2011). She then appears, looks directly into the camera, and says: 'And that's what's really exciting. Not knowing what's gonna happen.' She continues in a manner that suggests that simply being at the occupation has opened her to this unknowingness and to ongoing participation, even somewhat against her will: 'To come down here at first, I was sceptical, and now over the last couple of weeks, just seeing everybody's dedication and drive, it's inspiring, you can't help it.' Another occupier echoes this unknowingness, drawing a line from the Civil Rights Movement to Occupy to make the point that no one can know precisely what is to be done:

> When Rosa Parks refused to give up her seat on the bus, or when four black students sat down at a lunch counter in 1960, no one knew what would happen. No one expected that four years later there'd be a comprehensive Civil Rights Act. Or that one year after that there would be the Voting Rights Act. (David, 2011)

Activism, he proposes, unfolds on an unpredictable terrain and thus cannot be orchestrated from a position of certitude. The ramifications of a given political action or movement take time to manifest and certainly cannot be known in advance, a perspective that challenges those who might wish to pronounce its shape, trajectory and consequences from the outset. 'Even if nothing else happens here, even if everyone goes home today, it's enough,' he continues, 'because what started here is going to continue in other ways and I think it's going to continue in other ways we can't predict' (David, 2011).

Another participant who had flown to New York to 'stand shoulder to shoulder' with activists after seeing officers of the New York Police Department 'use military tactics against my fellow citizens' sounded similar themes of activists inhabiting unknowingness and figuring it out as they go:

> We celebrated our first month's anniversary yesterday. We're trying to figure out exactly where to go and what to do. You know, this is kind of like, you know we were gonna have a mom–and–pop store to sell a few hamburgers and all of a sudden we find out there's an international demand for them.

Sporting grey hair and wearing a suit and tie, he seems unfazed by that uncertainty, indicating instead the tremendous pull of participatory democracy:

> This is the proudest I've ever been to be an American in my life. ... I'm astounded, I mean I'm amazed. I walked in ... my first day here was Tuesday ... and the general assembly was just starting. And I watched. My jaw was just dropping ... pure democracy. And I'd never seen it before, I never thought I would see it. It was like magic. I just was in awe. (David, 2011)

These activists' expressions of not knowing what is to be done, their sense about the indeterminacy and unpredictability of activism, their awe about what transpires in the midst of the action, contrasts starkly with TINA, establishment and armchair activist knowingness. Activism necessarily unfolds in conditions of uncertainty – there is no knowing what is to be done in any a priori sense. How, then, do progressive and left activists inhabit that uncertainty and figure out what to do even so?[13] What does that feel like, and what are some effects?

On 2 November 2011, the day of Occupy Oakland's general strike, two painted signs at the entrance to the Occupy encampment formed a diptych: 'You have left home' and 'Welcome to life'.[14] These two signs convey something of the affects that circulate around moving forward with uncertainty. 'You have left home' addressed those camping out, but I also read it as a proposition that anyone participating in Occupy was leaving behind the comfort and security that derive from familiarity and knowing what to expect. 'Life', in contrast to home, throws curve balls and is unpredictable. This welcome mat seemed like an invitation to inhabit the uncertainties entailed in activism, an assertion that this direct, engaged mode of politics would rejuvenate, even electrify, those who participate. 'Welcome to life.'

While the uncertainties and ambiguities of activism generate anxiety among many – for example, establishmentarian commentators but also armchair activists – progressive and left activists themselves often seem able to inhabit those perhaps destabilizing but also exhilarating emotional states. Indeed, continuing with Occupy, one of its notable qualities was a widespread appreciation among participants that nobody knows precisely 'what is to be done' to bring about fundamental social change. Author and activist Naomi Klein put it this way in an interview with another Occupy organizer, Yotam Marom: '[N]obody knows how to do what we're trying to do. ... No movement has ever successfully challenged hyper-mobile global capital at its source', and that's what Occupy was trying to do (Klein and Marom, 2012). '[W]hat we're talking about is so new that it's terrifying.' How, then, to contend with that affectively charged unknowingness? Klein advised activists to 'admit that they're terrified and that they don't know how to do what they dream of doing', suggesting next that inhabiting unknowingness encourages healthy debate about what then to do rather than purist, correct line posturing to fill what might feel like a void. She cautioned, if people do not admit that they do not know exactly what to do and how to do it, and if they do not admit the terrifying nature of that unknowingness,

> their fear – or rather our fear – will subconsciously shape our politics and you can end up in a situation where you are saying, 'No, I don't want any structure,' or, 'No, I don't want to be making any kind of policy demands or have anything to do with politics,' when really it's that you're just completely scared shitless of the fact that you have no

idea how to do this. So maybe if we all admit we are on unmapped territory, that fear loses some of its power.

Marom agreed: 'Yeah, that's really important. We're all just making it up.'

In offering advice, Klein indicated her own concern about how activists move forward on unmapped territory. She knows that activist uncertainty sometimes masks itself in performances of knowingness, and how destructive that can be within a movement.[15] (More on that later.) But the very fact of this conversation between Klein and Marom, along with other Occupy activists' comments about not knowing what is to be done, indicate an activist culture that differs in striking ways from the forms of knowingness I detailed earlier. The ethos of Occupy, and many other progressive and left movements, encourages a mode of activism that figures it out as you go.

Marom suggested that Occupy challenged an additional form of knowingness when he described a shift he and others experienced just weeks into the movement, from world-weary certitude that fundamental social transformation was impossible to a sense that 'winning is possible, there is an alternative, it doesn't have to be this way' (Klein and Marom, 2012). What he and others had 'known' prior to Occupy – that there is no alternative to capitalism – had stopped activists and those who might become activists before they even got started. Occupy loosened the hold of TINA knowingness and its decomposing effects, effectively offering a way forward: 'It feels like something has been opened up, a kind of space nobody knew existed, and so all sorts of things that were impossible before are possible now. Something just got kind of unclogged.' Inhabiting the more open space of Occupy, Marom drew a lesson about knowingness and its limitations for activism: 'All of this was impossible a few months ago. All of this was inconceivable. And I felt that very personally and I was cynical.' Cynicism of the TINA variety knows with pessimistic certitude that any truly significant social transformation is impossible, meaning there really is no reason to collectivize. Marom continued: 'I learned a lot from that. Turns out we know very little about what is possible. And that's really humbling and important and it opens a lot of doors' (Klein and Marom, 2012).

Something gets opened when you break through TINA knowingness and also when you reject the notion of a blueprint telling activists what is to be done and how. Far from paralysing, that space of unknowingness in fact acts as a crack in the reigning reality that has been naturalized and inevitabilized, a crack that activists can try to enlarge. What previously could not even be imagined suddenly seems within the realm of possibility, and activists can get down to the business of collectively figuring out a way forward.

That figuring out happens through collective doing and assessing as you go. Which is to say, *there is a need to do in order to know what to do*. History cannot tell us precisely what is to be done, it cannot provide, in Salar Mohandesi's words, 'models to mechanically follow or avoid', because conditions differ across time and space (Mohandesi, 2017). Neither can theory provide a roadmap; there are necessary gaps between theory and practice. Even our own rich experiences cannot tell us precisely what is to be done; experience necessarily unfolds within specific conditions, and what it teaches in one moment may be less relevant in another. Doing, which includes engaging in a concrete analysis of the conditions you are facing, trying stuff out, and assessing as you go – attuned doing, critical doing, reflective doing – is the only way to figure out what then to do.

What informs that doing is not a priori knowing but learning along the way. Sociologist Aldon Morris writes that the Civil Rights Movement's modes of protest evolved through time, 'making use of trial and error' (Morris, 1999: 524). Organizer Shyam Khanna suggests Occupy learned from the fact that the Student Nonviolent Coordinating Committee was unencumbered by 'dogmas or established political ideology' and adopted a 'try-and-let's-see style of organizing, open to experiments and learning from experience' (Khanna, 2013, quoted in Dixon, 2014: 228). Black Lives Matter co-founder Alicia Garza notes that she and others in that movement similarly have 'learned by making mistakes' (Chatelain, 2015, quoted in Taylor, 2016: 171–172).

Learning here has multiple temporalities, all critical for activism: learning in the moment, on the fly; learning after a cycle of movements (for example, the 1968 or 2011 cycles); learning in the sense of trying to grasp the concrete conditions a movement is facing; learning from history. Study groups, a vital left institution, are where a lot of this learning happens, as well as during meetings, after meetings and, importantly, amid the action.

Inhabiting uncertainty and figuring it out as you go is an activist mode that invites collectivization: a brainstorm likes people being in the room together and riffing off one another's ideas. In contrast, a disposition of knowingness aligns with individualism: the subject who knows establishes distance between oneself and those who are not yet sure what is to be done, and that distancing potentially decomposes a collectivity, or precludes its coming into being in the first place. In a similar vein, not knowing opens oneself to being affected, and changed, by others; knowing, in contrast, can make one impermeable, closed off to being affected.[16] With regard to movement dynamics and the prospects for collectivizing, the stakes here are high.

I hope it is clear that the not knowing I am talking about is not the same thing as not knowing anything.[17] On the contrary, not knowing what is to be done is full rather than empty, brimming with unpredetermined potential. Attuned to the conditions of the moment and pulling from accumulated wisdom, not knowing here entails sensing your collective way into, around and through a plethora of possibilities, with all of the unpredictability therein, and figuring it out as you go. 'Walking, we ask questions', is the way the Zapatistas put it. Inhabiting unknowingness and uncertainty is generative, providing a space where, through trying stuff out, you come to better understand your own and others' desires, intelligences and capacities.

Political activism often means moving beyond what seems possible into an as yet unknown. It requires thinking and feeling your way, collectively, without a blueprint, embracing experimentation, and realizing that mistakes, alongside learning, will necessarily occur. Brainstorming, imagining anew, inventing, messing up and trying again, improvising: learning through doing is at the heart of activism and is the way that activists inhabit uncertainty and figure out what to do even so.

Pulling from her own political history, Angela Davis advocates this sort of active experimentation, even as she acknowledges that mistakes will be made:

> We often leapt into action even when we had no idea whether our strategies would work. I think you need to give yourselves permission to think and act in different ways, to take risks ... even when you may not be sure of the outcome. I can tell you many success stories from the sixties and seventies, but I can also tell you as many stories that did not end so triumphantly. (Davis and Martínez, 1994)

Chicana feminist writer and activist Elizabeth 'Betita' Martínez similarly suggests that inhabiting unknowingness offers a way forward: 'Let's experiment, we don't have to have all the answers; we certainly don't have to have the ideology down. ... [L]et's see some things that are wrong and try to change them, and take risks.' Indeed, both historically and in the present, acting without certainty about the effects of one's actions is the only way forward: 'The seven African American students who sat down at that Woolworth's lunch counter [in 1960] had no idea they were going to start a huge movement, a nationwide movement' (Davis and Martínez, 1994). Not knowing did not stop them and it should not, Martínez suggests, stop activists today.

I realize that the picture I am drawing of activists embracing uncertainty, experimentation and learning from mistakes counters a standard narrative that renders progressives and leftists as rigid, unnuanced and self-righteous in their knowingness. We often encounter activists through their actions, and actions in a sense convey a version of knowingness: 'What we are doing is what we think is to be done, at least in part, right now.' But that more or less provisional knowingness differs from the certitude I have described insofar as it does not preclude experimentation or learning from mistakes. Still, I would not deny that left knowingness sometimes prevails, and with bad consequences, including silencing those in the movement who feel unsure about the way forward but come alive amid a more open-ended discussion. Not hearing from those who are uncertain is to a movement's detriment.[18] Max Elbaum's history of the New Communist Movement during the late 1960s through the late 1970s is, in part, a cautionary tale. He describes how a tendency toward 'mechanical formulas and organizational narrow-mindedness' – what Elbaum names 'left purism' and I would characterize as a form of left knowingness – took hold amid 'narrowing opportunities for political advance' (Elbaum, 2018: 196, 200).[19] But Elbaum also documents something more complex that I suggest characterizes the left more generally: an oscillation between knowingness and experimentation. He notes that prior to the 'quest for Marxist orthodoxy' taking hold, the New Communist Movement was 'infused with energy and innovation' and characterized by 'free-wheeling discussion', 'lots of practical experimentation', 'an explosion of forums, study groups and written polemics' and 'a lively intellectual life' (Elbaum, 2018: 161–162). More generally, while it is true that activists sometimes do inhabit knowingness, it is all too easy to overlook the questioning, probing, brainstorming, debating, learning and experimenting that frequently characterize activist scenes.

This activist disposition of not knowing precisely what is to be done, and of acknowledging as much, may have existed earlier but it seems to have taken stronger hold in the later 20th century, especially after the revolutions of 1989 forced many on the left to come to terms with, in South African Communist Party member Joe Slovo's words, the 'crimes and distortions in the history of existing socialism, its economic failures and the divide which developed between socialism and democracy' (Slovo, 1989). That confrontation with the perversions and failures of actually existing socialism wrenched open the question of how best to move forward to a world beyond capitalism. Again, that's not to say that left knowingness has disappeared; it certainly makes an appearance among armchair activists and those selling newspapers at leftist events who, as Alicia Garza puts it, 'tell you what you should think and how you should make revolution happen now' (Wong, 2014). But today, many social movements self-consciously approach their activism with an attitude of not knowing in advance what is to be done. Socialist and scholar Keeanga-Yamahtta Taylor indicates that activists in the present phase of the Black freedom movement, for example, have such an open, exploratory approach, writing, 'No one knows what stage the current movement is in or where it is headed' (Taylor, 2016: 218). Anarchist and scholar Chris Dixon names activism with this disposition of unknowingness 'another politics', that is, an alternative to 'correct line politics', one based 'not so much on certainties as on common questions' about movement building toward fundamental social change (Dixon, 2014: 221).

Conclusion: The pull of knowingness, the potentialities of uncertainty

In October 2011, 'Comrades from Cairo' sent a letter of solidarity to Occupy. It offered advice, but in a very different register and from a different location than that of the more familiar armchair activist. They proposed collective experimentation and watching out for one another as the vital elements for forging a way forward in the uncertain battle to overthrow existing power relations and build a just and joyous world:

> To all those in the United States currently Occupying parks, squares and other spaces, your comrades in Cairo are watching you in solidarity. Having received so much advice from you about transitioning to democracy [perhaps armchair activist advice], we thought it's our turn to pass on some advice. ... [W]e stand with you not just in your attempts to bring down the old but to experiment with the new. ... [Our] advice to you is to continue, keep going and do not stop. Occupy more, find each other, build larger and larger networks and keep discovering new ways to experiment with social life, consensus, and democracy. Discover new ways to use these spaces, discover new ways to hold on to them and never give them up again. Resist fiercely when you are under attack, but otherwise take pleasure in what you are doing, let it be easy, fun even. We are all watching one another now, and from Cairo we want to say that we are in solidarity with you, and we love you all for what you are doing. (Comrades from Cairo, 2011)

I hear my own romantic yearnings as I type out their words, and a part of me self-admonishes because, after all, everybody knows that the Occupy movement largely disappeared, and we all know what happened to the Egyptian revolution of 2011, and we all know that authoritarianism has taken hold across the globe. In this context, where despondency understandably might overwhelm, it is tempting indeed to find and hold on to some authoritative roadmap that instructs progressives and leftists on what is to be done. Alicia Garza encountered her own search for such a blueprint when she first read Elbaum's (2018) *Revolution in the Air*. 'As a young organizer I read this book as if each page should contain a ready-made solution to the challenges I was grappling with' (Garza, 2018: ix). Amid the overwhelmingness of what is wrong with this world, who would not want a ready-made solution? Garza counters her own desire for certainty with lessons learned from activist practice: 'It's through the experience of making mistakes, of taking risks and having our efforts fail, that we can assess with clear eyes what went wrong, what went right, what the opposition is up to, and what to do or not to do the next time' (2018: x). This sort of conscious doing amid uncertainty – attuned, critical, reflective doing – helps to clarify what then to do.

'I do not have a bad opinion of doubt', writer and novelist Eduardo Galeano (1986) proclaimed, praising a disposition of uncertainty that acknowledges doubts and indeed uses them to forge a path forward that actually can transform the world:

I think doubt has been a factor in the movement of history. I have grown to appreciate doubt more and more and, at the same time, to distrust those *compañeros* who only offer certainty. They seem too much like the wooden men which the Popul Vuh in Mayan mythology describes as one of the mistakes the gods made when they attempted to create man and didn't know how to construct him and finally they made him out of corn and he came out alright. But one of those attempts consisted of creating him out of wood. The wooden man was just like a man except that no blood ran through his veins; he had no spirit or courage and didn't speak a word. I believe he had nothing to say because he had no courage and therefore was never discouraged. The proof that one has courage lies in the fact that one can be discouraged.

A disposition of knowingness disallows fear of the unknown and doubts about what is to come, thereby precluding discouragement, but courage as well. Galeano's story suggests that the fears and doubts evoked by not knowing can prompt enquiry and study, efforts to figure out what then to do. He points to the generative potential, indeed the revolutionary potential, of a disposition of unknowingness:

[T]he proof that one can arrive at certainties that are truly capable of transforming reality lies in the ability to entertain fertile doubts before arriving at certainty; doubts that buzz around in one's head, one's conscience, one's heart, in the imagination, like tenacious flies. We need neither fear doubt nor discouragement: they are proof that our endeavors are human. And we are fortunate that these endeavors are human. Otherwise, these would be the endeavors of false men, men of wood, that is to say bureaucrats, dogmatic men, people who choose models over reality. Discouragement and doubt indicate that one sees reality as it really is. (Galeano, 1986: 14–15)[20]

The complexity of reality, Galeano suggests, should give us all pause, allowing discernment in determining a way forward.

In a moment like the present when most people have very little control over their daily lives and billions live in poverty, when white supremacy, misogyny and xenophobic-inspired authoritarianism are on the rise globally, and both capitalism and climate catastrophe seem to be moving at a juggernaut pace, in a moment when, for many on the left, things seem overwhelmingly bad and there is a great deal of disorientation and confusion, it is tempting to find and hold on to some authoritative blueprint that lays out what is to be done to bring about genuine social transformation. In such a moment, it is all the more vital to hold open a space for not knowing and figuring out what to do even so.

Notes

1. An extended version of this chapter, including images, has been previously published: Gould, D. (2019) 'On (not) knowing what is to be done (in 17 affective registers)', *Emotions and Society*, 1(1): 15–43.
2. The '17 affective registers' in the title is more metaphor than actual. I have not done the arithmetic and thus do not know how many affective registers these discourses engage. Indeed, they are not discrete and quantifiable in any event. My point is there are many. My archive draws from US political discourses on the right, centre and left, and from different moments from the second half of the 20th century through the present.
3. Such mischaracterizations of Black Lives Matter have seriously dangerous consequences. In August 2017 the Federal Bureau of Investigation's (FBI) Domestic Terrorism Analysis Unit created a new investigatory classification – 'black identity extremists' – which rationalizes surveillance of Black Lives Matter, writing 'The FBI assesses it is very likely Black Identity Extremist (BIE) perceptions of police brutality against African Americans spurred an increase in premeditated, retaliatory lethal violence against law enforcement and will very likely serve as justification for such violence' (Winter and Weinberger, 2017). In Aaron J. Leonard's words, 'The designation, coming on the heels of the July 2016 shooting of police officers in Dallas in the wake of a Black Lives Matter (BLM) protest, has the effect of conflating a social justice movement with an individual act of violence and opens the BLM to further repressive scrutiny' (Leonard, 2018).
4. The claim that Occupy's purpose and goals were unclear is repeated so frequently it makes one wonder how hard it could be to ascertain what the protests were about. Protesters were, after all, occupying not just any old place, but Wall Street. Any of the following would be accurate encapsulations of what Occupy was protesting: US plutocracy, corporate domination of US politics, the bail out of Wall Street over Main Street, the domination of the wealthy 1 per cent over the 99 per cent, vast and growing economic inequality.
5. An editorial in the *Los Angeles Times* noted as much a bit over two weeks into the occupation of Zuccotti Park: 'The pundit class has largely ignored, dismissed or mocked the Occupy Wall Street protest' (*Los Angeles Times*, 2011a).
6. NPR similarly tried to discredit Occupy by suggesting protesters were complicit in capitalism because they used the bathroom in a McDonald's and relied on Verizon to livestream their protests. See Adler (2011).
7. My account corroborates Ost's (2004) research that shows that power centres are not simply arenas of cool, rational calculation. Where he emphasizes elite mobilizations of anger, my argument draws our attention to the way power's performances of knowingness involve feelings such as condescending self-confidence and contempt for others.
8. Shilts was more a journalist than an activist, but in the straight world he came to be seen as a partisan and spokesman for the gay community, and from that perspective, a gay activist.
9. Rich is talking about a crude Marxism here, but her point is relevant to any dogmatic correct-line politic.
10. As Rebecca Solnit (2003) notes, 'Despair presumes it knows what will happen next'.
11. For more on widespread union support for Occupy, verbal as well as material, see Eidelson (2011), Patterson (2011) and Wallsten (2011). For an analysis that explores the complexities of the relationship between Occupy and the US labour movement, see Balderston (2012).
12. Black Lives Matter founders describe their approach to leadership as follows: 'we resist the urge to consolidate our power and efforts behind one charismatic leader' and instead 'center the leadership of the many who exist at the margins', thereby nurturing a movement that is 'full of leaders' (Tometi et al, 2015). Their approach echoes the bottom-up form of leadership that Ella Baker cultivated throughout her life

and is premised on what Black freedom activist and historian Barbara Ransby (2015) describes as 'a confidence in the wisdom of ordinary people to define their problems and imagine solution'.
[13] In this chapter, I am considering uncertainty among progressive and left activists only.
[14] This section draws on Gould (2012).
[15] I have been on both sides of this: there are times when I have masked my own uncertainty with knowingness as well as times when I have seen how destructive that can be within an activist scene.
[16] Brennan (2004: 11–12, in particular) helped me think about the value of permeable ways of being.
[17] As well, this form of not knowing differs from the unknowingness that is born of denial, disavowal, wilful ignorance, turning away and other refusals to contend with historical and ongoing domination.
[18] How movements deal with participants' mistakes and other shortcomings matters too, as writer and activist adrienne maree brown (2015) reminds us: 'When the response to mistakes, failures and misunderstandings is emotional, psychological, economic and physical punishment, we breed a culture of fear, secrecy and isolation.'
[19] Elbaum importantly reminds that 'voluntarism, dogmatism, sectarianism and undemocratic practices are afflictions that can be rationalized by a multitude of ideological prescriptions, not just Marxism-Leninism' (Elbaum, 2018: 325).
[20] I was alerted to Galeano's text by Mary Patten (2011: 61) who similarly urges radical movements to embrace the potentialities of doubt.

References

Adler, M. (2011) 'Will Wall Street Protests Grow into a Movement?' NPR, 4 October. Available at: www.npr.org/2011/10/04/141033126/wall-street-protesters-gain-momentum

Balderston, B. (2012) 'Occupy Oakland and the labor movement', *New Politics*, 14(1) Summer. Available at: http://newpol.org/content/occupy-oakland-and-labor-movement

Bellafante, G. (2011) 'Gunning for Wall Street, with Faulty Aim', *New York Times*, 23 September. Available at: www.nytimes.com/2011/09/25/nyregion/protesters-are-gunning-for-wall-street-with-faulty-aim.html

Birmingham News (1963) 'White Clergymen Urge Local Negroes to Withdraw from Demonstrations', 13 April. Available at: https://bplonline.contentdm.oclc.org/digital/collection/p4017coll2/id/746/rec/1

Blake, J. (2016) 'Is Black Lives Matter blowing it?' CNN, 2 August. Available at: www.cnn.com/2016/07/29/us/black-lives-matter-blowing-it/

Bosman, J. (2014) 'Lack of Leadership and a Generational Split Hinder Protests in Ferguson', *New York Times*, 17 August. Available at: www.nytimes.com/2014/08/17/us/lack-of-leadership-and-a-generational-split-hinder-protests-in-ferguson.html

Brennan, T. (2004) *The Transmission of Affect*, Cornell University Press.

Brown, A.M. (2015) 'What Is/Isn't Transformative Justice', Blog, 9 July. Available at: http://adriennemareebrown.net/2015/07/09/what-isisnt-transformative-justice/

Burnett, E. (2011) 'Seriously, Protesters?!' CNN, 3 October. Available at: www.youtube.com/watch?v=SRGns6LaJgA

Chatelain, M. (2015) '#BlackLivesMatter: An Online Roundtable with Alicia Garza, Dante Barry, and Darsheel Kaur', *Dissent*, 19 January. Available at: www.dissentmagazine.org/blog/blacklivesmatter-an-online-roundtable-with-alicia-garza-dante-barry-and-darsheel-kaur

Comrades from Cairo (2011) 'From Egypt to Occupy: "Keep Going and Do Not Stop"', 24 October. Available at: https://southissouth.wordpress.com/2011/10/24/from-egypt-to-Occupy-keep-going-and-do-not-stop/

David, E. (2011) *Where Do We Go from Here?* [video]. Available at: https://vimeo.com/30778727

Davis, A.Y. and Martínez, E. (1994) 'Coalition building among people of color: a discussion with Angela Y. Davis and Elizabeth Martínez', *Inscriptions* 7. Available at: https://culturalstudies.ucsc.edu/inscriptions/volume-7/angela-y-davis-elizabeth-martinez/

Dixon, C. (2014) *Another Politics: Talking across Today's Transformative Movements*, University of California Press.

Eidelson, J. (2011) 'Labor and Progressive Groups Join Occupy Wall Street in Solidarity March', *AlterNet*, 5 October. Available at: www.alternet.org/story/152619/labor_and_progressive_groups_join_occupy_wall_street_in_solidarity_march?utm_source=feedblitz&utm_medium=FeedBlitzRss&utm_campaign=alternet

Elbaum, M. (2018) *Revolution in the Air: Sixties Radicals Turn to Lenin, Mao and Che* (2nd edn, with foreword by Alicia Garza), Verso.

Estep, T. (2016) 'Protests continue; Atlanta police chief worries; Andrew Young labels some protesters "brats"', *The Atlanta Journal-Constitution*, 10 July. Available at: www.myajc.com/news/local/protests-continue-atlanta-police-chief-worries/XzPghrFzSVfQkvPmTMTMlM/

Farber, D. (2011) 'Does Occupy Wall Street Need to Get Specific?' *CBS News*, 14 October. Available at: www.cbsnews.com/news/does-occupy-wall-street-need-to-get-specific/

Feldman, J. (2015) 'Don Lemon to #BlackLivesMatter Organizer: You Can't Affect Change by just "Yelling"', 2 September. Available at: www.mediaite.com/tv/don-lemon-to-blacklivesmatter-organizer-you-cant-affect-change-by-just-yelling/

Friedman, M. (1979) Appearing on *The Phil Donahue Show*, www.youtube.com/watch?v=RWsx1X8PV_A (1:00–1:38).

Galeano, E. (1986) 'The proof that one has courage lies in the fact that one can be discouraged', *NACLA: Report on the Americas*, 20(5): 14–19.

Garza, A. (2018) 'Foreword'. In M. Elbaum, *Revolution in the Air*, Verso, pp ix–xvi.

Gitlin, T. (2012) 'Occupy's Expressive Impulse', Possible Futures: A Project of the Social Science Research Council, 21 May. Available at: www.possible-futures.org/2012/05/21/occupys-expressive-impulse/ (last accessed 1 May 2019).

Goodman, S. (2011) 'An Open Letter to NPR on Covering Wall St Protests', *Huffington Post*, 28 September. Available at: www.huffingtonpost.com/sandy-goodman/npr-occupy-wall-street_b_986021.html

Gould, D. (2012) 'Occupy's political emotions', *Contexts*, 11(2): 20–21.

Gresham, G. (2011) 'Occupy Wall Street: The First Quarter and Beyond', *Huffington Post*, 16 December. Available at: www.huffingtonpost.com/george-gresham/occupy-wall-street-the-fi_b_1152334.html

Hall, C. (2011) *Bill Clinton to David Letterman: Occupy Wall Street Needs to Be for Something*, Mediaite, 13 October [video]. Available at: www.mediaite.com/tv/bill-clinton-to-david-letterman-occupy-wall-street-needs-to-be-for-someting/

Hall, S. (1974) 'Deviance, Politics, and the Media'. In P. Rock and M. McIntosh (eds) *Deviance and Social Control*, Tavistock, pp 261–305.

Harsanyi, D. (2018) 'Marching in the Streets Is Not an American Virtue', *The Federalist*, 26 March. Available at: http://thefederalist.com/2018/03/26/marching-not-an-american-value/

Khanna, S. (2013) 'Mississippi Goddam: SNCC, Occupy, and Radical Community Organizing', *Tidal: Occupy Theory, Occupy Strategy*, 4: 13.

King, Jr, M.L. (1963) 'Letter from a Birmingham Jail', 16 April. Available at: www.africa.upenn.edu/Articles_Gen/Letter_Birmingham.html

Klein, N. and Marom, Y. (2012) 'Naomi Klein Talks to Occupy Organizer Yotam Marom: Why Did Occupy Take Off and What Happens Now?' *The Nation*, 16 January. Available at: https://www.thenation.com/article/archive/why-now-whats-next-naomi-klein-and-yotam-marom-conversation-about-occupy-wall-street/

Krauthammer, C. (2011) 'The Scapegoat Strategy', *Washington Post*, 13 October. Available at: www.washingtonpost.com/opinions/the-scapegoat-strategy/2011/10/13/gIQArNWViL_story.html?utm_term=.157aa14adc75

Lawler, K. (2011) 'Fear of a Slacker Revolution', Possible Futures: A Project of the Social Science Research Council, 1 December. Available at: www.possible-futures.org/2011/12/01/fear-slacker-revolution-occupy-wall-street-cultural-politics-class-struggle/ (last accessed 1 May 2019).

Leonard, A.J. (2018) 'Despite its Trump Probe, the FBI Is No Friend to Justice', *Truthout*, 10 April. Available at: https://truthout.org/articles/despite-its-trump-probe-the-fbi-is-no-friend-to-justice/

Life (1967) 'Dr King's Disservice to His Cause', 21 April, 62(16) [editorial].

Long, C. (2011) 'Wall Street Protest's Success Not Easily Measured', *Associated Press/Deseret News*, 1 October. Available at: https://www.deseret.com/2011/10/1/20220026/wall-street-protest-s-success-not-easily-measured/

Los Angeles Times (2011a) 'Occupy Wall Street's Message', 4 October [editorial]. Available at: http://articles.latimes.com/2011/oct/04/opinion/la-ed-protest-20111004

Los Angeles Times (2011b) 'How Occupy Wall Street Can Change its "Flea Party" Image', 13 October. Available at: https://opinion.latimes.com/opinionla/2011/10/how-occupy-wall-street-can-change-its-flea-party-image-the-conversation.html

Marans, D. (2017) 'The Biggest Moment of Nancy Pelosi's Town Hall Almost Didn't Happen', *Huffington Post*, 2 February. Available at: www.huffingtonpost.com/entry/nancy-pelosi-town-hall_us_58937228e4b06f344e407154

Mohandesi, S. (2017) 'Back in Black', *Viewpoint Magazine*, 8 February. Available at: https://viewpointmag.com/2017/02/08/back-in-black/

Morris, A.D. (1999) 'A retrospective on the civil rights movement: political and intellectual landmarks', *Annual Review of Sociology*, 25: 517–539.

New York Post (2016) 'It's Time for "Black Lives Matter" to Grow Up', 18 July [editorial].

New York Times (1967) 'Dr. King's Error', 7 April [editorial].

New York Times (1990) 'AIDS and Misdirected Rage', 26 June [editorial].

Ost, D. (2004) 'Politics as the mobilization of anger: emotions in movements and in power', *European Journal of Social Theory*, 7(2): 229–244.

Patten, M. (2011) *Revolution as an Eternal Dream: The Exemplary Failure of the Madame Binh Graphics Collective*, Half Letter Press.

Patterson, M. (2011) 'Unions Heart Occupy Wall Street', Capital Research Center, 2 December. Available at: https://capitalresearch.org/article/unions-heart-occupy-wall-street/

People (2015) 'Oprah Winfrey's Comments about Recent Protests and Ferguson Spark Controversy', 1 January. Available at: http://people.com/celebrity/oprah-on-recent-protests-and-ferguson/

Ransby, B. (2015) 'Ella Taught Me: Shattering the Myth of the Leaderless Movement', *Colorlines*, 12 June. Available at: www.colorlines.com/articles/ella-taught-me-shattering-myth-leaderless-movement

Rich, A. (1979) *On Lies, Secrets, and Silence: Selected Prose 1966–1978*, W.W. Norton.

Saslow, E. (2015) 'The Public Life and Private Doubts of Al Sharpton', *Washington Post*, 7 February. Available at: www.washingtonpost.com/sf/national/2015/02/07/the-public-life-and-private-doubts-of-al-sharpton/?tid=a_inl&utm_term=.c9946e646046

Schumacher-Matos, E. (2011) 'Newsworthy? Determining the Importance of Protests on Wall Street', NPR, 26 September. Available at: www.npr.org/sections/ombudsman/2011/09/26/140815394/newsworthy-determining-the-importance-of-protests-on-wall-street

Shear, M.D. and Stack, L. (2016) 'Obama Says Movements Like Black Lives Matter "Can't Just Keep on Yelling"', *New York Times*, 23 April. Available at: www.nytimes.com/2016/04/24/us/obama-says-movements-like-black-lives-matter-cant-just-keep-on-yelling.html

Shilts, R. (1989) 'Politics Confused with Therapy', *San Francisco Chronicle*, 26 June, p A4.

Slovo, J. (1989) 'Has Socialism Failed?' South African Communist Party, January. Available at: www.marxists.org/subject/africa/slovo/1989/socialism-failed.htm

Solnit, R. (2003) 'Acts of Hope: Challenging Empire on the World Stage', TomDispatch.com, 19 May. Available at: www.tomdispatch.com/post/677/rebecca_solnit_on_hope_in_dark_times

Somashekhar, S. (2015) 'Protesters Slam Oprah over Comments that They Lack "Leadership"', *Washington Post*, 2 January. Available at: www.washingtonpost.com/news/post-nation/wp/2015/01/02/protesters-slam-oprah-over-comments-that-they-lack-leadership/?noredirect=on&utm_term=.9cce6e1cf1d2

Sorkin, A.R. (2011) 'On Wall Street, a Protest Matures', *New York Times*, 3 October. Available at: https://dealbook.nytimes.com/2011/10/03/on-wall-street-a-protest-matures/?ref=business

Taylor, K.-Y. (2016) *From #BlackLivesMatter to Black Liberation*, Haymarket Books.

Time (2018) 'Former Sen. Rick Santorum said Kids Should Be Learning CPR Instead of Protesting Gun Violence', 26 March. Available at: www.youtube.com/watch?v=T1WM0iqAfq0

Tometi, O., with Garza, A. and Cullors-Brignac, P. (2015) 'Celebrating MLK Day: Reclaiming Our Movement Legacy', *Huffington Post*, 18 January. Available at: www.huffingtonpost.com/opal-tometi/reclaiming-our-movement-l_b_6498400.html

Volsky, I. (2011) 'Gingrich: Occupy Wall Street Should "Go Get a Job Right After You Take a Bath"', *Think Progress*, 19 November. Available at: https://thinkprogress.org/gingrich-occupy-wall-street-should-go-get-a-job-right-after-you-take-a-bath-22ef9fd583b3/

Wallsten, P. (2011) 'Occupy Wall Street and Labor Movement Forming Uneasy Alliance', *Washington Post*, 20 October. Available at: www.washingtonpost.com/politics/occupy-wall-street-and-labor-movement-forming-uneasy-alliance/2011/10/19/gIQAkxo80L_story.html

Wall Street Journal (2011) 'Not All the Rage', 3 October [editorial], A16.

Winter, J. and Weinberger, S. (2017) 'The FBI's New US Terrorist Threat: "Black Identity Extremists"', *Foreign Policy*, 6 October. Available at: https://foreignpolicy.com/2017/10/06/the-fbi-has-identified-a-new-domestic-terrorist-threat-and-its-black-identity-extremists/

Wong, J. (2014) 'As Ferguson "Weekend of Resistance" Begins, Organizers Weigh How to Turn a Moment into a Movement', *In These Times*, 10 October. Available at: http://inthesetimes.com/article/17243/from_a_moment_to_a_movement

Yakas, B. (2011) 'Video: Giuliani Thinks Occupy Wall Street Is "Millstone" around Obama's Neck', *Gothamist*, 5 November [video]. Available at: http://gothamist.com/2011/11/05/video_giuliani_thinks_occupy_wall_s.php

3

Facing Defeat: Rosa Luxemburg in Dialogue with Prefigurative Politics

Maša Mrovlje

Introduction

Hopes associated with the recent spate of resistance mobilization around the world – such as the Occupy movement, Arab Spring uprisings and Black Lives Matter protests – seem to have given way to disappointment. The consolidation of oppressive practices in the wake of protests has been so forceful that even supportive observers are tempted to ask the devastating question: Has it all been in vain?

Scholars aiming to challenge the defeatist readings of these 'failures' often resort to a prefigurative approach to revalue their achievements (Graeber, 2013; Sande, 2013; Cidam, 2021; Goldman, 2023). Even if these resistances have failed to produce any 'demonstrable' outcomes, these scholars argue, they have prefigured alternative futures by showing that a different way of being together is possible.[1] In this respect, prefigurative approaches echo the sensibility of Rosa Luxemburg, a foremost revolutionary thinker who sought to come to terms with the inherent fallibility of revolutionary politics and, in response, reconsidered revolutionary action beyond the instrumental logic of success. On her account, revolutionaries driven by calculations of usefulness are prone to lapse into defeatism in the wake of failure. In contrast, Luxemburg adopted the view of revolution as a path of learning from failure and outlined how experiences of failure, though devastating, can build forms of revolutionary consciousness and collective action that make possible radical change.

This chapter explores how Luxemburg's practice of learning from failure can enrich prefigurative engagements with failure. Thereby, I contribute to recent scholarship that has sought to reclaim the value of Luxemburg's thought (and practice) for prefigurative politics. Luxemburg may not appear to be a natural ally of prefiguration; indeed, her revolutionary writings were critical of initiatives that were oriented solely to prefiguring change, rather than advancing the bigger goal of creating a radical alternative to the capitalist system (Luxemburg, 2004a; Sandoval, 2016: 109). However, scholars of Luxemburg and prefigurative politics have recently emphasized that not only does Luxemburg embrace 'a degree of prefigurative thinking' (Hutchings, 2021: 63) but her thought can also strengthen and supplement prefigurative approaches and initiatives (Sandoval, 2016; Sande, 2022).

The purpose of this chapter is to extend this bourgeoning dialogue between Luxemburg and prefigurative politics to the challenge of responding to failure, and examine failure as a prominent site of ambivalence that the resisters must negotiate and work through rather than disavow. In line with the focus of the edited collection, I approach ambivalence as a simultaneous experience of contradictory feelings about resistance that may result in hesitation, doubt or even disengagement, yet that may also serve as an opportunity for critical self-examination and recuperation. I explore how ambivalence manifests itself in the challenge of responding to failure, which necessarily involves negotiating and working through difficult and contradictory feelings of hope and despair, of possibility and loss, of commitment and uncertainty, or hopelessness and resilience.

I argue that while prefigurative approaches recognize the fallibility of political action and foreground the necessarily experimental nature of revolutionary practices, they also focus primarily on prefiguring positive practices and examples. Luxemburg's practice of learning from failure, in contrast, allows for a deeper recognition of both the crushing impact of failure and its potentially productive political value. It enjoins the revolutionaries to accept ambivalence and confront the contradictory feelings of loss, hopelessness, uncertainty, commitment and resilience as an inevitable part of their involvement in revolutionary politics. I suggest Luxemburg's learning from failure valuably complements the focus on prefiguring positive futures, offering prefigurative politics additional and perhaps more robust resources to weather disappointment and face defeat without lapsing into defeatist narratives. In addition, it shows how ambivalence can become a space of self-examination, learning and possibility.

Before proceeding with the argument, two qualifications are in order. First, while the terms prefiguration, prefigurative politics or prefigurative approach are usually associated with the anarchist tradition of political thought, they have been invoked in different ways and contexts since the late 1970s. The term itself is usually traced to Carl Boggs and what he, in a 1977 article, called 'the prefigurative tradition' of political thought (Boggs, 1977). This tradition referred to different anarchist, syndicalist and council communist workers' movements of the 19th and 20th centuries as well as 'New Left' movements of the 1960s and 1970s. These movements shared a critique of instrumentalism they associated with orthodox Marxism and sought to embody in their practices the radically different forms of society they wished to bring about (Sande, 2022: 7–8). In past decades, the term has been used more broadly, in reference to a wide variety of social movements – the alter-globalization movements of the 1990s and early 2000s, autonomous movements in Latin America, and occupation movements of the 2010s, such as Occupy Wall Street, 15-M, and the Arab Spring uprisings – that adopted horizontal organizational models and democratic decision-making practices and attempted to construct an alternative future in the here and now (Sande, 2022: 8–9). It is this broader usage of the term that I employ in this chapter.

Second, in line with prefigurative politics and Luxemburg's sensibility, I refrain from assessing the 'success' or 'failure' of an initiative or movement from an external vantage point, by referring to a set of abstract ends, goals or outcomes it achieved or failed to achieve. Rather, I adopt an experiential understanding of failure, relying on the perspective of theorists or activists involved in these initiatives and what they themselves perceived to be the key failures of revolutionary politics. These, as we shall see, can be traced to external factors, for instance when resistance is defeated because oppressive regimes have doubled down on their repressive or unjust policies in the face of protest, or to some internal aspect of resistance that has betrayed its principles, reproduced oppressive patterns of interaction or been torn apart by inter-factional strife.

Prefigurative responses to failure

Scholars of resistance have often resorted to prefigurative approaches to contest the defeatist readings of failed resistances or uprisings. For instance, these critics argue that those who bemoan the 'failure' of the Occupy movement or the 2011 Arab Spring uprisings base their judgement on these movements' demonstrable outcomes. Yet reducing the meaning of such events to a set of ends or goals they (failed to) achieve not only risks misrecognizing or obscuring the aims, grievances and hopes of the actors involved in these initiatives. It may also miss the significance of the radical alternatives to the status quo that they actualized in the very act of struggle (Sande, 2013: 226).

Prefigurative approaches to 'failed' resistances, in contrast, focus on the positive practices, initiatives and examples these movements embodied or prefigured. In a highly influential intervention, David Graeber shed light on the successes of the Occupy movement (Graeber, 2013). Those critics that have pronounced Occupy 'dead' and a 'failure' failed to appreciate the radical break with the status quo and the possibility of radical futures that the movement instituted and made possible. As a result of Occupy, Graeber continues, hundreds of thousands of people 'now have direct experience of self-organisation, collective action, and human solidarity' (Graeber, 2013: 8). And 'once people's political horizons have been broadened, the change is permanent' (Graeber, 2013: 8). The democratic, horizontal practices of Occupy have laid 'the groundwork for a genuinely democratic culture' and introduced 'the skills, habits, and experience that would make an entirely new conception of politics come to life' (Graeber, 2013: 8).

Similarly, Mathijs van de Sande resorts to a prefigurative approach to contest the defeatist readings of the 2011 Egyptian Revolution as unsuccessful or ineffective (Sande, 2013). The occupation of Tahrir Square during the revolution may not have produced clear outcomes such as a new programme or party, but it allowed the protesters to experiment with alternative ways of living in the here and now. Tahrir Square 'housed a complete alternative "society-under-construction", which functioned as a social laboratory, as a place where alternatives could be formulated and experimented with' (Fahmi, quoted in Sande, 2013: 234). In this sense, the organization of Tahrir Square was 'more than a means to an end'; it embodied the ideal of a new political community, 'a space of freedom where equality and democracy was lived' (Sande, 2013: 236).

Key to prefigurative approaches to instances of failed resistance, then, is challenging abstract assessments of events in terms of their 'outcomes', 'successes' or 'achievements' (Sande, 2013: 233). Prefigurative politics entails a break with 'consequentialist' readings of political action, where the ends are key to discerning the meaning of an event and are usually evoked to legitimize the means employed (Sande, 2013: 233). Instead, the alternative practices and non-hierarchical relations of power these movements embodied – such as democratic decision-making procedures, horizontal modes of organization, and the communal use of property – are read as an accomplishment in themselves. For such practices turned equality into 'a present, if fragile and always contested, fact, a lived experience, rather than a distant goal or a future agenda' and 'demonstrated, if for a fleeting moment, that another way of being and relating to one another is possible' (Cidam, 2021: 35, 4).

This emphasis on the prefigurative dimension of failed resistances offers three interrelated ways of braving disappointment. First, it counters the 'sense of failure', the sense of 'the complete ineffectiveness of political action against the system' which tends to be used by those in power to discourage any future protest (Graeber, 2013: 164). Against this sense of failure, the emphasis on the prefigurative dimension of 'failed' resistances affirms the belief that radical alternatives to the existing system are possible and that the status quo can indeed be changed. On this understanding, even an uprising that failed to bring about any immediate result can effect a change in what is deemed possible and prepare the 'conditions for something new to emerge' in the future (Gordon, 2021: 78). In the face of defeat, resisters can thus find solace in the awareness that their efforts were not in vain: that they might be taken up again in the future and serve as an inspiration for new challenges to the status quo.

Second, and relatedly, a prefigurative reading of past 'failures' draws attention to the changes in individual and collective consciousness, to experiences of democratic, free and equal ways of being with others that make it impossible to go 'back to one's previous life and see things the same way' (Graeber, 2013: 8). Such experiences – even if they failed to translate into lasting change – seem to produce a residue of hope and purpose that resisters can draw upon to brave disappointment and sustain their revolutionary commitment in the face of defeat.

Third, the experimental character of prefigurative politics embraces failure as an inevitable part of revolutionary action. Prefigurative approaches to change are not about realizing a pre-defined programme or idea. Rather, they resemble an experimental practice, where the means and ends are constantly tested, debated and re-evaluated (Sande, 2013: 232). This means prefiguration does not start from a presumption of certainty about the rightness of a certain idea or programme. It accepts that a radically different society can only come into being through a process of trial-and-error that will necessarily entail failure. As Graeber put it with regard to the anti-globalization movement: 'none of us know how far these principles can actually take us, or what a complex society based on them would end up looking like' (Graeber, 2002: np). The creation of a culture of equality and democracy 'among people who have little experience of such things is necessarily a painful and uneven business, full of all sorts of stumblings and false starts' (Graeber, 2002: np). An awareness that the establishment of radical alternatives from within the oppressive present can only be a work in progress makes it easier to accept, and even expect, failure.

Prefigurative approaches, then, effectively counter defeatist readings of failed resistance. Yet their response to failure rests primarily on teasing out the positive examples and practices that the failed resistance prefigured. These positive examples and practices are, in a way, evoked as a counterweight to the sense of failure and disappointment. However, what remains insufficiently developed is a more profound exploration and revaluing of failure as a learning experience crucial to the development of revolutionary consciousness and collective power. Here is where Luxemburg can prove a valuable ally and resource.

Luxemburg's learning from failure

Like prefigurative approaches, Luxemburg recognized failure as an inevitable part of any revolutionary politics that seeks to build radical alternatives to the oppressive present. Yet she also developed the crucial role of failure as a simultaneous place of both loss and possibility. Here, I argue Luxemburg's engagement with failure develops prefigurative approaches to failure in two ways.[2]

First, it is one of Luxemburg's strengths to acknowledge the crushing impact of failure, not only on revolutionaries' psyche, but on their continued ability to hope and persist in the struggle. Luxemburg thought failure was unavoidable, but this does not mean she remained impervious to disappointment, despair and hopelessness in its wake. To the contrary, she was often in despair, enraged, horrified, 'almost broken' by what she interpreted as major setbacks of revolutionary politics (Rose, 2011: 15).

This aspect of her thought is most evident in her letters and correspondence with trusted comrades. Luxemburg's key moment of disappointment concerned the refusal of the German Social Democratic Party (SPD – *Sozialdemokratische Partei Deutschlands*) to oppose the First World War. This was a moment that brought Luxemburg close to attempting suicide (Arendt, 1968: 52). For her, it represented a culmination of the reformist politics within the party. It confirmed her growing awareness that the majority of the party members were not at all interested in a revolutionary overthrow of the existing system, but were content to adopt the framework of parliamentary reform (Luxemburg, 2004b: 386).

In several letters she wrote in months following SPD's fateful decision to confirm the war budget, Luxemburg voiced her profound disappointment, despair and shame. In her letter to Hans Diefenbach of 1 November 1914, for instance, she writes of the 'mood of despair', of the feeling of 'wanting to tear one's hair out', and of the 'scarcely endurable' 'pain' as 'former "friends" commit ever new villainies and vile actions' (Luxemburg, 2013: 361). In the face of disappointment, Luxemburg tried to find personal consolation in her 'modest personal needs': 'a good book, a walk in the meadows ... and last of all there is music' (Luxemburg, 2013: 361). So, too, she often sought refuge in 'the deep, elemental, hidden wellsprings of history' (Luxemburg, 2013: 392) as 'the last place of hope' (Blättler and Marti, 2005: 97). As she writes to Marta Rosenbaum in 1917, during her imprisonment, 'I absolutely do not become disheartened' since 'history itself always knows best what to do about things, even when the situation looks most desperate' (Luxemburg, 2013: 392).

In addition, especially in her letters from prison, Luxemburg frequently referred to sightings of animals, impressions of nature, or the garden she managed to cultivate in her cell, as harbingers of a better world capable of lifting her spirit. Those experiences evoked in her the sense of a harmonious universe that helped her recover a sense of hopefulness about the future (Michaelis, 2011: 218–219). In her letter to Mathilde Wurm of 16 February 1917, for instance, she asserts: 'I feel at home in the entire world, wherever there are clouds and birds and human tears' (Luxemburg, 2013: 397). Or, as she writes to Sophie Liebknecht on 2 August 1917, the way to ward off despair and gloom is to 'link up with the cheerfulness and beauty of life which are always around us everywhere, if one only knows how to use one's eyes and ears, and thus to create an inner equilibrium and rise above everything petty and annoying' (Luxemburg, 2013: 456).

Luxemburg's personal efforts to cultivate a hopeful disposition in the face of defeat bring home the weight of failure and show how reclaiming or sustaining commitment in the face of failure is a challenging and arduous task. Yet Luxemburg's theoretical and political writings also develop the potential of failure as a site of learning and possibility, revealing how experiences of failure can build forms of revolutionary consciousness that make socialism possible. I consider this as her second key contribution to prefigurative engagements with failure.

Luxemburg clarifies how failure develops forms of revolutionary consciousness capable of realizing a socialist society in her *Reform or Revolution* (Luxemburg, 2004a), her response to Eduard Bernstein's theoretical argument for reformism in *Evolutionary Socialism* (Luxemburg, 2004a). There she challenges Bernstein's argument that the conditions for a revolution are not yet ripe and that any attempt to realize it 'prematurely' will end in failure. For Luxemburg, this view rested on a misunderstanding of the revolutionary process. It postponed the goal of building socialism until conditions are opportune as if the socialist transformation of society 'can be realized in one act, by a victorious blow of the proletariat' (Luxemburg, 2004a: 159). In Luxemburg's view, in contrast, revolution resembles 'a long and stubborn struggle in the course of which, quite probably, the proletariat will be repulsed more than once' (Luxemburg, 2004a: 159). But these experiences of failure are not something to avoid; they are key moments driving the revolution forward. As Luxemburg writes, it is the very experience of failure that allows the working class to 'acquire the degree of political maturity' and create 'the *political* conditions of the final victory' (Luxemburg, 2004a: 159).

On this account, even a revolutionary action that has failed – and here Luxemburg is in agreement with prefigurative politics – can 'provoke and determine the *point* of the final victory' (Luxemburg, 2004a: 159). But, in Luxemburg's view, this is not only because the positive experiences of democratic political action and solidarity that the workers enacted during the uprising can be seen to prefigure the contours of the future socialist society. More crucially, failure helps the working class develop forms of collective consciousness that they will need to persist in the struggle and ultimately allow it to emerge victorious (Luxemburg, 2004a: 165).

The seemingly 'paradoxical idea of succeeding by failing' (Michaelis, 2011: 208) is what, for Luxemburg, distinguishes a true revolutionary from a reformer. A true revolutionary, for Luxemburg, is not driven by calculations of usefulness, but a principled adherence to a socialist transformation of society that precisely cannot depend on future success (Luxemburg, 2013: 384). The risk and likelihood of failure is a distinguishing feature of the socialist revolution as a revolution oriented to a radical transformation of society, and it is through experiences of failure that revolutionaries can grasp this distinct character of socialist revolution (Michaelis, 2011: 205). Luxemburg's notion of learning from failure, thus, denotes a deeper, more fundamental process of changing consciousness to accept the difficulty of societal transformation and the need to persist in the struggle over long periods of time. By clarifying the nature of revolutionary change, in other words, experiences of failure develop resilience. As Michaelis writes, 'it is the continuous forging and reforging of this dedication on the anvil of failure to which the process of revolution is devoted and on which alone, in the end, the victory of this revolution depends' (Michaelis, 2011: 206).

In addition, experiences of failure build revolutionary forms of consciousness because they serve as opportunities for self-examination and thus for the development of adaptability in response to the changing historical situation. In the 'Junius Pamphlet', Luxemburg argues that even the worst capitulation of the SPD – its refusal to oppose the First World War – can be turned into a positive learning experience. The 'shame and misery' that this terrible betrayal of socialist principles brought upon the working class 'will not have been in vain' if the workers are willing to learn from it (Luxemburg, 2004c: 321).

For this learning to be possible, this concrete instance of failure needs to be viewed in its 'objective historical significance' (Luxemburg, 2013: 361) – as a testimony to the errors of leadership, a testimony to the fallacy of reformism that has led to this catastrophe, and a testimony to the fallacy of the workers' forfeiting of their own capacities for critical judgement in front of the rule of necessity. What Luxemburg hopes the workers will gain from this experience of failure and self-examination was the awareness of themselves as agents of the revolution, responsible for themselves and their history. For then it can become clear to them that socialism will not 'fall as manna from heaven', but will emerge only as a result of 'a long chain of powerful struggles' in which the proletariat will 'become instead of the powerless victim of history, its conscious guide' (Luxemburg, 2004c: 321).

Further, experiences of failure enhance revolutionary consciousness by building the capacity for self-rule. Luxemburg developed this argument in her criticism of the revolutionary politics of Lenin and the Bolsheviks. Luxemburg was critical of the Bolshevik tendency to try to secure the success of the revolution by resorting to dictatorial means and eliminating spaces for democratic participation of the people. Socialist transformation, for Lenin, required adherence to a set of prescribed rules enacted by the party leadership. Thus, Luxemburg argues in 'The Russian Revolution', Lenin sought to eliminate the possibility of failure (Luxemburg, 2004d: 305). Yet he has thereby also swept from under the proletariat's feet the mainspring of radical change: the capacity for self-rule of the people, which can only come about through experience of error and failure (Luxemburg, 2004d: 305–306).

For Luxemburg, experiences of failure are crucial for building the capacity for self-rule because they can cultivate democratic dispositions and practices as well as the creativity necessary for confronting the difficulties of revolutionary action. Here, Luxemburg echoes the crucial realization of prefigurative politics that the people's capacities for self-rule cannot 'simply be handed down by an enlightened elite' but 'must be developed by the masses themselves through their practices' (Raekstad, 2018: 365). For people to be able to develop these capacities, the organizational means of revolutionary action must, 'to a significant extent, prefigure the social organisation aimed for in a free and democratic society' (Raekstad, 2018: 365). Luxemburg similarly argues that dictatorial rule will not be able to effect the required 'spiritual transformation in the masses degraded by centuries of bourgeois class rule' and inspire 'social instincts in place of egotistical ones' (Luxemburg, 2004d: 306). The practical realization of socialism, she continues, 'lies completely hidden in the mists of the future' and can only be shaped 'in the school of public life itself', through the broadest democratization of political action (Luxemburg, 2004d: 305–306). But, in contrast to prefigurative approaches, Luxemburg also clarifies how these social instincts can only be developed through experiences of failure as the essential condition of bringing into being new, non-exploitative relations between people (Luxemburg, 2004d: 305).

As Luxemburg emphasizes in 'Organisational Questions of Russian Social Democracy', 'the mistakes that are made by a truly revolutionary workers' movement are, historically speaking, immeasurably more fruitful and more valuable than the infallibility of the best possible "Central Committee"' (Luxemburg, 2004e: 265). This is because it is through failures that the working class can acquire 'the most intensive political training' and 'the accumulation of experience' (Luxemburg, 2004d: 305) that will enable it 'to solve inevitable problems and hiccups' on the way to revolutionary transformation (Raekstad, 2018: 367).

Such learning from failure can entail various forms of learning and enhance the capacity for self-rule in different ways. For instance, experiences of failure can inspire resisters to cultivate forms of solidarity and build institutions that are capable of coping with the inherent fallibility of revolutionary politics. This may entail democratic and inclusive practices and decision-making procedures that protect freedom 'for the one who thinks differently' and keep open a space for experimentation and creativity (Luxemburg, 2004d: 305). As Luxemburg insisted, it is only 'unobstructed' public life that 'is capable of correcting and opening new ways' (Luxemburg, 2004d: 306). On the one hand, the active participation 'of the broadest masses of the people' can control and correct 'all the innate shortcomings of social institutions' (Luxemburg, 2004d: 302). On the other hand, a democratic exchange of diverse experiences and different opinions 'brings to life creative force' and enables 'new forms and improvisations' (Luxemburg, 2004d: 306). In this sense, experiences of failure are not only something that we need to accept and brave on the path to revolutionary societal transformation. They can also help cultivate the sense of what a successful transformation might look like, and develop the habits and dispositions necessary to bring it about.

Coda

The effort to reclaim the potential of Luxemburg's practice of learning from failure should not be taken to imply that learning from failure is a straightforward, easy or, for that matter, necessarily successful undertaking. Luxemburg's own personal battles with despair, anxiety and depression mirror the experience of many activists who may find it impossible to recover, move on and persist in their commitment in the wake of defeat (Lindsey, 2019). Indeed, for resisters whose hopes and dreams for the future have been dramatically shattered, it can be extremely 'painful, even traumatic, to dwell on the past' (Lindsey, 2019). As Lindsey writes with reference to the betrayed promise of the 2011 Arab Spring, 'the scale and ferocity of the defeat of progressive forces has left the losers with little time or space to ponder their mistakes or delusions, let alone to share their thoughts publicly. Even privately, such discussions can be difficult, given the intensely personal disagreements over where things went wrong' (Lindsey, 2019).

And yet, as Yasmin El-Rifae emphasizes, it is necessary to reckon with what happened – a reckoning that can only start from the experience of failure, loss and defeat (El-Rifae, 2013). In this chapter, I have tried to show how Luxemburg's learning from failure can serve as an inspiration to activists who may find it difficult to find solace in memories of alternative futures they enacted during the uprisings. Her approach to failure as a site of both loss and possibility foregrounds the need for activists to collectively sustain and work through, rather than suppress or disavow, their ambivalent thoughts and feelings that arise in the aftermath of defeat. It powerfully speaks to practical on-the-ground efforts of activists to come to terms with and meaningfully respond to failure – even if the positive outcome of such efforts cannot be assured.

One such example are the cooperative initiatives that emerged in the wake of the 2011 Egyptian Revolution and that sought to prefigure an alternative future in the here and now, rather than waiting for it to be realized in the distant future. Several of these initiatives persisted after the defeat of the revolution, affirming Luxemburg's reconsideration of failure as an opportunity for self-examination and the development of resilience. MH, a representative of one such cooperative, thus reflected on the victory of the counter-revolution: 'We will keep going for our dream with the same spirit and enthusiasm, no matter the failures, because when we fail we will get the chance to know what needs correction' (Maarek and Awad, 2018: 208). Similarly, several activists responded to the many failures, dark turns and missed opportunities during the period of revolutionary change between 2011 and 2013 by calling for vigilance. Alaa Abd El-Fattah – a prominent activist and one of the leading voices of the 2011 uprising imprisoned for criticizing the military abuses against the protesters – related how miserable he felt in jail, but at the same time argued that the sense of being 'let down' by the regime should translate into a stubborn will to persist in resistance (Abd El Fattah, 2011). The awareness of the ways that state institutions betrayed the revolution, he felt, should inspire the revolutionaries to keep the pressure on the new decision makers through direct political action and persist in their struggle for the revolution's original goals of bread, freedom and social justice (Abd El Fattah, 2011).

Another example of learning from failure was an attempt by the activists involved in the Occupy movement to counter the ways in which Occupy's practices ended up reproducing the existing patterns of systemic oppression. For instance, several activists expressed their disappointment with 'colonial, white supremacist and heteronormative dynamics' as well as 'an underlying current of classism and unequal power' in forms of organization and decision making (Markoff et al, 2021: 12–13). In response, the activists developed novel 'democracy-enhancing' decision-making practices and procedures that were meant to address gender, racial and other inequalities within the movement (Kinna et al, 2019: 373–374; Markoff et al, 2021: 13–15). Even if these practices were not always successful in challenging unequal relations of power, they powerfully reflect Luxemburg's insights about how experiences of failure can enhance the people's capacity for self-rule.

These on-the-ground exercises in learning from failure suggest time is ripe for prefigurative approaches to engage more systematically with both the crushing impact and the potential productive value of failure. In this endeavour, Luxemburg's learning from failure can serve as an important theoretical resource, confronting head on the ambivalences and uncertainties of revolutionary politics and valuably complementing the existing focus on prefiguring positive futures.

Notes

[1] Here, it might be useful to distinguish 'institutional' outcomes from non-instrumental and immediate 'social' outcomes such as shifts in public discourse, social attitudes, or an increase in the latent mobilization capacity of societies. I thank the editors for drawing my attention to this distinction.

² This analysis builds on my previous work on Luxemburg's distinct way of engaging with failure as an inevitable part of revolutionary politics (Mrovlje, 2023) but focuses specifically on the relationship between Luxemburg's learning from failure and prefigurative approaches.

References

Abd El Fattah, A. (2011) 'Half an Hour with Khaled', *Al Shorouk*, 19 December 2011. Available at: www.jadaliyya.com/Details/24901

Arendt, H. (1968) 'Rosa Luxemburg, 1871–1919'. In *Men in Dark Times*, Harcourt, Brace & Company, pp 33–56.

Blättler, S. and Marti, I.M. (2005) 'Rosa Luxemburg and Hannah Arendt: against the destruction of political spheres of freedom', *Hypatia*, 20(2): 88–101.

Boggs, C. (1977) 'Marxism, prefigurative communism and the problem of workers' control'. *Radical America*, 6 (Winter): 99–122.

Cidam, C. (2021) *In the Street: Democratic Action, Theatricality, and Political Friendship*, Oxford University Press.

El-Rifae, Y. (2013) 'Dispatches', *Cairo, Again*, blog, 17 August 2013. Available at: https://cairoagain.wordpress.com/2013/08/17/dispatches/

Goldman, L. (2023) *The Principle of Political Hope: Progress, Action, and Democracy in Modern Thought*, Oxford University Press.

Gordon, L.R. (2021) *Freedom, Justice, and Decolonisation*, Routledge.

Graeber, D. (2002) 'The new anarchists', *New Left Review*, 13 (February): np.

Graeber, D. (2013) *The Democracy Project: A History, a Crisis, a Movement*, Spiegel & Grau.

Hutchings, K. (2021) 'Revolutionary Thinking: Luxemburg's Socialist International Theory'. In P. Owens and K. Rietzler (eds) *Women's International Thought: A New History*, Cambridge University Press, pp 52–71.

Kinna, R., Prichard, A. and Swann, T. (2019) 'Occupy and the constitution of anarchy', *Global Constitutionalism*, 8(2): 357–390.

Lindsey, U. (2019) 'Lessons of Defeat: Testimonies of the Arab Left', *The Point Magazine*, 18 (January). Available at: https://thepointmag.com/politics/lessons-of-defeat-testimonies-of-the-arab-left/

Luxemburg, R. (2004a) 'Social Reform or Revolution'. In P. Hudis and K.B. Anderson (eds) *The Rosa Luxemburg Reader*, Monthly Review Press, pp 128–167.

Luxemburg, R. (2004b) 'Selected Correspondence, 1899–1917'. In P. Hudis and K.B. Anderson (eds) *The Rosa Luxemburg Reader*, Monthly Review Press, pp 380–395.

Luxemburg, R. (2004c) 'The Junius Pamphlet: The Crisis in German Social Democracy'. In P. Hudis and K.B. Anderson (eds) *The Rosa Luxemburg Reader*, Monthly Review Press, pp 312–341.

Luxemburg, R. (2004d) 'The Russian Revolution'. In P. Hudis and K.B. Anderson (eds) *The Rosa Luxemburg Reader*, Monthly Review Press, pp 281–310.

Luxemburg, R. (2004e) 'Organizational Questions of Russian Social Democracy'. In P. Hudis and K.B. Anderson (eds) *The Rosa Luxemburg Reader*, Monthly Review Press, pp 248–265.

Luxemburg, R. (2013) *The Letters of Rosa Luxemburg*, edited by G. Adler, P. Hudis, and A. Laschitza, Verso.

Maarek, E.A. and Awad, S.H. (2018) 'Creating Alternative Futures: Cooperative Initiatives in Egypt'. In C. de Saint-Laurent, S. Obradović and K.R. Carriere (eds) *Imagining Collective Futures: Perspectives from Social, Cultural and Political Psychology* (Palgrave Studies in Creativity and Culture), Springer International Publishing, pp 199–219.

Markoff, J., Lazar, H. and Smith, J. (2021) 'Creative Disappointment: How Movements for Democracy: Spawn Movements for Even More Democracy'. In D. Pettincchio (ed) *The Politics of Inequality* (Research in Political Sociology, Vol. 28), Emerald Publishing Limited, pp 237–262.

Michaelis, L. (2011) 'Rosa Luxemburg on disappointment and the politics of commitment', *European Journal of Political Theory*, 10(2): 202–224.

Mrovlje, M. (2023) 'The Disappointment of Rosa Luxemburg: Rethinking Revolutionary Commitment in the Face of Failure'. *Philosophy & Social Criticism*, 0(0). https://doi.org/10.1177/01914537231184406

Raekstad, P. (2018) 'Revolutionary Practice and Prefigurative Politics: A Clarification and Defense', *Constellations*, 25(3): 359–372.

Rose, J. (2011) 'What More Could We Want of Ourselves!' *London Review of Books*, 16 June, sec. 33(12). Available at: www.lrb.co.uk/the-paper/v33/n12/jacqueline-rose/what-more-could-we-want-of-ourselves

Sande, M. van de (2013) 'The prefigurative politics of Tahrir Square: an alternative perspective on the 2011 revolutions', *Res Publica*, 19: 223–239.

Sande, M. van de (2022) *Prefigurative Democracy: Protest, Social Movements and the Political Institution of Society* (Taking on the Political), Edinburgh University Press.

Sandoval, M. (2016) 'What would Rosa do? Co-operatives and radical politics', *Soundings*, 63(63): 98–111.

4

Orchestrating the Furies: Anzaldúa's Evolving Conception of Ambivalent Political Struggle

Alyson Cole

Introduction

For most of us, with perhaps the exception of those Eric Hoffer (1951) classified as 'true believers', ambivalence is an inescapable condition of life; impulses are always mixed, or feelings doubled. Even if inevitable, ambivalence is still commonly regarded as undesirable, 'a potentially dangerous state of mind, which could thwart your goals and potentially get you in trouble' (Brogaard and Gatzia, 2020). Political scientists who study electoral politics and social movements tend to adopt this normative framing, casting ambivalence as cognitive indeterminacy that leads to 'action paralysis', and insisting that overcoming ambivalence is a prerequisite for political participation (see, for example, Connell et al, 1999; Gainous et al, 2010: 337; Miller and Peterson, 2004: 848).[1] In our current political climate, ambivalence feels especially taxing and potentially defeatist: social media amplifies the tone and pace of politics, narrowing possibilities for sustained exchange and nuanced expression; while widespread and deepening polarization increases the pressure to summon certitude and 'pick a side'. Divided rather than unified, hesitant and reflective rather than confident, the liminality of ambivalence seems to render us precarious, unsure whether even collectively we can alter enduring injustices. Ambivalent activism, therefore, would appear to be oxymoronic.

This chapter aims to trouble such presumptions about the emotional inclinations or affective dispositions necessary for politics. Dispensing with positivist premises about actors who know their ultimate objectives before they engage in politics, enter politics to realize those ends, and then assess success by measuring an action's impact on public policy, we look instead to the *doing* of politics, to how political participation impacts the participants themselves. After all, those who join in political struggle rarely do so with the expectation of guaranteed outcomes or closure (Hall, 1986). Moreover, participation itself often transforms actors' sense of themselves and the purpose of their activism (McAdam et al, 2009). Ambivalence has been considered an obstacle to political action by observers who conceive of it as a condition of static antimonies, misreading stasis as the lack or termination of movement. However, as Tina Campt has suggested (in a different context), stasis is an 'effortful equilibrium achieved through a labored balancing of opposing forces and flows' (2017: 51–52). Indeed, it is this effort to sustain that balance that causes many who experience ambivalence to find it an uncomfortably frictious state until they recognize it as molten and generative, and that without friction there is no movement.

As an inherent part of the emotional life of injustice, ambivalence might be better understood as a dissident epistemology of the sort Alison Jaggar called 'outlaw emotions', 'observations that challenge dominant conceptions of the status quo' (1989: 161), which contribute to feelings that mobilize insurgencies from below. The question then becomes whether ambivalence undermines and obstructs or enables and sustains affective networks of solidarity, the feeling with/for others, that are essential to the process of building new worlds. By drawing on feminist theorist Gloria Anzaldúa's account of the continuously reconfigured assemblages ('*todas las partes de nosotros valen*') created at borders, within and between subjectivities (1987: 88), I explore how psychic division, ontological ambiguity and political conflict might be appreciated as conditions of political possibility rather than conditions to transcend.

Ambivalent meanings

The word 'ambivalence' migrated into the English language from the German *Ambivalenz*. Combining the Latin *ambi* (both, around, or in more than one way) and *valentia* (strength), Paul Eugen Bleuler coined the term in his 1910 study of key symptoms of schizophrenia. Within a matter of years, 'ambivalence' entered common usage to designate a more general state of emotional dividedness (OED: 2023). While Bleuler held that all three forms of ambivalence (emotional, intellectual and volitional) also occur to some degree throughout the population (Berretta et al, 2015), the negative connotations of ambivalence as neurotic conflict linger in ordinary use even today. Simply put, ambivalence is conceived of as something to disavow and surmount, not to cultivate.

Despite a proliferation of scholarship on emotion and affect over the last two decades within and beyond the social sciences, including the role of polyvalent emotions in contentious politics (see, for example, Gould, 2009; Jasper, 2011), insufficient attention has been given to ambivalence. For example, in her pivotal work on negative affects, *Ugly Feelings* (2007), Sianne Ngai analyses a variety of non-cathartic emotions, such as envy, disgust and irritation, all of which she characterizes as 'ambivalent' (Ngai, 2007: 10). Ngai, like others who excavate the archive of negativity, uses the term to denote the obliqueness of such feelings (in contrast to the more unequivocal emotion-driven politics of the past) and to highlight how they might be deployed for both progressive and reactionary purposes (Ngai, 2007: 3, 7). Nevertheless, ambivalence remains adjectival in her study, it is not a feeling or cognitive state worthy of investigation itself.

Akwugo Emejulu's exploration of ambivalence as a 'misfeeling', a configuration of refusal to adhere to the demands of emotional management advancing capitalist productivity (2022: 4), is a notable exception. Emejulu theorizes ambivalence as constituting a necessary and defiant hiatus when working against injustice. But she still maintains that 'ambivalence must be resolved before action can take place' (2022: 5). Like Emejulu, I view ambivalence as fertile ground for restructuring feelings and engaging in political thought. But I propose that ambivalence is more than a prelude to action. Ambivalence constitutes a praxis integral to political activism, though one that straddles agency/passivity, inoperative/productive dichotomies. By de-emphasizing the idea of ambivalence as incompatibility or dissonance, we can reconceive of ambivalence as the product of the politically fecund effort to hold divergent views and feelings, not something to overcome but instead the basis of our shared condition and an essential aspect of political struggle. Rather than assuming that ambivalence should or can be settled prior to action, we need instead to understand better how to act *with* ambivalence. Audre Lorde encouraged us to 'learn to orchestrate the furies so they do not tear us apart' (1981: 9). Anzaldúa, I hope to demonstrate, comes to formulate ambivalence as the orchestration.

Building bridges with Anzaldúa

How we live with precarity varies considerably depending on our circumstances, which makes collective contestation even more challenging (Waite, 2009: 426).[2] As Lauren Berlant observed, there is a fundamental 'class incoherence' to the range of 'populations claiming precarity' (Berlant, 2011: 2). Previous forms of political organizing, whether alliances of international solidarity or the mutual recognition of identity politics, presumed a stable ground that precarity dislocates (Neilson and Rossiter, 2008: 65). Given persistent and growing economic, social and political instability, Brett Neilson and Ned Rossiter recommend that political actors reimagine how activism takes shape, and that, like precarity itself, 'effective political organisation must ... be composed in transborder ways' and through 'heterolingual modes of address' (2008: 65). Their intuition that political mobilization now necessitates transborder movement and heterolingual speech resonates with the content, genres and multi-lingual prose of Anzaldúa's work. In all these modes, she grapples with how to engage politically within the shifting, liminal spaces of precarity, how the subversive potential of ambivalence might be deployed in politics. While Anzaldúa is best known for her writing on hybridity, specifically 'mestiza consciousness', toward the end of her life she turned to theorize another figure, the Nepantlera (derived from a Nahuatl word meaning in-between). Her account of the Nepantlera provides a critical resource for reflecting on how integral ambivalence is to activism that embraces the unruliness of politics, forsaking certitude in pursuit of continually expanding inclusivity. As we will see, for the Nepantlera, ambivalence is less a condition of dividedness or confusion than part of an evolving process of working toward disalienation in concert with others.

Over the course of her writing, Anzaldúa theorizes the divides (geographic, national, racial/ethnic, gendered, sexual and linguistic) that create and prolong precarity for some by marking them as Other. Her testimonial accounts of residing in the 'vague and undetermined place[s]' at and between borders underscore how precarity moves in and through transient, colonized, hybridized populations (Anzaldúa, 1987: 3). She traces the ambivalence precaritization breeds and exacerbates, as well as the precariousness of ambivalence itself. The borderland 'is a constant state of transition', she asserts. 'Ambivalence and unrest reside there and death is no stranger' (1987: 3–4). To depict different postures of inhabiting ambivalence while engaging politically, Anzaldúa sketches three archetypes –Shiva, Mestiza and Nepantlera. Each of these totem figures wrestles with the impediments of being cast as the Other, the innate tensions of hybridity, and the pull of contentious politics. But they respond to their situation differently: Shiva rejects ambivalence as a mistaken projection imposed by others; Mestiza sublimates ambivalence; and Nepantlera accepts it. Through these varied approaches Anzaldúa tarries with two dimensions of ambivalence: ambivalence as an affective condition of the precariousness of hybridity, and ambivalence about ambivalence itself; that is, the challenge in devising how to address the ambivalence that hybridity engenders, and how to harness it for politics. Through the Nepantlera, Anzaldúa comes to theorize ambivalence as politically fertile, a resource to value. 'Transformations occur in this in-between space', she contends, 'an unstable, unpredictable, precarious, desconocida [unknown]' (2002: 1). She thus asks us to reconceive the plurality and mobility of ambivalence, which begins internally and continues as we join with others in struggle, by remembering that, as Sara Ahmed later put it, collective action 'does not stand still, but creates and is created by movement' (Ahmed, 2017: 3).

Ambivalent archetypes: Shiva and Mestiza

Before turning to investigate her ideas more closely, I first consider how Anzaldúa constructs her texts to amplify and then transgress linguistic borders. *Mestizaje* (the Spanish term for mixture, especially regarding race) is not only a concept that Anzaldúa reclaims and reworks; her texts themselves serve as vivid illustrations of such fusions. Credited as pioneering the genre of *autohistoria-teoría* (which builds on older Latin American feminist forms of *testimonio*), she intermingles poetry, personal narrative, descriptions of food, landscapes and ancient mythology with political provocations, and an abundance of metaphors. Her prose also blends English with Spanish, Tex-Mex, Nahuatl and the 'bastard' language Chicano Spanish. 'I am my language', she insists. 'Until I am free to write bilingually and to switch codes without having always to translate … my tongue will be illegitimate … I will have my serpent's tongue' (Anzaldúa, 1987: 59). Anzaldúa invites readers to join her in straddling rifts, linguistic and otherwise, marshalling new approaches to reading and thought.

In her early writings, published in the anthology she co-edited with Cherríe Moraga, *This Bridge Called My Back: Writings By Radical Women of Color* (Moraga and Anzaldúa, 1983), Anzaldúa depicts bridging as a self-protective measure against the dismembering impulse of identity politics. ('They would chop me up into little fragments and tag each piece with a label' (1983: 205).) Such political and ultimately cognitive dividedness serves as the context in which Anzaldúa initially raises the issue of ambivalence: 'You say my name is ambivalence?' she asks (Moraga and Anzaldúa, 1983: 205). Rebuffing being so named as another form of misrecognition, she clarifies that she is multifaceted, not fragmented, and assents to being 'a fucking crossroad' (Moraga and Anzaldúa, 1983: 206). She is like the Hindu goddess Shiva, whose numerous appendages extend in every direction, reaching across racial, sexual and class ruptures. Separatist violence is imposed from without, even if it is eventually internalized. There is nothing ambivalent about plurality rightly understood: 'Only your labels split me' (Moraga and Anzaldúa, 1983: 205).

Anzaldúa returns to the issue of ambivalence in *Borderlands/La Frontera: The New Mestiza* (1987). Psychic dividedness remains a central theme, now expanded to include spatial/geographic as well as affective, cultural, linguistic and embodied manifestations. But in this book, Mestiza's hybridity substitutes for Shiva's pluralism. Whereas Shiva deflects ambivalence as the myopic projection of those who insist upon singular loyalties, Mestiza grapples with – and then overcomes – ambivalence. Mestiza endures a precarious existence in the borderlands, marked by destabilizing 'perplexity', 'insecurity and indecisiveness', as well as 'psychic restlessness' (Anzaldúa, 1987: 78). Tempting as the siren call of assimilation may be, such interpellation necessitates disavowing crucial aspects of history, both personal and political. Her impulse, therefore, is to resist. Defensively, Mestiza assumes a 'counterstance', endeavouring to revalue what the dominant culture disparaged. But like any reactive formation, the oppressor ultimately circumscribes such proud defiance, since 'all reaction is limited by, and dependent upon, what it is reacting against' (Anzaldúa, 1987: 79).

Even as Anzaldúa appreciates the counterstance as a form of resistance, she ultimately rejects it as a viable politics because it provides only an encumbered freedom. Achieving true freedom necessitates action rather than reaction, a transfiguration that requires expanded consciousness, emotional and political flexibility, 'coping' with precarious movement, and a 'tolerance for contradictions' (Anzaldúa, 1987: 79). Mestiza does not choose sides ('nothing is thrust out, the good, the bad, and the ugly, nothing rejected, nothing abandoned' (p 79)). Instead, she reassembles the divergent pieces. ('I gather the splintered and disowned parts of la gente mexicana and hold them in my arms' (p 88).) Mestiza, quite simply, transforms 'ambivalence into something else' (p 79).

At this point in theorizing ambivalence, Anzaldúa envisages a way to surmount it. She begins by describing the challenges that living with ambivalence presents, but concludes by switching terms, suggesting that Mestiza learns to fortify 'her tolerance (and intolerance) for ambiguity' (Anzaldúa, 1987: 82). Why might Anzaldúa replace ambivalence with ambiguity? After all, 'ambiguity' denotes a lack of clarity which, as Falguni Sheth contends, can 'in itself lead to a state of excruciation' for those marked as Other (Sheth, 2022: 25). Even if the change of terms was inadvertent,[3] it is significant. Some disruptive experience, perhaps the disunity of subjectivity itself, compels Mestiza to move beyond ambivalence. ('She can be jarred out of ambivalence by an intense, often painful, emotional event' (Anzaldúa, 1987: 79).) This rupture pushes Mestiza to reassemble her disparate allegiances and forge a 'synthesis', which, Anzaldúa underscores, constitutes more than 'merely coming together' or 'a balancing act' (p 79). The amalgamation Anzaldúa envisions here is partial, tenuous and otherwise devoid of the triumphalism associated with Hegelian dialectics: 'Every time she makes "sense" of something, she has to "cross over," kicking a hole out of old boundaries of the self and slipping under or over, dragging the old skin along, stumbling over it' (p 49). Nonetheless, by replacing 'ambivalence' with 'ambiguity', Anzaldúa allows for a resolution of ambivalence, a healing, even if only temporary, of the splitting.

Reconfiguring ambivalence: Nepantlera

Two decades after its initial publication, Anzaldúa co-edited a new version of her famous anthology, *this bridge we call home: radical visions for transformation*

(Anzaldúa and Keating, 2002).[4] As the revised title indicates, this compilation recasts bridging from a burden to shoulder to a space in which to reside, a place meriting the name 'home'. In the final chapter Anzaldúa introduces a new fluid figure, the Nepantlera. The Nepantlera represents a decisive development in Anzaldúa's understanding of ambivalence. Constructed rather like a self-help manual, the concluding essay outlines seven moments, without clarifying whether these are phases in thought, action, feeling or becoming. Anzaldúa often uses the word 'stages', but she also formulates these intervals in spatial terms and accentuates their multi-directionality. The most recurrent moment is *nepantla*, since it is both one of the seven as well as the place between them, a liminal position where opposing forces tug in different directions. Sometimes Anzaldúa likens nepantla to being 'suspended on the bridge' (Anzaldúa and Keating, 2002: 548); at other times, to being deep within a chasm that requires bridging (p 554); at still others, a birth canal (p 554). The multiple pathways and varying movements of the Nepantlera also vary temporally, defying linear chronology by continually oscillating in and out, like a Deleuzian folded force. 'All seven are present within each stage,' she specifies, 'and they occur concurrently, chronologically or not' (p 545).

Whereas Anzaldúa's account of Mestiza charted a teleological progression of expanding consciousness, Nepantlera undergoes a process characterized by simultaneity and rhizomatic 'zigzagging' (Anzaldúa and Keating, 2002: 545). More than the direction of movement distinguishes these two figures, however. The Nepantlera, she clarifies, evolves from consciousness to 'conocimiento' (from awareness to knowledge/understanding), and from intersectionality to interrelatedness.[5] Conocimiento emerges from accepting rather than resisting one's vulnerability; a willingness to remain open to being affected and to affecting in turn on numerous levels, by 'your surroundings, bodily sensations and responses, intuitive takes, emotional reactions to other people and theirs to you, and ... the images your imagination creates' (Anzaldúa and Keating, 2002: 542). In contrast to Mestiza who painfully labours to synthesize and create new narratives ('a dry birth, a breech birth, a screaming birth' (Anzaldúa,1987: 49)), Nepantlera knows there can be no definitive account and forsakes the goal of closure. The point is the process itself, the always-precarious and unending effort to stretch toward increasing inclusivity (Anzaldúa and Keating, 2002: 562). 'You realize that "home" is that bridge, the in-between place of nepantla and constant transition, the most unsafe of all spaces. You remove the old bridge from your back, and though afraid, allow diverse groups to collectively rebuild it' (p 574). Nepantlera, in other words, is another way to depict the precarity of ambivalence, to theorize being 'torn between ways' and in continuous transition (p 547).

Nepantlera initially finds the agonism of politics profoundly disorienting. Much like Mestiza, at first, she suffers from 'double vision'. Eventually, however, Nepantlera realizes that double vision can become 'doble saber (double knowledge)', a more capacious epistemological perspectivalism that allows her to stitch together, like 'Shelley's Frankenstein monster' (Anzaldúa and Keating, 2002: 549, 561), an assemblage of affiliations with others. Boundaries, borders, cracks, divisions and differences are no longer covered over, but instead 'serve as gateways' (p 561). Consciousness transforms into knowledge through engagement with others; intersectionality is not a subject position that one inhabits, but a relational practice.[6]

This Bridge We Call Home is not the first time Anzaldúa employed the concept of nepantla. It also appears in *Borderlands* (Anzaldúa, 1987). But in that text, nepantla designated a state experienced by Mestiza, not a persona in her own right (Anzaldúa, 1987: 78). When the Nepantlera emerges as the central character in place of the Mestiza, I suggest, Anzaldúa aims to theorize a different posture toward ambivalence. Recall that Mestiza also acquiesces to the painful echoes of misrecognition in her effort to work toward a similarly inclusive positioning (as does Shiva, 'that which is insulted I take as part of me' (Anzaldúa, 1983: 206)). Mestiza exposes herself to different, even antagonistic, views and ideas: 'She surrenders all notions of safety, of the familiar. Deconstruct, construct. She becomes Nahual, able to transform herself into a tree, a coyote, into another person' (Anzaldúa, 1987: 83). Ultimately, however, Mestiza blends, fuses, synthesizes and reconciles: 'Soy un amasamiento. I am an act of uniting and joining that not only has produced both a creature of darkness and creature of light, but also a creature that questions the definitions of light and dark and gives them new meaning' (p 81). Through an arduous process of kneading and massaging, Mestiza blends these differences into a unified whole; whereas the Nepantlera only sutures (like Dr Frankenstein) the precarious assemblage.

Ultimately, these figures represent divergent conceptions of sovereignty: Mestiza still strives for it, while Nepantlera accepts non-sovereignty. Unlike Anzaldúa's account of the Mestiza, moreover, which ends with returning to the Rio Grande Valley (Anzaldúa, 1987: 89–91); and, short of that, a plan to build a new home on whatever terrain she might lay claim to ('If going home is denied me then I will have to stand and claim my space, making a new culture—una cultura mestiza—with my own lumber, my own bricks and mortar, my own feminist architecture' (Anzaldúa, 1987: 22)), the Nepantlera has no final destination, certainly no stable base or territory. Nepantlera acutely feels the disquiet of ambivalence, but she commits herself to engaging in the process of political reparation rather than the pursuit of an idealized closure. She finds home in the diaspora (Anzaldúa and Keating, 2002: 574). Nepantla is ambivalence, a space in-between and a never-ending practice, a constantly moving process: 'its own space and ... [the] transition between each of the others' (p 546).

For Nepantlera, tarrying with ambivalence no longer occurs primarily as a cognitive endeavour ('consciousness'), nor is it about coping, as it was for Mestiza. It is rather the proposition that negative space enables the political. Nepantlera disavows the fixity of coherent identities or other forms of stability and imagined security. She moves beyond the Hegelian constitution of the subject, accepting that the world is fragmented and shifting in 'variations of intensities, assemblages set by affinities, and complex synchronizations' (Braidotti, 2012: 305). Nepantlera does not seek belonging or grounding (no need for lumber, bricks and mortar to make her home), but to engage in a process of becoming, a becoming with others through shared political struggle.

In-between politics

This chapter has argued that the figure of the Nepantlera represents Anzaldúa's proposition for how we might accept ambivalence and exercise it as a form of refusal – the in-between as a politics. As we have seen, the other figures of ambivalence, Shiva and Mestiza, reject or remake ambivalence 'into something else'. They serve as mediators engaged either in a balancing act or one of merging and submerging. Mestiza resides at the intersection of identities; she 'has gone from being the sacrificial goat to becoming the officiating priestess at the crossroad' (Anzaldúa, 1987: 80). Nepantlera, by contrast, exists in, works from and exposes the fissures. She does not attempt to ground herself in the centre but creates a home within the always-unstable in-betweens, unattached to any specificity, ethnic or otherwise. She endures ambivalence, occupies it, and uses it to transform all sides and herself. Her ambivalence manifests as 'nimble and strategic practices that undermine the categories of the dominant' (Campt, 2017: 32), thereby circumventing the trap of reactive resistance. A reparative impulse motivates Nepantlera, but it is not to restore the original, heal the splitting, resolve the differences, or curtail the motion. In this way, Anzaldúa suggests that political activism requires working with, not surmounting, inevitable ambivalence. The Nepantlera serves as an illustration of how we might accept fragmented multiplicity and, more importantly, how the tensions themselves can be politically productive.

This is an alternative conception of ambivalent activism, one tied to, instead of evading, precarity. Rather than conceiving of ambivalence as an attitudinal void obstructing political engagement, Anzaldúa envisions it as a critical, liminal affect generative of politics. Political ambivalence, so understood, is less about the presence of irreconcilable dividedness, or an absence of conviction, than an excess of intensely held, complex commitments and emotions. Polyvocal and polyvalent, it is the 'too-muchness' of ambivalence that makes it seem politically untenable to some.[7] But Nepantlera's multidimensionality, her multifarious feelings about the society that excludes and degrades her, compel rather than thwart her politics. It is the instability of ambivalence that opens the possibility for connecting with others and, more generally, for developing an awareness of how often political options are falsely circumscribed and dichotomized, pushing us into hierarchized Manichean either/or thinking in the search for certainty, stability, security and closure. She thus enacts a conception of non-sovereignty that seeks not to resolve contradictions, but to sustain them.

Anzaldúa's Nepantlera serves as a vital provocation encouraging activists to expand our thinking, to keep in view a broader field of social reality and holistic analysis, and to grapple with holding onto more than one 'truth' at a time by embracing the unruliness of abundant thoughts, feelings and coalition politics. Like Nepantlera, we might learn to adopt ever-changing positions that neither aspire to overcome ambivalence, nor fully embrace contingency, disruption and fragmentation. Instead, she invites us to think about them as conditions of possibility by providing a process-oriented account of both inner life and intersectional politics with a plurality of others. Through the figure of the Nepantlera, Anzaldúa reminds us that acting with ambivalence means accepting the precarity of ambivalence and of political struggle, as well the ambivalence of precarity.

Notes

1. A perceptive critique of the scholarship on political behaviour suggests that political scientists tend to conflate ambivalence and indifference. Yoo's study provides compelling evidence that ambivalence does not lead to action paralysis, while indifference does (Yoo, 2010).
2. This chapter draws from my previous work on Anzaldúa (Cole, 2017).
3. *Common Errors in English Usage* reports that English-speakers regularly confuse 'ambivalence' and 'ambiguous', likely due to the shared prefix (Brians, 2003). A similar conflation of *ambivalencia* and *ambiguedad* is not uncommon among Spanish-speakers.
4. Many of the original contributors to *This Bridge Called My Back* are included in *This Bridge We Call Home*, as well as trans, male and white writers. Such expansiveness was integral to Anzaldúa's project of reconceiving the politics of difference, also indicated by the change in the title from a possessive singular ('my') in the first *Bridge* to a collective pronoun ('we') in *Home*. 'Though most people self-define by what they exclude,' she explains in the preface, 'we define who we are by what we include – what I call the new tribalism' (Anzaldúa and Keating, 2002: 3).
5. When Anzaldúa first employs the term *conocimiento* in the opening lines, she includes a footnote on the etymology of the word from Latin, its meaning in Spanish (knowledge, skills), and her distinctive use of conocimiento to denote the impulse to act on what one knows (Anzaldúa and Keating, 2002: 577). But note that her English translation of conocimiento varies within the book and even within the 'now let us shift' chapter. At various junctures its meaning is 'understanding' (p 4), 'reflective consciousness' (p 542) or 'awareness' (p 545).
6. It is noteworthy that Anzaldúa's Nepantlera seems to anticipate Puar's (2012) criticisms of intersectionality by providing an alternative framing.
7. I am borrowing Bordo's (2003) conception of 'too-muchness', though she uses it in the context of explicating women's subordination.

References
Ahmed, S. (2017) *Living a Feminist Life*, Duke University Press.
Anzaldúa, G. (1983) 'La Prieta'. In C. Moraga and G. Anzaldúa (eds) *This Bridge Called My Back: Writings by Radical Women of Color*, 2nd edition, New York: Kitchen Table/Women of Color Press, pp 198–209.
Anzaldúa, G. (1987) *Borderlands/La Frontera: The New Mestiza*, Aunt Lute.
Anzaldúa, G. (2002) 'Preface: (Un)natural bridges, (Un)safe spaces'. In G. Anzaldúa and A.L. Keating (eds) *this bridge we call home: radical visions for transformation*, Routledge, pp 1–5.
Anzaldúa, G. and Keating, A.L. (eds) (2002) *this bridge we call home: radical visions for transformation*, Routledge.
Beretta, V., Alameda, L., Empson, L.A. and Tozzi, A.S. (2015) 'Ambivalence according to Bleuler: new trajectories for a forgotten symptom', *Psychotherapies*, 35(1): 5–19.
Berlant, L. (2011) 'Austerity, Precarity, Awkwardness'. *Presentation at the Annual Meeting of the American Anthropological Association*, Montreal, Canada, 15–20 November.
Bordo, S. (2003) *Unbearable Weight: Feminism, Western Culture, and the Body*, University of California Press.
Braidotti, R. (2012) *Nomadic Theory: The Portable Rosi Braidotti*, Columbia University Press.
Brians, P. (2003) *Common Errors in English Usage*, William, James & Co.
Brogaard, B. and Gatzia, D. (2020) '5 Kinds of Ambivalence That May Explain Why You Are Stuck', *Psychology Today* [online], 16 August. Available at: www.psychologytoday.com/us/blog/the-mysteries-love/202008/5-kinds-ambivalence-may-explain-why-you-are-stuck (accessed 28 January 2024).
Campt, T. (2017) *Listening to Images*, Duke University Press.
Cole, A. (2017) 'Precarious politics: Anzaldúa's reparative reworking', *Women's Studies Quarterly*, 45(3/4): 77–93.
Connell, S., Fien, J., Lee, J., Sykes, H. and Yencken, D. (1999) 'If it doesn't directly affect you, you don't think about it': a qualitative study of young people's environmental attitudes in two Australian cities', *Environmental Education Research*, 5(l): 95–113.
Emejulu, A. (2022) 'Ambivalence as Misfeeling, Ambivalence as Refusal', *Post45*, 27 October. Available at: https://post45.org/2022/10/ambivalence-as-misfeeling-ambivalence-as-refusal/ (accessed 28 January 2024).
Gainous, J., Martinez, M.D. and Craig, S.C. (2010) 'The Multiple Causes of Citizen Ambivalence: Attitudes about Social Welfare Policy', *Journal of Elections, Public Opinion and Parties*, 20(3): 335–356.
Gould, D. (2009) *Moving Politics: Emotion and ACT UP's Fight Against AIDS*, University of Chicago Press.

Hall, S. (1986) 'The problem of ideology: Marxism without Guarantees', *Journal of Communication Inquiry*, 10(2): 28–44.

Hoffer, E. (1951) *The True Believer: Thoughts on the Nature of Mass Movements*, HarperCollins.

Jaggar, A.M. (1989) 'Love and knowledge: Emotion in feminist epistemology'. *Inquiry*, 32(2): 151–176.

Jasper, J.M. (2011) 'Emotions and social movements: twenty years of theory and research', *Annual Review of Sociology*, 37: 285–303.

Lorde, A. (1981) 'The uses of anger', *Women's Studies Quarterly*, 9(3): 7–10.

McAdam, D., Tarrow, S. and Tilly, C. (2009) 'Comparative Perspectives on Contentious Politics'. In M.I. Lichbach and A.S. Zuckerman (eds) *Comparative Politics: Rationality, Culture, and Structure*, Cambridge University Press, pp 260–290.

Miller, J.M. and Peterson, D.M. (2004) 'Theoretical and empirical implications of attitude strength', *The Journal of Politics*, 66(3): 847–867.

Moraga, C. and Anzaldúa, G. (eds) (1983) *This Bridge Called My Back: Writings by Radical Women of Color* (2nd edition), SUNY Press.

Neilson, B. and Rossiter, N. (2008) 'Precarity as a political concept, or, Fordism as exception', *Theory, Culture & Society*, 25(7–8): 51–72.

Ngai, S. (2007) *Ugly Feelings*, Harvard University Press.

Oxford English Dictionary (OED) (2023) 'ambivalence (n.)', July [online]. Available at: https://doi.org/10.1093/OED/6723001131 (accessed 28 January 2024).

Puar, J.K. (2012) 'I would rather be a cyborg than a goddess: becoming-intersectional in assemblage theory', *philoSOPHIA*, 2(1): 49–66.

Sheth, F.A. (2022) *Unruly Women: Race, Neocolonialism, and the Hijab*, Oxford University Press.

Waite, L. (2009) 'A place and space for a critical geography of precarity?', *Geography Compass*, 3(1): 412–433.

Yoo, S.J. (2010) 'Two types of neutrality: ambivalence versus indifference and political participation', *The Journal of Politics*, 72(1): 163–177.

PART II

Activism as Ambivalent Praxis

5

An Activism of the In-between

Melody Howse

Dedicated to the work and memory of
Biplab Basu 1951–2024, rest in power.

Introduction

Things can fall apart in activist spaces; they start with such energy and fire but they can burn themselves out. This momentum is necessary, it brings together people, in turn changing minds and actions. But very few can sustain their engagement in activist organizations: to perpetually live in the fight is to feel constantly at war. It is exhausting. It causes pain and at times it clouds some of the beauty that exists within and outside of these spaces of opposition and change. There is a demand made of people who engage with activist practices in a sustained and long-term way that is not required of others. These activists are meant to be solid, unwavering, endless wells of energy, knowledge, time and money. Such expectations inevitably come at a price: the price of putting not just your body, but your mental and emotional health on the line. There is real risk in the work of activism with state surveillance and harassment by your political opponents, where not just yourself but your family and friends can be targets for violence. Some activists see these costs as just part of the job. You give your all for the cause. But what I want to think about here is, if we cannot necessarily protect ourselves from external risks, how do we stop using each other up in a cycle of burning out the people who are giving their time to support movements and organizations? How do we keep ourselves in one piece?

Akwugo Emejulu and Leah Bassel have written extensively about the practices that are prevalent within activist organizations (Emejulu and Bronstein, 2011; Emejulu and Bassel, 2021; Emejulu and Van der Scheer, 2022), including the way in which tiredness and exhaustion is a badge of honour we wear. It is a way to identify who is in it for real and who is in it for the optics. Are you tired? How tired? You are exhausted – then you are the real deal. Emejulu and Bassel (2021) named this kind of signalling the 'politics of exhaustion'. I paraphrase and oversimplify their detailed and insightful work, but the point remains, not only are we burning ourselves out, but we are also demanding that burn-out from others as a mark of their legitimacy. This is a capitalist mode of thinking, that if you are not working yourself to the bone, then you are not working hard enough, that you are worthless. It is a way of engagement that that does not benefit us. Our movements and organizations need to go the distance, they need to be more effective than as a vector of temporary change; they need to be a source of sustained pressure to actualize real and lasting change. I think here about the tireless work of activist organizations in Berlin making that sustained change such as 'Reach Out Berlin', 'Sudan uprising', or the work of International Women's★ Space (IWS★), and Women in Exile whose work never stops. It cannot because their goals are far bigger than any one individual and yet all of their work takes time, money, energy and commitment.

The need for dedication will not change in relation to most activist organizations. But I want to think around this idea of 'burning out' and consider how an in-between status, an ambivalent state of being in and out of activist organizations, where one engages with activist practices in a different way, could sustain not just organizations but individuals too. I am questioning the relationship between the sheer exhaustive physical and mental embodied state we call 'burn out' and the generative space of ambivalence. That space where one can dis/re-engage, where priorities are redefined by a different set of needs than merely coping with living under constant pressure. The realities of 'burn out' in organizing spaces brings me to a place of ambivalence where reconsidering and redefining how we organize and why we organize takes a different, more contemplative, slower and perhaps restrained form, one that is guarding the what is left of our energy as a practice of care, a tactical retreat and a pivot to a different, maybe temporary mode of engagement, but a mode of engagement that operates in the space of ambivalence. To riff off Bassel and Emejulu's (2021) 'Politics of Exhaustion' I am considering how a 'politics of the in-between' might be the modality of an ambivalent activism as a sustainable practice. To explore this further, I return to the point that got me thinking this way. Back to the place where things started to fall apart.

Impasse

This situation took place within a Black-led social justice organization in Berlin. But it is a familiar experience found in many organizations all over the city, if not all over the world. What is relevant is not the organization itself, but the challenges we faced and how that moved my thinking toward a different type of activist practice. I am imagining a practice that can help us step forward and back depending on needs, meaning not only the needs of organizations but of the individual. This is an idea that seems counter-intuitive to an activist practice where there is oftentimes a demand for selflessness. Many organizations fall victim to their own internal politics, but here was a situation that was both internally and externally complex. That meant in the end, many of my fellow activists and I had to watch as something that had taken years to build and grow, stalled and eventually crumbled. This ruination was not the fault of one factor, but a catalogue of issues that came together to create the perfect conditions to remove an organization from the Berlin activist scene. I say remove, as ultimately outside intervention was the death knell, but we were already stalling on our own.

Like all activist organizations, retention had been a perpetual problem, enticed by spectacular events and demonstrations, prospective members felt moved to join and offer their time and skills. There was a willingness that at times either was not utilized properly by us or was overly exploited because we had an unrealistic idea about what the work entailed. We live in the time of social media, and for some of our new members, the image of being an activist outweighed the realties. Some were surprised to learn that demonstrations were not as spontaneous as they appeared. It took more to mobilize people than a one-off Instagram story, tweet or Facebook post, although social media engagement is crucial to contemporary activist work. It took careful planning and considered action to make a protest space that was safe and inclusive. We had to pay attention to seemingly small but essential details, such as: registering the demonstration with the police, finding volunteer wardens, and then training them on not just safety issues, but how to de-escalate conflict, and what to do if a protester or someone from the organizing team got arrested. It takes logistics and contacts that we as organizers developed over years. But keeping people engaged outside of such spectacular event-based organizing would prove difficult, and in the end a core team emerged, a group of about five people doing the majority of the work. With so much labour falling on the shoulders of only a few, resentment and frustration grew, and people's commitment to the organization started to waiver.

There is a common misconception that often surrounds small organizations: they are imagined as much larger than they are and supposed as having funding to support and respond to all relevant causes and issues. This would be an ideal scenario, but the reality is that often these spaces are self-funded with members pouring their own money into events to ensure everything that is needed can be acquired. This expectation of small organizations is something that many have no other option than to try to live up to. It takes time to build trust with different community groups and to establish an organization. No one wants to let people down. This is an external pressure that small organizations must navigate, they need to stay current and responsive to fulfil their role in the community. But the time taken to do these unpaid and necessary jobs, to keep not only in contact with other organizations, but with the community while providing assistance and support, is work that goes unrecognized and unvalued by many people. The community needs help, and as an organization we were committed to providing that help, irrespective of the damage of constantly providing for others without considering our own care and well-being.

This requirement to find a way to get work done regardless of your own situation extended to everyone, including those in unofficial positions of leadership, those few who were the glue that kept things going, and who shouldered a much heavier burden than many understood. Putting themselves under pressure, putting their own health at risk and their bodies on the line, becoming an unintentional example of how to employ practices that sidelined their own needs. Inside these organizations this is just sometimes how it is, work needs to be done by whoever is willing to do it. But when issues arise it is the structure of that organization and its ability to resolve conflict and to adapt to the changing landscape that predicates whether it will survive or fail. Inside many activist spaces there has been a backlash against hierarchies. Jo Freeman (1971) famously wrote on this topic in 'The Tyranny of Structurelessness' in relation to the American Women's Liberation Movement of the 1970s. People want to work with and not for one another and so the emergence of flat hierarchies have become a norm. In my experience, these are utopian ideals – aspirational and admirable but, in reality, very difficult to put into practice. Flat hierarchies, in fact, as Freeman noted, do not necessarily serve us well in times of trouble. While I applaud the desire to redistribute power and the refusal to reproduce capitalist structures within many activist organizations, these flat hierarchies require consensus, and I learned that calls for 'consensus' could be weaponized for people's personal agendas. Consensus became a roadblock that would eventually defeat us.

Dependencies

The potentially negative dimensions of maintaining a flat organizational structure revealed themselves at a time when we were already overworked, when many of us needed a break to recharge after months of intense activity. Although social media can promote unrealistic expectations and impressions, nonetheless, it provides critical channels through which activist organizations plan and share information. Without the affordances of social media platforms, many of our most important contemporary social movements would have been hampered, some may have never got off the ground. Therefore, we had been steadily building an online community and had established a Facebook page that was constantly updated, serving the needs not only of our organization, but many other Black-led organizations in the city, forming an information bridge between many of the city's disparate activist groups and initiatives. The page became a central hub of information and exchange that had taken dedication, time, care and attention to establish. Part of the reason our Facebook page became such an important point of exchange between activists in the city was because of its shareable resources, such as ethical community guidelines we developed for posting. We offered guidance on (1) how to deal with trolls and hate speech which constantly slid into our inbox and as replies on posts; (2) how to respond to triggering situations, such as instances of police violence, with compassion and care; (3) opensource resources for how to organize demonstrations safely; (4) resources informing people of their rights when dealing with the police; and (5) how to safely film the police. Our digital community was vital to us, it was our eyes and ears, and the place where people could easily find us.

One morning that changed, when logging into the admin page, I suddenly found I could not get past the login stage. Instead, there was an error message stating that the page had been suspended as it contravened Facebook's policies. There was a flurry of phone calls between the admins, no one could log in and no one had prior warning of the page suspension. It was a moment of paralysis that exposed underlying issues and tensions. In her book *Twitter and Tear Gas: The Power and the Fragility of Networked Protest* (2019: xix), Zeynep Tufekci talks about the practices and trajectories of modern protest, how digital connectivity has the capacity to reshape 'how movements connect, organize and evolve during their lifespan'. Until now, we had mostly had positive experiences with Facebook and had come to rely on this communication channel. However, here we were, faced with a situation that on reflection we should have seen coming. Facebook has a so-called 'real name policy'. (Perhaps from your own experience on the platform you will know that this policy is loosely enforced.) As a platform, it relies on community enforcement, meaning that someone must flag the name as being 'not real' and then a process of verification begins, in the meantime the page is blocked from activity. We were aware that some right-wing extremist groups and individuals considered our organization as a hate group, some going as far as to refer to it as a terrorist organization.

These claims are, of course, unfounded; supporting the Black community and challenging structural violence did not make our organization any such thing. But global tech corporations must respond to such accusations with action. It did not matter that this online trolling had been directed at the organization since its inception, or that there were people who administered these pages who faced a daily onslaught of online abuse from accounts that rarely saw any repercussions for their actions. Being in a visible role for an organization that some find divisive can be hazardous. To do this task is to make yourself vulnerable, therefore as admins of the Facebook page we had not given our real names as a matter of safety. There had been previous experiences of people being doxed and physically harassed by strangers who had found their home addresses using their real name online. To name oneself publicly online was to open oneself up to potential danger and it would not just be ourselves that we were exposing but also our families. Therefore, the choice to use well-established social media handles that could be verified through our social media footprint became a solution to the 'real name' problem. Anyone wanting to verify if any of us were real or not, just had to perform a simple search and there were a slew of posts and connections that could easily be traced showing personal interactions. But this would ultimately be our downfall; someone unknown to us and with no warning had flagged us to Facebook, and our lack of 'real names' meant that the platform had a 'legitimate' reason to suspend our page. We had had our organizational head cut off, and in the 'attention economy' (Tufekci, 2019) that is something that needed to be remedied quickly. Contact with Facebook proved unfruitful, no one was ever able to get past standard replies and with no funds or lawyers to contest the decision, we had to make a choice about what to do next.

Such a decision needs to be a collective one; that, at least, is the rationale of a non-hierarchical organization. It might have made more sense for the administrators of the page to mobilize other social media streams and jump from one platform to another, alerting everyone to what had happened and to rally support. Instead, we found ourselves in an endless cycle of committee meetings, where no decision on the future of the group ever materialized. There always seemed to be one person missing, one voice that we had to consider and who, seemingly, we could not make a decision without. This became about the needs and requirements of a few, a way to hold power over the future of the organization even if unintended. A blind adherence to consensus as an ideal, no matter the consequence, because 'no other means could possibly be anything but oppressive' (Freeman, 1971: 1). In the end this indecision became an insurmountable roadblock and a way to disable our part in a movement. What had been instigated by a random individual, was ultimately destroyed by an inability to accept leadership in a moment of crisis.

Activism of the in-between

Such an impasse created frustration: how could we move forward, adapt and respond if we could not agree on how to do it. It felt like a war of attrition, and I wondered why we could not get past it, what was standing in our way other than a desire not to upset the balance of the group? According to Freeman (1971: 2):

structurelessness becomes a way of masking power ... as long as the structure of the group is informal, the rules of how decisions are made are known only to a few and awareness of power is limited to those who know the rules. Those who do not know the rules and are not chosen for initiation must remain in confusion, or suffer from paranoid delusions that something is happening of which they are not quite aware.

This statement from more than 50 years ago resonates with what we were experiencing. In the end, a few of us who had been working together for years and who all felt similarly about our need to try a different tack at this moment of deadlock walked away. We could, of course, regroup and start again, but we were tired and a little disillusioned.

It was an experience that made me reconsider how I would engage in activist spaces in the future. To do that, I looked to those who have managed to sustain their engagement over years in these spaces and have avoided burning themselves out in the process. Collective and self-care are non-negotiable factors I have come to value in activism. There is often a well-intentioned discourse about the importance of care in activist spaces, but the reality is that the work can be gruelling, and caring for ourselves and each other is the first thing to be cast aside in the endless pursuit of getting the work done. We are all guilty at times of ignoring our own and others' needs to meet a deadline or to respond to a situation. But this care and attention toward yourself and your needs is something I have learned must be guarded; you are no use to anyone when you are depleted. Taking time out of these activist spaces is essential to remind you why they are necessary, and to see the impact they can have on the wider community, something often obscured when you are consumed by the daily grind of organizational dynamics.

Through this experience, a politics of the 'in-between' has emerged for me; I have learned to shift and drift between spaces, to pull back and recharge. It is a practice that is mindful of what sometimes must occur for change to happen and recognizes how tensions and conflicts of interest that inevitably occur can create new openings. In such moments the only answer is the pause, that breath that is protective as well as regenerative. It is a practice that I have honed over the past few years and makes me rethink what activism is. It is essential to question what activism is and who activists are. I invite a widening of the concept of 'activism', as well as our understanding of the people who do 'activist' work. I am advocating for the unseen labourers to countless causes and movements. I am also advocating for those who take any and all opportunity to make and affect change even on a small scale. For me an activist practice now looks like the books I choose to put on a syllabus, the discussions I start in the classroom as well as the more practical work of being a community researcher, which can mean providing research support for a policy paper or grant-writing skills for an organization. It is a practice that is accountable but not over committed. This has meant having the capacity to both step forward and pull back depending on the situation and the position in which I find myself. This might seem contradictory, we know that organizations do not run on whim, but on the energy and the hard work of dedicated individuals. But this ambivalent approach to activist practice has its place, and perhaps at least for me at this present moment, it is the only sustainable practice that I have.

In pursuing a practice such as this, that is in and out of place, shifting between roles and expectations, there is much to lose and much to gain. You lose the close-knittedness of working with a dedicated group over a long period of time, those deep connections that make you feel as if anything is possible if we just keep going. But conversely, I gain the space to be realistic about what I can offer and what capacities I have. I get to prioritize differently so that I can reclaim my health that, over time, has deteriorated due to my dogged neglect of myself in service of others. Activist spaces have their own problems as I have illustrated, but they are necessary and without them we would all be worse off. They are also tiring spaces – it is emotional and physical work – where this expectation to live, breathe and sleep 'the cause' can be the very thing that turns away those we desperately need to sustain our collective ambitions and work for a new world.

Ambivalent futures

An activism of the in-between, and an advocacy of an ambivalent activism, is a call for a more human approach to how we treat each other in activist spaces. We cannot always give our all, as in the end there will be nothing left to give. Ideals and goals are essential for how we imagine the future, but at the same time without being able to adapt to situations we find ourselves in, moments that could be easily navigated become insurmountable due to utopian social relations and unrealistic organizational structures. I am not necessarily advocating for traditional top-down leadership in these spaces, but in times of crisis we have to look to each other to find the solution and be open to taking risks, as the bigger risk is apathy and frustration where, in the end, we all lose. This perhaps is also a call for flexibility; these ideal structures work at the best of times, but we need to be open to changing our approach at the worst of times.

In relation to the burn-out that so many face and the expectations put on those who are tirelessly running and contributing to organizations, we need to make more room for activists to recharge, to allow space for ambivalence as a regenerative practice and not see it as a lack of commitment. There must be a different understanding that allows people to step forward and pull back depending on capacities and situation without such movement being perceived by comrades as abandonment. Such judgemental thinking stops people returning to these spaces when they feel ready to re-engage. I am conscious that this call for flexibility runs counter to organizational needs, where the formation and role of a core group is a way to maintain continuity, focus and knowledge that has been amassed over time. However, this dedicated core that is the fire which provides the steam on which a movement runs, can itself be extinguished, if we do not care for those doing this work. By this I mean not to disavow the role of such dedicated activity, but to reiterate that even those at that centre must be allowed to step back to recharge. If not, the price can be fatal; we have lost too many people who have dedicated their lives to fighting injustice, through the sheer toll – physical, psychological and emotional – that this work can take. I think here of the gaping hole left by the recent passing of my friend, mentor and community leader Biplab Basu in Berlin.

Therefore, changing how we consider these roles is essential if we really want to care for one another. It begs the questions: how could an activist organization look if centralized knowledge could be shared? How can we maintain that necessary continuity of skills and participation without requiring self-sacrifice? One answer that a fellow activist suggested is a temporal solution, asking for commitment for a limited time, so as not to reach the point of burn-out, as well as the rotation of roles that require sustained commitment among a larger group. Thereby, both sharing knowledge and skills while creating the flexibility to prevent an individual or group from carrying the organizational burden alone. No doubt, every organization will have its own answers to these questions, but perhaps what is fundamentally needed is a shift in thinking. Within any proposed solution, flexibility must be inherent since circumstances change. Organizations need to build in resilience to account for these inevitable and unpredictable changes, instead of adhering to rigid ideals that can inadvertently do us a disservice.

Thankfully, some organizations are already embracing ambivalent activism, making room for different types of engagement that takes seriously the differing capacities of activists. By changing how we conceive of activism and what we expect from those who contribute, it is possible to create the psychological security needed to know that if it is too much then one can walk away, while at the same time inviting those who can participate to do so on terms that are sustainable for them. This, then, is a call for a more sustainable activist practice, a 'care-full' practice that does not require the sacrifice of individuals in which we do more harm to each other than the injustices we are fighting. Care must look like something different; it needs to reflect the real and changing needs of individuals and in doing so we can create wider and stronger networks that we can all call on in times of need.

References

Emejulu, A. and Bronstein, A. (2011) 'The politics of everyday life: feminisms and contemporary community development', *Community Development Journal*, 46(3): 283–287.

Emejulu, A. and Bassel, L. (2021) 'The politics of exhaustion', *City*, 24(1–2): 400–406.

Emejulu, A. and van der Scheer, I. (2022) 'Refusing politics as usual: mapping women of colour's radical praxis in London and Amsterdam', *Identities*, 29(1): 9–26.

Freeman, J. (aka Joreen) (1971) 'The tyranny of structurelessness', Available online: https://www.jofreeman.com/joreen/tyranny.htm (last accessed 18 April 2025).

Tufekci, Z. (2017) *Twitter and Tear Gas: The Power and Fragility of Networked Protest*. New Haven, CT: Yale University Press.

6

Resisting with People I Do Not Like: Exploring the Internal Tensions Among Queer Activists in Lagos, Nigeria

Adebayo Quadry-Adekanbi

Introduction

When I began researching queer activism in Lagos, the last thing I expected to find was a complex dynamic of interpersonal conflicts between various activists. What struck me as particularly noteworthy was that I, as a researcher, also found myself getting drawn into these conflicts and developing what I perceived as negative emotions toward some Lagos queer activists. I felt inconvenienced by them. I felt frustrated and stymied in my interactions with them. My feelings of inconvenience toward these activists does not mean I dislike them as individuals. Many of them have proven to be remarkably amiable, at least on a surface level. Rather, my ambivalence toward them was more about the personas they constructed for themselves vis-á-vis their personal politics within queer activist spaces. I noted the contradiction between what they said and what they did. The stark differences between how they portrayed themselves on social media and their problematic behaviours in the queer activist spaces in the city. Despite these contradictions, many of these activists have done and continue to do important and influential work, particularly within a context of institutionalized queerphobia and violence.

As I explored various spaces within queer activism in Lagos, I began to experience ambivalence. Rothman et al (2017: 33) define ambivalence as 'the simultaneous experience of positive and negative emotional or cognitive orientations toward a person, situation, object, task, goal, or idea and the feelings of tension and conflict that result'. This ambivalence emerged as a complex and confusing feeling for me because I recognized the importance of the work being done, yet found myself uncomfortable with how it was being carried out. I gradually began to understand the roots of this ambivalence – it stems, at least in part, from the reality that many activists do not actually like each other, or rather, they *believe* that they do not, and do not always recognize that this is a consequence of their realities, and is almost inevitable. Activists are often forced into community with people they do not agree with, or with whom they share personal conflicts and tensions, simply because the urgent nature of queer activism supposedly requires *collective action*. As a result, they are compelled to navigate this ambivalence to get the work done.

However, I argue that the issue goes beyond mere interpersonal dislike; it is fundamentally rooted in the experience of *inconvenience*. Activists are inconvenienced by one another, by themselves, and by the broader context in which their queerness exists. Berlant (2022) discusses inconvenience as a fundamental aspect of coexistence, requiring people to adjust to the presence of others and to the world. Berlant conceptualizes inconvenience as a force that prompts subtle shifts in how people process their surroundings, often manifesting through fleeting micro-incidents, such as glances, physical contact or heightened sensory awareness of sharing a space with others. Inconvenience is not limited to external events; it can also emerge internally, triggered by affective responses to thoughts or memories. It evokes a range of emotions: irritation, discomfort, enjoyment or indifference, and shapes how people interact, negotiate relationships and navigate social hierarchies. In this way, inconvenience is ordinary and pervasive, and highlights the constant adjustments people must make in response to their environments.

Within the queer activist community in Lagos, inconvenience operates on multiple levels. Activists are inconvenienced by the state, which punishes and marginalizes them, and by a world that dismisses or relegates queer African perspectives. They are also inconvenienced by themselves – by the internalized pressures of self-surveillance and the weight of navigating their queerness in an oppressive context. Finally, they are inconvenienced by each other, as they contend with tensions, conflicts and personal grievances within the shared spaces of activism. This layered inconvenience gives rise to feelings of tension, conflict and, ultimately, ambivalence – an ambivalence that becomes an inescapable condition of their work.

This chapter aims to explore the ambivalences that exist due to the queer Nigerian activist community being inconvenienced by each other. I argue that activists find themselves constrained by structural inequalities that compel many to prioritize their individual well-being over collective interests and needs which, in turn, hinders solidarity and creates a messy dynamic of inconvenience and tension. Rather than seeking to resolve this messiness, I argue that these ambivalences are an essential part of queer activism in the city, and that we should not seek to resolve these feelings of inconvenience but instead consider what this emotion signals about the social relations in queer spaces. As Berlant (2022: 2) highlights: 'Mostly, people are inconvenient, which is to say that they have to be dealt with. "They" includes you.' Essentially, we are all in it. Berlant notes that inconvenience is a mutual experience: just as we find others inconvenient, they also find us inconvenient.

During my time in Lagos, an activist expressed feeling disliked by me, which gave me pause. Despite my genuine regard for them, the expression of my inconvenience toward their actions created an impression that I did not like them. Reflecting on this, I began to scrutinize my interactions with other activists. How many others perceive my expressions of inconvenience as personal dislike? How many were inconvenienced by my interactions with them as a researcher in this space? Recognizing the inconveniences caused by others helps us understand the dynamics of our relationships. Acknowledging these inconveniences requires us to shift our attention and reorganize ourselves. In this chapter, I argue that embracing the ambivalent feelings of inconvenience can spark a process of reflection that can help activists understand our boundaries, vulnerabilities and ways of relating to others. Engaging with ambivalence can foster empathy, resilience and a deeper understanding of ourselves and others.

Context: queer activism and institutionalized queerphobia in Nigeria

Queer activism in Nigeria takes shape amid state-sponsored violence against queer people. Legislative measures contributing to the criminalization of queer people encompass statutes such as the Criminal Code Act, the Penal Code and the Sharia Penal Code, each operating within distinct regional contexts in Nigeria (Arimoro, 2018). The Criminal Code Act, applicable in southern states, proscribes acts deemed 'against the order of nature', with punitive measures including imprisonment. Similarly, the Penal Code delineates offences such as cross-dressing and non-heteronormative conduct, with penalties ranging from imprisonment to fines. The Sharia Penal Code, adopted by select northern states, imposes severe punishments, including stoning to death, for acts classified as 'sodomy' or lesbianism.

The Same Sex Marriage Prohibition Act 2014 (SSMPA) stands out for its draconian measures. Reflecting the British colonial legacy, the SSMPA defines marriage in a manner reminiscent of Lord Penzance's formulation (*Hyde v Hyde*, 1886, LRIP and D, 130), underscoring the enduring colonial influence of historical legal paradigms. At the heart of the SSMPA lies a comprehensive proscription of same-sex unions and related activities. Provisions within the act criminalize not only same-sex marriages but also the establishment and operation of LGBTQ+ organizations and clubs. Punishments prescribed by the SSMPA include lengthy terms of imprisonment, up to 14 years, highlighting the punitive stance adopted toward queer people by Nigerian authorities.

These legal frameworks delineate societal norms and boundaries, shaping people's identities and interactions. The state-sanctioned discrimination against queer Nigerians perpetuates a cycle of marginalization and violence, both institutionally and within society at large. Queer people are compelled to engage in self-surveillance and regulation, often effectively internalizing the norms dictated by governing bodies (Bacchi, 2009). This phenomenon underscores the subtle yet pervasive influence of dominant ideologies on people's behaviour and societal dynamics. Consequently, queer people are subjected to heightened vulnerability, with instances of violence against queer people often going unreported, and often encouraged, due to the explicit endorsement of such actions by the state. Recent incidents, such as the mass arrest of 57 people at a party in Egbeda, Lagos, under the pretext of disrupting a 'homosexual initiation', underscore the pernicious effects of these legal frameworks on the lived experiences of queer communities (The Initiative for Equal Rights, 2020).

Social attitudes, deeply rooted in conservative religious and cultural beliefs, also contribute significantly to the challenges faced by queer people. The stigma and discrimination amplify the urgency of activism while simultaneously creating fault lines within the movement. Queer activists must contend with trying to escape oppression while experiencing internal dissent arising from differing perceptions of how to confront the oppression they experience in their milieu. While the harmful environment compels them to unite against a common adversary, this shared struggle becomes a double-edged sword, simultaneously forging solidarity but also highlighting internal schisms.

Methodology

This chapter is grounded in my empirical research conducted for over a year between October 2022 and December 2023. I used a combination of semi-structured interviews and participatory observation methods within the dynamic context of queer communities in Lagos, Nigeria. During this time, I engaged with various spaces in Lagos that queer activists occupy. I spoke to members of non-governmental organizations (NGOs) that serve queer people and observed their programming and activities. I interviewed 20 people through semi-structured interviews and conducted two focus group discussions with an average of three to four people. I formally engaged with 27 people through interviews and many others through informal conversations during participatory observations and navigating spaces in Lagos. The participatory observations took me from various queer-centred events and parties to spaces queer people occupy that were not necessarily labelled as queer. I walked the streets of Lagos with queer people to understand how they navigated these spaces, and I worked with various queer-centred organizations on their programming, to get an insider perspective on the activities that they engaged in.

Using participatory and group observation strategies allowed an immersive understanding of activists' behaviours and actions (Arksey and Knight, 1999). Semi-structured interviews with the activists facilitated an in-depth exploration of the observations, avoiding preconceived assumptions and ensuring a nuanced comprehension of the participants' perspectives (Arksey and Knight, 1999; Naples and Sachs, 2000). The triangulation of participatory observation and semi-structured interviews enhanced the robustness of the study, offering a comprehensive and multidimensional analysis of the experiences and actions of activists in Lagos.

The participatory observation allowed me, as a queer, Yoruba, Nigerian researcher, to navigate the dual position of insider and outsider (Ellis et al, 2011). While my positionality offered an intimate understanding of the context, the interviews were conducted to extend findings beyond my subjective experiences. Ethnography complemented this by broadening the scope to include the practices, values and beliefs of queer people. These observations and interactive interviews, often occurring within established relationships (Adams, 2008), encouraged collaborative and meaningful dialogue on sensitive topics, while group interviews highlighted shared and conflicting perspectives within the community (Merton et al, 1990). These methods allowed a nuanced understanding of the multiplicities and social realities of queer people.

Ethical considerations and positionality were integral to the research process. Recognizing the risk of reductive portrayals, participants were engaged as co-producers of knowledge to affirm their agency and ensure representation of their realities (Walford, 2007). This approach not only mitigated the risk of data extraction but also framed the research as a socially conscious act that amplifies silenced experiences, encourages empathy and challenges traditional research paradigms. Relational ethical considerations have also encouraged maintaining full anonymity for all participants, and a removal of all identifiable data points.

On the inconvenience of queer activists

Tensions among activists are undeniable (Eschle, 2001). Ambivalence, then, is an inescapable part of activism. Berlant (2022) explores how inconvenience in relationships is a key part of living together, requiring people to adapt to others and their environment. Inconvenience is an 'affective sense of the familiar friction of being in relation' (Berlant, 2022: 2). In this context, it refers to the challenges and tensions that arise when working with people one may not like or agree with. Among queer activists in Lagos, this could be anything from classism to transphobia. Berlant stresses that humans are always connected to others and their environment, meaning they must continually adapt and react to what is happening around them. Queer activists in Nigeria are not simply inconvenienced by the legal impediments to queer rights that they are fighting against, and the sociopolitical milieu of Nigeria, but they are also contending with inconveniences that they experience from being among each other in a space of inconvenience, insecurity and precarity. These are the ambivalent conditions to which they must adapt.

The ability to navigate these inconveniences requires accepting them as an inevitable part of activist life. Embracing inconvenience means acknowledging and engaging with differences, disagreements and unresolved tensions within the activist community. Navigating interpersonal dynamics and collective action within Lagos' queer activist scene needs to confront the discomfort and ambivalences that exist and see these inconveniences as opportunities for growth and collective action. As Berlant (2022: 8) argues:

> If there is an inconvenience drive, can consciousness of it become a resource for building solidarity and alliance across ambivalence, rather than appearing mainly as the negative sandpaper of sociality? Is it possible to turn ambivalence from the atmosphere of negativity it currently brings with it into a genuinely conflicted experience that allows us to face up to the phenomenality of self-disturbance in the space of coexistence and even the desire to let in particular objects, or to protect them once they've gotten under the skin?

Ultimately, navigating inconvenience recognizes and prioritizes common goals of social change while acknowledging and addressing interpersonal tensions within the queer activist community in Lagos. By recognizing the complexity of human relationships in activism, activists are encouraged to approach disagreements with openness and dialogue. By doing so, they contribute to a more inclusive and effective activist scene in Lagos, fostering solidarity and collaboration despite personal conflicts.

Taking the inconvenience and ambivalence seriously is not a theoretical concern for activists since these dynamics have very real effects. For example, a queer activist I spoke to, who was seeking support for a project, refused to collaborate with another activist who would have been in a great position to help them due to past conflicts. Similarly, another activist, working on a project that could benefit from multiple resources and perspectives, felt unable to seek support from fellow activists due to perceived animosity.

These unresolved and unacknowledged conflicts hinder the potential for dialogue and openness that could encourage a unified approach and resource pooling. These unresolved tensions make tasks and organizing unnecessarily complicated, and often ineffective.

Despite the inevitability of tensions, ignoring them is counterproductive. As Eschle (2001: 74) mentions: 'Oppression and conflict within civil society and between social movement actors cannot simply be wished away or ignored, and neglect of this issue represents a central failing of post-Marxist versions of civil society.' It is important to critically analyse why activists do not get along, how it impacts the advocacy, and the systemic factors contributing to them not getting along. Schulman (2016) advocates for a proactive approach among communities, wherein mutual accountability, constructive questioning and intervention facilitate open dialogue during disagreements (Fischer, 2020). It is within these thoughts I situate this chapter.

The sources of inconvenience

As I looked closer into this issue of inconvenience among queer activists in Lagos, I discovered that this problem manifests in two related ways: on institutional and individual levels. On an institutional level, inconveniences rear their heads when considering the structure of queer activism in Lagos, particularly within the framework of NGOs. Despite activists' intentions, the dynamics of state-sponsored oppression combined with the constrained organizational structures in which they are enmeshed mean that activists are overly concerned with the maintenance and sustainability of NGOs, such as applying for funding and ensuring their own and their organizations' survival, which crowds out the time commitments to the cause they started out to fight against. These organizational dynamics breed competition and conflict between activists and negatively impact trust and solidarity (Bassel and Emejulu, 2017).

Munshi and Willse (2017) mention that a difference need to be made between the people themselves and the institutions they exist within. Of course, institutions influence what people do, but they do not change the inconveniences caused by people's actions. Moreover, some of these activists and the consequences of their actions go beyond the institution and seep into broader activist milieu. I especially critique individuals alongside institutions because individuals often distance themselves from the problems they aim to solve, lacking self-awareness and accountability of their participation in the problem. They use the institution as a shield to justify their actions, often unaware of their power and agency. Therefore, it is important to highlight how deeply embedded the inconveniences of the institution are in individual actions. This will encourage a shift from institutions to what Berlant (2022) describes as *infrastructure*, where the individual can coexist with tensions and conflict without sacrificing a common and unified front. I will explore this later in the chapter.

The institutional: NGOs vs solidarity

Unpacking contemporary queer activism in Lagos requires an exploration of the 'NGOization' of activism. NGOization refers to the 'institutionalisation, professionalisation, depoliticisation and demobilisation of movements for social and environmental change' (Choudry and Kapoor, 2013: 1). This is characterized by grassroots movements, rooted initially in community-based initiatives and solidarity, evolving into formalized NGOs to secure external funding and institutional legitimacy and recognition from political actors (Paternotte, 2016). While this funding and institutional recognition can be important for sustaining activism and achieving goals, it introduces tensions between the movement's grassroots origins and the bureaucratic demands imposed by neoliberal formal NGO structures (Alvarez, 2009). This NGOization dramatically restructures how activism is organized, financed and perceived, particularly in the context of queer activism amid state-sponsored violence. NGOs are often viewed as expressions of community interests, conduits for community support, and they attract financial and labour contributions in the name of communal welfare. Queer activists in Lagos commonly engage with NGOs as their first foray into activism, emphasizing these organizations' pivotal role in community representation and power.

Critiques of NGOs in Lagos are important, considering how NGOs often serve 'to displace, destroy or neutralise social movements fighting for economic and social injustice throughout the Third World' (Choudry and Kapoor, 2013: 5). Capitalist interests and state co-optation of non-profits, too, often steer activists toward professionalization and individual career achievements rather than mass-based movements for radical social change (Smith, 2017). Additionally, the lure of funding prompts some social movements organizations and networks to mirror and reproduce capitalist structures rather than confront them. NGO professionals use 'knowledge to restructure collective non-capitalist forms of organisation into hierarchical strata, detaching them from the movements they originate in and connecting them to the relations of ruling' (Smith, 1987: 216–217).

Considering that queer people face legal, social and political barriers to their existence in Nigeria, NGOs serving them are often dependent on overseas funding, particularly from Western governments and philanthropists. As such, their programmes prioritize the interests of overseas donors rather than those of local communities. In Lagos, activists mention that they feel compelled to align their work with the criteria, interests and metrics of Western funding bodies, limiting their flexibility to address local issues and the diverse spectrum of queer identities and needs. Various queer people I interviewed mentioned being turned away from receiving support from NGOs because they do not meet the funding criteria – criteria often set by Western funding bodies. As such, the NGOization of activism contributes to a narrower, externally imposed vision of what queer activism in Lagos is and could be.

The NGOization of activism is further exacerbated by activists opting to become paid employees, assuming roles as 'professional' community representatives with the prospect of receiving financial remuneration. As Choudry and Kapoor (2013) mention, 'professional staffers tend to represent their organisations in public as spokespeople, at negotiating tables, and in partnership structures, whereas they could instead support mobilisation on the ground, and help movement activists to develop leadership skills and represent their movements as they see fit'. This promotes the idea of treating social justice organizing like a career, implying that one should only engage if there is pay involved (Smith, 2017). An activist I spoke to mentioned being upset with queer people and other activists because they do not feel like the work they do is appreciated. They mention how they are beginning to transition their 'activism career' into a 'pleasure activism' that prioritizes themselves and immediate communities in ways that allow them to reap the rewards of their work. This logic ignores the fact that mass movements depend on the participation of a dedicated cadre of activists who may not receive payment (Smith, 2017) nor see the fruits of their labour in their lifetimes. Adopting a careerist approach to activism means relying on a few people to do the work of many, which is unsustainable.

This tricky terrain for activists is made more complex by the high unemployment rate in Nigeria, particularly among young people, as the labour market struggles to accommodate them (Salami, 2013; Adelowokan et al, 2019). In 2020, Nigeria's national unemployment rate was 33.3 per cent, while Lagos has an unemployment rate of 37.1 per cent (National Bureau of Statistics, 2022). Additionally, 63 per cent of Nigerians, or 133 million people, face multidimensional poverty, which impacts access to education, healthcare, adequate housing and a life free from violence. With high levels of poverty and unemployment, NGO activism is a gateway to an improved quality of life as it provides a career path and an opportunity to ascend the socio-economic ladder. This activism reflects a desire to achieve upward social mobility regardless of whether it is beneficial to the 'community'.

Numerous new NGOs are emerging in Lagos, supposedly serving queer people, as activists-cum-professionals aim to legitimize their self-appointed roles and pursue their careers. Every few months, an activist shares a 'life update', urging people to follow the social media pages of newly established organizations, of ambiguous origins, focusing on queer liberation, healthcare provision and advancing rights, yet lacking clear aims and actionable steps for achieving these goals. This ambiguity often persists to facilitate flexibility in applying for funding and supporting individual career ambitions.

The individual: 'life update!'

The tensions between queer activists often begin with a substantial change in lifestyle among a few individuals upon entering the NGO space. Many former activists move to the Island (the financial and cultural hub of Lagos, including many affluent neighbourhoods), begin patronizing high-end establishments and become friends with socialites and people in positions of power. Numerous activists face allegations of neglecting the issues they claim to care about once they attain a certain level of comfort and security through their NGO work. Whether relocating to prosperous neighbourhoods, gaining the ability to migrate to Western countries or securing lucrative employment, they are accused of prioritizing personal well-being over the various pressing needs of the queer community that they initially sought to serve.

While this shift to affluent and supposedly safer spaces can be understood as an attempt to access a certain degree of safety their newly found class position can provide, most of their subsequent work remains concentrated in this purportedly safe, upper-middle class, exclusionary space. Consequently, these activists cease to advocate for the safety and survival of *all* queer people wherever they live in the city. Activists begin to centre their new neighbourhoods, exclusively serving those who can access their newly established 'safe space'. For instance, a substantial number of events targeting queer people by NGOs and activists in Lagos occur on the Island, particularly in areas such as Ikoyi, Victoria Island or Lekki. These events often happen at consulates, diplomatic buildings, gated high-rise estates or expensive restaurants, where access is restricted, logistically challenging, or expensive for Mainland and/or working-class attendees. Many newly formed NGOs purportedly supporting all queer people also operate exclusively in these areas under the guise of safety and security. Implicit in this conversation is the understanding that safety is contingent upon the class position of these spaces, and what activists on the Island avoid acknowledging is their implicit endorsement of the classist politics that make these supposedly safe spaces safe in the first place.

Queer activists frequently rationalize their actions by emphasizing their marginalization, suffering, and their need to 'survive'. Choudry and Kapoor (2013) mention: 'The dominant notion of "civil society" emphasises rights of individuals to pursue their self-interest rather than collective rights and upholds the interests of states and capital.' They use the issues that poor queer Nigerians face to access funding and resources but then only support the most privileged queer people in the city by concentrating their work in the most affluent neighbourhoods.

This model fosters a culture of competition over collaboration and solidarity (Smith, 2017). This competition leads to the incessant need to be the 'first' to do something, whether that means erasing past efforts or perpetuating voyeuristic and simplistic portrayals of non-Western homophobia. Nowhere is this more evident than in the way Nigeria has celebrated Pride for the 'first time' every couple of years for the past few years. In recent memory, Nigeria allegedly celebrated its 'first Pride' in 2019 (Bamidele, 2019). A few years later, Nigeria celebrated its 'first Pride' in 2022 (Kachi, 2022). The claim of the 'first Pride' event in 2022 is even more laughable, considering that it was not even the first Pride event that season. Unsurprisingly, this competition for attention and funding creates deep conflicts within activist circles, leading to public confrontations as activists-professionals scramble to assign blame and dodge accountability. As an activist mentioned to me, 'Everybody wants to be a star ... an average queer activist in Nigeria just wants to be the Messiah'. This undermines the fluidity necessary for real social transformation. As organizations and activists focus more on attracting funders and bolstering their social and financial capital than on grassroots organizing, they resort to niche marketing and publicity ploys, fragmenting the movement rather than fostering broad-based social change.

From institution to infrastructure: toward a heterotopia

Within the complexities of queer activism in Lagos, it is important to differentiate between *infrastructure* and *institutions* to highlight how these concepts shape social dynamics and collective action (Berlant, 2022). As discussed, institutions, such as NGOs, exert significant influence on queer activism in Lagos. These are formalized organizations that encompass established rules, decision-making processes and hierarchies that guide how the movement functions. In contrast, infrastructure encompasses the essential framework, resources and support systems that empower activists to unite, organize and mobilize for change. It includes physical spaces, digital platforms, communication networks and logistical arrangements facilitating collaboration and coordination. Infrastructure underpins the operational aspects of resistance efforts, providing the necessary tools for communication, action planning and collective organizing.

There are various examples of infrastructure being established successfully among queer activists in Lagos. This is especially seen in their ability to build coalition and strategic alliances to enhance their collective impact, recognizing the importance of such collaborations. The shared objective of resisting state-sponsored violence serves as the common ground for these coalitions, enabling activists to pool resources, share expertise and collectively address multifaceted challenges, despite various members not liking or agreeing with each other. This strategic alignment strengthens advocacy efforts and creates a unified front that garners increased national and international attention.

For instance, a coalition successfully challenged a specific provision in the SSMPA bill, Section 4(1), that criminalizes the registration of LGBTQ+ organizations, as this was found to violate constitutional guarantees of freedom of expression and association. The 15-plaintiff coalition comprised eight organizations and seven key stakeholders and activists. In my discussions with these coalition members, I understood that it involved a lot of negotiation and compromise. It was not fixed in time and space, necessitating activists to set aside personal differences for the collective cause. These groups gathered human rights lawyers and organizations and challenged the bill at Nigeria's Supreme Court. Notably, even in this space, internal politics and tension were reported, ranging from attempts to claim credit for the work to conflicting views on how the news of the success should be disseminated. These conflicts and tensions are inevitable. However, the ultimate success of these coalitions lies in their recognition of the benefits of collaboration and their knowledge of when to disband and go on about their businesses after these successes have been reached. By leveraging diversity in skills, experiences and perspectives, they forge a more robust and comprehensive resistance against state-sponsored violence, and disband when necessary.

To counter the competition that NGOization promotes, various queer activists in Lagos are also establishing new funding infrastructures. Some are organizing market stalls and entrepreneurship events for queer activists to sell their merchandise to raise money to do their work and to live, without relying on grants and institutional funding. There are also various queer activist collectives organizing physical spaces for queer people to gather, party and experience joy. This is especially noticeable in the thriving rave and nightlife scene in Lagos. Interestingly, as one rave space becomes increasingly expensive, mainstream and commercialized, another pops up with more affordable pricing and accessibility. The infrastructure can be reinvented and shifted as necessary because it sits outside of institutions.

Furthermore, with online spaces such as X (formerly known as Twitter) being increasingly used by queer people to combat erasure (Onanuga, 2020), it has also provided room for queer people to hold queer activists accountable. Through hashtags, threads and retweets, they engage in dialogue that critiques mainstream activism. Also, by sharing personal experiences and insights with queer activists, queer people on X expose activists and push them to confront blind spots and address systemic issues such as transphobia and classism within the movement. This online discourse fosters accountability and encourages activists to continuously evolve their advocacy efforts to serve various queer communities better.

These infrastructures exist within what Foucault (1986) discusses as a heterotopia, which offers a lens to understand the dynamics of resisting within the Nigerian queer activist space, particularly concerning inconveniences and interactions with people one may not like. Heterotopias are alternative spaces or sites that exist alongside and challenge dominant societal norms and institutions. These spaces, such as community centres, online platforms or gatherings, provide avenues for resistance that differ from traditional institutional frameworks. Within these heterotopic spaces, people can navigate and challenge power dynamics, hierarchies and exclusions in mainstream society or activist circles. They offer flexibility, adaptability and inclusivity, allowing for the accommodation of diverse perspectives and preferences. By engaging in resistance within heterotopic spaces, Nigerian queer activists can find avenues for collaboration, dialogue and empowerment, even with people they may not like or those who inconvenience them.

A heterotopia encourages the acknowledgement of ambivalence (Berlant, 2022). It stresses recognizing the diversity of perspectives, experiences and identities within the activist community. Embracing this perspective could help queer activists in Lagos approach relationships with openness and understanding because it highlights transitional spaces where norms are challenged, and new possibilities arise. This perspective encourages viewing conflict as an opportunity for growth and transformation. Engaging openly among themselves, even those they disagree with or do not like, can reshape dynamics, build solidarity and pursue collective goals for social change.

Conclusions: On queer solidarity

Ambivalence produces and operates across both *inner conflict* (within activists) and *interpersonal conflict* (between activists). On one level, *inner conflict* arises as activists navigate the tension between recognizing the necessity of collective action and feeling discomfort, irritation or disagreement about the methods, dynamics or people involved in the work. This internal ambivalence is compounded by the oppressive sociopolitical context that forces activists into a position where their queerness must be carefully surveilled and managed. This creates a complex negotiation, where activists feel compelled to suppress or manage personal grievances and conflicts to prioritize the collective cause. On the other hand, this inner ambivalence often spills into *interpersonal conflict*. Activists, who are already inconvenienced by their precarious social and political positioning, experience further friction when forced into community with others they do not fully agree with, like or trust. This inconvenience manifests in moments of tension, disagreement and outright conflict between activists, which are shaped by pre-existing personal dynamics, differing strategies or unresolved issues. Thus, ambivalence creates a circular dynamic: it fuels *inner conflict* as activists struggle with their own discomforts and tensions, which then exacerbates *interpersonal conflict* as these feelings bleed into their interactions with one another. At the same time, the tensions between activists reinforce and deepen the internal ambivalence they feel about the collective work, creating a loop that is difficult to escape.

Taking ambivalence seriously, that is, accepting unresolvable conflict and contradiction as an inevitable part of activism, can be a productive mode of engagement. It can support challenging individuals to confront their perceptions of entitlement and agency, especially when working with like-minded others for social change. Frequently, marginalized communities, such as queer Nigerians, are viewed primarily as a singular group with their individuality stripped from them. It is important to reconceptualize Nigerian queer identities to take individuality seriously in tandem with, and not in competition with, queer solidarity. Queer activists can collectively hold themselves accountable for actions that cause tension and inconvenience while preserving space and recognition for individual aspirations, joys and loves. Efforts to engage with the queer activist space in Lagos should recognize it as a network of diverse identities rather than as singular entities that must always get along and like each other. Rather than perceiving interpersonal tensions as inherently harmful, it is crucial to view conflict as opportunities for growth, dialogue and the fortification of the movement. Like Berlant (2022), I also propose a shift toward ambivalence and pursuing love and social change without guarantees. This means addressing the unpredictability of actions and coping with the inconveniences created in pursuit of social transformation. It raises questions about motivations for activism, restructuring social norms and building a collective for a better world. It prompts a reassessment of power dynamics and norms in activism.

The reasons for queer activists not liking each other in Lagos are many, and much more than has been explored here. Despite the shared struggle against oppressive legal frameworks and societal prejudices, navigating relationships within the queer activist space presents complexities stemming from ideological differences, past relationships and resource scarcity, exacerbated by the competitive nature of NGOs. Berlant (2022: 10) mentions this: 'Just because we are in the same room does not mean that we belong to the room or to each other.' Just because these activists have a common enemy in a common space does not mean they are for each other. My research into queer activism in Lagos led me to unexpected encounters with a complex web of inconveniences. These inconveniences, while sometimes rooted in personal dislikes, are deeply intertwined with the broader struggle for queer rights in Nigeria. They emphasize the need to consider activists' political positions and approaches within the movement. Amid these challenges, infrastructures emerge as spaces for collaboration and resistance. Coalitions and strategic alliances amplify advocacy efforts, challenging dominant norms and fostering inclusivity. By embracing these inconveniences and engaging with diverse perspectives, queer activists in Lagos can navigate interpersonal tensions and foster solidarity.

References

Adams, T.E. (2008) 'A review of narrative ethics', *Qualitative Inquiry*, 14(2): 175–194.

Adelowokan, O.A., Maku, O.E., Babasanya, A.O. and Adesoye, A.B. (2019) 'Unemployment, poverty and economic growth in Nigeria', *Journal of Economics and Management*, 35(1): 5–17.

Alvarez, S. (2009) 'Beyond NGO-ization? Reflections from Latin America', *Development*, 52(2): 175–184.

Arimoro, A.E. (2018) 'When love is a crime: is the criminalisation of same sex relations in Nigeria a protection of Nigerian culture?', *Liverpool Law Review*, 39(1): 221–238.

Arksey, H. and Knight, P. (1999) *Interviewing for Social Scientists*, Sage.

Bacchi, C.L. (2009) *Analysing Policy: What's the Problem Represented to Be?* (1st edition), Pearson Australia.

Bamidele, M. (2019) 'Bisi Alimi Organises LGBT Event in Lagos', *The Guardian Nigeria* [Online]. Available at: https://guardian.ng/life/bisi-alimi-organises-first-ever-lgbt-event-in-lagos/ (accessed 20 May 2024).

Bassel, L. and Emejulu, A. (2017) *Minority Women and Austerity Survival and Resistance in France and Britain*, Policy Press.

Berlant, L. (2022) *On the Inconvenience of Other People* (1st edition), Duke University Press.

Choudry, A. and Kapoor, D. (2013) 'Introduction'. In A. Choudry and D. Kapoor (eds) *NGOization: Complicity, Contradictions and Prospects*, Zed Books, pp 1–23.

Ellis, C., Adams, T.E. and Bochner, A.P. (2011) 'Autoethnography: an overview', *Historical Social Research*, 36(4): 273–290.

Eschle, C. (2001) 'Globalizing Civil Society? Social Movement and the Challenge of Global Politics from Below'. In P. Hamel, H. Lustiger-Thaler, J.N. Pieterse and S. Roseneil (eds) *Globalization and Social Movements*, Palgrave, pp 61–85.

Fischer, M. (2020) 'Good Conflict: The World Is Consumed by Violent Fights and Hostile Disagreements. Sarah Schulman Sees a Way Out of Them', *The Cut*, 2 August. Available at: www.thecut.com/2020/08/sarah-schulman-conflict-is-not-abuse.html (accessed 12 December 2023).

Foucault, M. (1986) 'Of other spaces', *Diacritics*, 16(1): 22–27.

Hyde v Hyde (1886, LRIP & D, 130).

Kachi, E. (2022) 'Lagos, Nigeria, Prepares for the Country's First-ever Pride', Xtra, 20 June. Available at: https://xtramagazine.com/power/activism/lagos-nigeria-first-ever-pride-225266 (accessed 20 May 2024).

Merton, R., Fiske, M. and Kendall, P. (1990) *The Focused Interview: A Manual of Problems and Procedures* (2nd edition), Free Press.

Munshi, S. and Willse, C. (2017) 'Foreword'. In: INCITE! (ed) *The Revolution Will Not Be Funded: Beyond the Non-Profit Industrial Complex*, Duke University Press, pp xiii–xxii.

Naples, N.A. and Sachs, C. (2000) 'Standpoint epistemology and the use of self-reflection in feminist ethnography: lessons for rural sociology', *Rural Sociology*, 65(2): 194–214.

National Bureau of Statistics (2022) *Nigeria Multidimensional Poverty Index (2022)*, National Bureau of Statistics.

Onanuga, P.A. (2020) 'Queer Nigerian Twitter Can Challenge Homophobia and Assert Sexual Agency', blog. Available at: https://blogs.lse.ac.uk/africaatlse/2020/10/29/queer-nigerian-twitter-social-media-challenge-homophobia-and-assert-sexual-agency/ (accessed 23 November 2021).

Paternotte, D. (2016) 'The NGOization of LGBT activism: ILGA-Europe and the Treaty of Amsterdam', *Social Movement Studies*, 15(4): 388–402.

Rothman, N.B., Pratt, M.G., Rees, L. and Vogus, T.J. (2017) 'Understanding the dual nature of ambivalence: why and when ambivalence leads to good and bad outcomes', *The Academy of Management Annals*, 11(1): 33–72.

Salami, C. (2013) 'Youth unemployment in Nigeria: a time for creative intervention', *International Journal of Business and Marketing Management*, 1(2): 18–26.

Schulman, S. (2016) *Conflict Is Not Abuse: Overstating Harm, Community Responsibility, and the Duty of Repair* (1st edition), Arsenal Pulp Press.

Smith, A. (2017) 'Introduction: The Revolution Will Not Be Funded'. In: INCITE! (ed) *The Revolution Will Not Be Funded: Beyond the Non-Profit Industrial Complex*, Duke University Press, pp 1–18.

Smith, D. (1987) *The Everyday World as Problematic: A Feminist Sociology*, University of Toronto Press.

The Initiative for Equal Rights (2020) 'A Timeline of the "Egbeda 57" Case'. Available at: https://theinitiativeforequalrights.org/acquit57/ (accessed 3 March 2022).

Walford, G. (2007) 'Classification and framing of interviews in ethnographic interviewing', *Ethnography and Education*, 2(2): 145–157.

7

Ambivalent Activism: Recontextualizing Mental Health Politics

Hel Spandler, Dina Poursanidou and Sonia Soans

Introduction

Mental health activism is a heavily contested field which can include protests, campaigns and politics involving patients/user/survivors, family members/carers, professionals/practitioners, all with various and sometimes conflicting agendas. This chapter explores ambivalent activism as an antidote to a specific manifestation of contemporary mental health politics, characterized by polarized debates about contentious issues in the field, such as psychiatric diagnosis and medication.

We use the idea of an ambivalent politics to refer to the need to provide a space for seemingly contradictory feelings, thoughts and attitudes toward madness and related interventions/systems. This aligns with a Mad Studies perspective which 'cultivates critical ambivalence to reckon with the simultaneous harm and benefit that may accompany madness ... [and] respects and sometimes harnesses "mad" feelings like obsession and rage as stimulus for radical thought and action' (Bruce, 2021: 9). Moreover, the ambivalence toward mental health systems is often articulated by Mad activists and survivors. For example, in a blog entitled '5 Ways Your Critiques of Psychiatry Might Be Ableist', Sam Dylan Finch reflects, 'while psychiatry has certainly done its fair share to traumatise me, I also wouldn't be here without it' (Finch, 2018). This goes to the heart of the many paradoxes about mental health care that an ambivalent politics seeks to address.

Like other forms of activism, motivations for mental health activism usually stem from anger and hurt at perceived injustices. It often arises from direct or indirect contact with mental health systems which can be experienced as abusive and neglectful (Spandler, 2016). It is important to be clear that we are *not* ambivalent about these injustices, which are frequently real and deeply felt. On the contrary, we are acutely aware of the damaging effects of oppression and discrimination on people's mental health; the often-traumatizing effects of mental health systems on people who use them, as well as people who work in them; and the impact of psychophobia and sanism[1] (LeBlanc and Kinsella, 2016; Beresford and Russo, 2021).

At the same time, we *are* profoundly ambivalent about the various explanatory frameworks, alternative solutions and political strategies proposed and deployed to challenge these injustices. As such, we are frequently left with uncertainty, confusion, anxiety and discomfort. However, rather than seeing this as a problem, we see it as a resource that can be helpful and productive (Breslow, 2021). While it is not always an easy position to adopt, we think ambivalence helps to ensure that our activism does justice to the complex, contested and contextualized nature of mental health challenges and debates. Therefore, this chapter outlines our motivations, justifications and methods for promoting ambivalent mental health activism, and uses our involvement in *Asylum: The Radical Mental Health Magazine* as an exemplar.[2]

We have different biographical, social and cultural backgrounds, both in terms of our relationship to mental health (as service users, allies and researchers) and our location and life histories. However, we share a connection with England, where most of this chapter is focused, and where *Asylum* magazine is based. Dina was born in Greece and moved to England in the 1990s; Hel grew up in England where they still live; and Sonia was born in India, lived in England for several years, and now lives in India. Our ambivalence was formed out of our individual and collective reflection on our experiences in these different contexts.

For example, Dina's profound ambivalence about her own madness, mental health service use (which involved involuntary hospitalization) and recovery (Poursanidou, 2013) took shape in the context of a radical 'Mad Pride' politics which developed in response to the historical subjugation and oppression of people with psychosocial disabilities.[3] Her mental health crisis represented a major biographical disruption that had catastrophic consequences for every aspect of her life and left her feeling bitter and angry, fearful, sad and with an acute sense of loss. Dina experienced profound feelings of humiliation and shame in relation to her madness, as well as a deep sense of failure, injustice and stigmatization. At the same time, she recognized that the crisis opened up opportunities for personal growth and transformation, affording her hope and new insights into the human condition.

Hel's ambivalence was formed in the context of witnessing family, friends and colleagues using/surviving and working in mental health systems. Hel has simultaneously held seemingly contradictory feelings toward both madness and mental health/psy systems (including anger, rage, regret, fear, longing, desire and gratitude). Initially, Hel was drawn toward anti-psychiatry and various critiques of psychiatry. However, over the years, diverse encounters with mental health systems and witnessing people being both helped and harmed by psychiatric interventions *and* by critical alternatives, brought the realization that a progressive politics of mental health needed to hold a space for diverse and sometimes seemingly contradictory perspectives (Spandler, 2018, 2023).

Sonia studied psychology and worked for a brief period in mental health services in India, where her training viewed the idea of 'mental illness' and psychological concepts as above reproach. When she studied in the UK she discovered more ostensibly critical and feminist approaches to mental health care. Although they provided alternative theoretical frameworks, it was her contact with service user/survivors that more profoundly challenged all these frameworks. Sonia's ambivalence comes from rejecting easy dichotomies around different mental health systems such as 'indigenous' versus 'biomedical' or 'Eastern' versus 'Western' approaches (Soans, 2022). To her, ambivalence means appreciating the complexities and contradictions within and between these different systems, and how different approaches can be experienced in multiple ways.

Using examples from the particularities of these different national contexts (England, Greece and India), we attempt to show how adopting an ambivalent political sensibility is critically important and necessary, especially in the context of acutely polarized debates which characterize mental health politics today. These debates frequently decontextualize mental health politics by disregarding situational nuances, and we suggest that ambivalence is a potential antidote to polarization as it goes hand-in-hand with the recontextualization of mental health politics.

Ambivalence and prefigurative mental health politics

Ambivalent mental health activism is a good example of what has been referred to as prefigurative politics (Raekstad and Gradin, 2020). Prefigurative politics tries to anticipate and model the kind of world we wish to see, in the here and now. This means that activism needs to be congruent with the world we are trying to create. By extension, mental health activism needs to embody the kinds of mental health support we would like to see in the world. For this, it seems important to take our lead from people who have used or survived mental health systems, and what they have found helpful and harmful.

Mental health system users and survivors have repeatedly criticized services for their tendency to diagnose and treat people according to systems and frameworks that very often disregard the complex reality of their suffering. Survivors often find that services deny their agency and autonomy and also discredit their perspectives, on the basis of their 'mental illness' and their collapse of rationality and 'insight' associated with it. Furthermore, what mental health system survivors often find most damaging in mental health services is mental health professionals' lack of humility, empathy and understanding of their situation, whatever their professed ideology. Therefore, what Jacob Breslow (2022) has referred to as the 'worrying politics of certainty' is especially important in mental health activism. However, there is a danger of an equally unambivalent politics of certainty which advocates alternative, seemingly more 'progressive' or even 'radical' values, models or frameworks. Unwittingly, these can be just as problematic as the politics of certainty which often characterizes mainstream diagnostic and treatment frameworks. There have been many examples of alternatives to psychiatry, from psychoanalysis onwards, that have been experienced as damaging and pathologizing, especially when they are presented as universal panaceas and seek to become established as new orthodoxies, without attention to the contexts in which they are implemented.

In a wider context of social and cultural normalcy, even seemingly radical proposals can be co-opted and used to oppress, silence and marginalize the very people who are supposed to benefit from them. For example, the international 'recovery movement', which was initially seen as a radical alternative to the therapeutic pessimism characterizing biomedical frameworks in psychiatry, has become a new orthodoxy in mental health services that fits the prevailing neoliberal austerity agendas. 'Recovery-orientated' approaches are used as a justification to refuse people long-term support, services and social security and promote individual responsibility; what the UK-based activist collective Recovery in the Bin has referred to as 'neo-recovery' (Recovery in the Bin et al, 2019). Another example is the way that 'trauma-informed' approaches have been applied and used (see Aves, 2022).

Considering all this, a politics of certainty forecloses our awareness of the possibility that alternative frameworks and theories might be damaging; shuts down alternative understandings; curtails the possibility of learning from our mistakes and from each other; and limits the possibility of progressive social change. By contrast, ambivalence keeps open the possibility of understanding how different approaches to mental health care can be potentially helpful or harmful in different sociopolitical contexts. It helps to cultivate an openness of mind, criticality and curiosity, and enables us to tolerate uncertainty and ambiguity while embracing complexity. This form of 'epistemic humility' (Ho, 2011) is so important in the mental health context where survivors frequently suffer 'epistemic injustice', meaning the discrediting of their capacity as credible knowers (Fricker, 2007). Indeed, it has been suggested that tackling epistemic injustice is a prerequisite for democratic practice in this context (Atterbury and Jones, 2022).

This approach helps to unsettle the (over) investments that activists often have in our own concepts, views and perspectives. It is likely to lower the tendency to be emotionally defensive about our own views and enhance our ability to be open to critique. Such emotional openness goes hand-in-hand with expanding the ability to show empathy and concern for those who may challenge our perspectives. Being open to challenge is, we suggest, essential for a prefigurative politics. After all, one of the main values of Mad and neurodiversity movements is their challenge to prevailing understandings of 'normality' and 'health' (Chapman, 2023; Frazer-Carroll, 2023).

Here, it is crucial to note the links between a politics of certainty and the acute polarization characterizing mental health politics in the UK, and internationally. This heightened polarization is most evident in social media debates about various issues in mental health care. Tony Roberts (2023), a mental health nurse and ally of mental health service users and survivors in the UK, who sadly passed away last summer, described the acute polarization prevailing in mental health – for example, between critical psychologists and biomedical psychiatry – as 'trench warfare' where mental health survivors get caught in the crossfire.

This also highlights the problem with the tendency among some activists to juxtapose 'critical/radical' versus 'traditional/mainstream' mental health perspectives. It assumes fixed radical or traditional positions, irrespective of sociopolitical and policy context, culture or material conditions. In practice, one seemingly 'radical' position might be progressive in relation to one context or concern, but 'traditional' or even reactionary in relation to other contexts and concerns. This is very apparent when it comes to diagnosis and medication, two long-standing issues that have concerned mental health activists. These are particularly illustrative examples of the need for ambivalent recontextualization, as we discuss next.

Resisting and reclaiming diagnosis

> Diagnosis wields immense power. It can provide us access to vital medical technology or shame us, reveal a path toward less pain or get us locked up. It opens doors and slams them shut. (Clare, 2017: 41)

Psychiatric diagnosis has been the focus of one of the most contested and polarized debates in UK mental health politics over the past few years. While being 'anti-diagnosis' is often read as being a progressive, critical and radical position in mental health, diagnostic politics is much more complex, nuanced and contextualized than it would often appear (Chapman, 2021; Frazer-Carroll, 2023). For example, some mental health activists campaign for the *abolition* of psychiatric diagnosis in its entirety whereas others focus specifically on abolishing particularly stigmatizing and damaging diagnoses (such as homosexuality or transsexuality in the past, or Schizophrenia and Borderline Personality Disorder in the present). Other activists might campaign for the *inclusion* of specific diagnoses, so they are officially recognized (such as 'Dissociative Identity Disorder' or 'Premenstrual Dysphoric Disorder'). Other activists might campaign for conditions to be taken out of the psychiatric lexicon and be placed in the category of physical illnesses (for example, in the case of Myalgic Encephalomyelitis/ Chronic Fatigue Syndrome or ME/CFS) while others might argue for a reclassification of diagnoses (for example, for 'Personality Disorder' to be reclassified as 'Complex Post-Traumatic Stress Disorder'). Even a diagnosis as stigmatizing, pejorative and problematic as Borderline Personality Disorder is contentious among survivors and activists. For example, some neuroqueer feminist activists see it important to acknowledge, and attend to the particular needs and sensibilities of people who might identify with the diagnosis and use it to recognize their 'borderline' experience (Johnson, 2021).

Similarly, while the neurodiversity movement argues that neurodivergence is best considered as a difference rather than an illness/disability, many neurodivergent people find that a diagnosis can help them understand and make sense of their behavioural and sensory differences, as well as enable them to access social adjustments and support. Indeed, many report seeing oneself through a neurodiversity lens as liberating (Widdowson, 2023). At the same time, the increase in autism-related and mental health diagnoses has created legitimate concerns about over-diagnosis, over-medicalization and pathologization of human diversity (Frances, 2013). However, acutely polarized positions which either idealize or reject diagnoses fail to appreciate that *both* concerns – over-medicalization/over-diagnosis *and* recognition of neurodivergence and distress – represent potentially valid standpoints.

A critique of diagnosis or 'medicalization' might be progressive in some contexts (for example, in relation to the over-diagnosis and over-medicalization of the experiences of trauma survivors). However, critiques of diagnosis may be reactionary in other contexts, for example, where autistic people need formal recognition of their disability to access support; where trans people need a diagnosis to access medical transition; where it is helpful to develop shared identities, alliances and support; or where psychiatric diagnosis might be a prerequisite to secure specific services or welfare support. Of course, this depends on the wider context within which support is developed, justified and provided. In neoliberal contexts, characterized by the decimation of state-funded mental health services and punitive welfare reforms, psychiatric diagnosis tends to be a necessary justification in order to obtain state welfare support. Both the UK and Greece are examples of such neoliberal contexts. Characteristically, a 'schizophrenia' diagnosis tends to secure the highest score in assessments for state disability pensions in Greece.

Felicity Callard refers to the 'indispensability of ambivalence' in debates about diagnosis, and maintains that we need to attend to voices seldom or never heard in these debates. Moreover, she suggests we need to have 'more open and balanced interrogations of the achievements and limits of diagnosis' in order to do 'justice to the multifaceted ways in which those in receipt of diagnoses live with, through, against and beyond them' (Callard, 2014: 530). In a similar vein, Akiko Hart (2018) makes a plea for mental health service users' autonomy and choice over the adoption or rejection of psychiatric diagnosis. And Merri Lisa Johnson (2021) suggests that activists need to complicate, without dismissing, psychiatric diagnoses, at the same time as complicating, without dismissing, critiques of those diagnoses.

Endorsing a simplistic pro- or anti-diagnosis position might close off the possibility of alliances with mental health activists who have been profoundly harmed by diagnosis frameworks, but also with disability activists who have been claiming or reconceptualizing notions of illness and disability to enable them to work for them in contemporary welfare systems (Frazer-Carroll, 2023). For example, people with chronic health conditions such as ME/CFS who are struggling to have their experiences bio-medically validated (Spandler and Allen, 2018) or people who require diagnosis to obtain support and environmental adjustments, such as neurodivergent people (Chapman, 2023). Progressive alliances are necessary for social movements, and by adopting a more ambivalent position toward issues like diagnosis, it is possible to forge alliances between the psychiatric survivor movement and the wider disability and emerging neurodiversity movements. Arguably, this enables activists to see beyond our usual allies and forge new and unexpected solidarities with diverse communities and movements.

Problematizing and democratizing medication

Psychiatric medication has been the focus of ferocious and highly polarized debates for decades in the UK. 'Psy' professionals subscribing to biomedical frameworks of mental health tend to overemphasize the efficacy and usefulness of psychiatric drugs without, at the same time, adequately acknowledging the significantly harmful (and at times even fatal) side effects of these drugs or the serious withdrawal effects characterizing attempts to reduce or discontinue them. On the other hand, critical mental health professionals and some activists tend to talk categorically about the harms of medication and the need to pursue alternatives. Both 'sides' of these debates have a tendency to express moral judgements about people who either take or do not take medication, assuming that one is inherently preferable to the other (depending on one's perspective). Many mental health service users find such judgements significantly shaming, especially when they are made as blanket statements that ignore the complexity of individual circumstances. This has led to the notion of the 'pill shaming' of people who take medication, and people who refuse medication being seen as treatment resistant.

The recent high-profile challenge to the 'chemical (serotonin) imbalance' theory of depression, the questions it raised regarding the high prescribing rates of antidepressants and the ensuing debate around their usefulness and efficacy (Moncrieff et al, 2023) represented a particularly illustrative example of heightened polarization to the politics of medication (Spandler, 2023). Similarly, a 'Beyond Pills' initiative was launched in the UK aiming to reduce the prescribing of antidepressants, which was accompanied by a letter in the *British Medical Journal*, making an 'evidence-based' call for the deprescribing (reduction and discontinuation) of antidepressants (Davies et al, 2023). The responses to the launch of the Beyond Pills initiative on social media and in mental health literature illustrate the acute polarization relating to psychiatric medication in the UK.

A more ambivalent approach to psychiatric medication would attempt to highlight and challenge the power of 'Big Pharma'; the over-prescribing of psychiatric drugs, and over-medicating certain groups of service users in particular contexts in the UK, for example, forensic mental health patients, many of whom are Black men, in long-term detentions in hospital under very restricted and coercive regimes (Jacob and Holmes, 2011). However, it would also recognize that some people are still not able to access medication that they might find helpful; and/*or* might not be able to access alternatives to medication, as there are limited meaningful alternatives available. For example, long-term psychotherapy is very rarely (if at all) offered on the NHS and private psychotherapy is an acutely expensive industry and can be equally – if differently – problematic and pathologizing for some clients.

An ambivalent approach might question who has the right to decide who is able to access medication, or alternatives. It would also challenge the assumed either/or, for/against, nature of these debates. This might also involve questioning the boundary between prescribed and 'recreational' drugs which, in turn, would open up a space for a more transparent discussion of, and challenge to, society's gatekeeping of access to substances that may be helpful or harmful. In other words, it might draw attention to the way society might over-prescribe some substances, but prevent access to others.

In this way, some survivors involved in Mad Pride activism have demanded more control over medication access, leading one commentator to argue that it might be possible to develop a 'radical pharmacology fit for Mad liberation' (Aftab, 2023) and another survivor activist arguing for Prescription Abolition. Prescription Abolition is the idea that individuals should be the ultimate decision makers over their own minds and bodies so that they, not medical professionals, 'critical' or otherwise, should make the ultimate decision about what medications to consume or not (Anon, 2018). Whether or not we agree with such a proposal, it certainly unsettles the usual pro- or anti-medication positions that tend to characterize contemporary mental health politics.

Global mental health contradictions

While most of our commentary so far has concerned the UK context, different concerns are likely to animate mental health activists in other national contexts. There has been a recent understandable growth in calls for decolonizing madness and psychiatry. However, activists often counterpose pre-colonial/indigenous systems of healing against 'Western' psychiatry. This can result in treating both systems as culturally homogeneous and it also tends to assume that psychiatry and the psy disciplines were entirely invented in the West, thus erasing the contributions and agency of other peoples.

Psychiatry, while largely created in Western nations and brought to the colonies, may have represented freedom from often harmful religious explanations and treatments of mental illness, at the same time as creating a new kind of oppression. Those involved in the so-called Global Mental Health Movement tend to suggest that 'underdeveloped' nations need to introduce modern psychiatric systems instead of antiquated and unevidenced systems of indigenous healing (Mills, 2013). While critics of this movement rightly highlight the problem with modern mental health systems in the West, they often suggest we need to embrace indigenous practices instead. However, pre-psychiatric forms of mental health care were far from idyllic and not always benign or free from oppressive power dynamics (Soans, 2022). The asylum in Erwadi, India, for instance, was run as an indigenous healing space, but became a site for abuse (Stephen et al, 2021). As this example indicates, while indigenous healing systems may represent spaces for more progressive alternatives to psychiatry to develop, they are also open to abusive and negligent practices. As well as endorsing abusive attitudes and practices toward mad and disabled people, some indigenous practices also reinforce culturally oppressive ideas of gender, sexuality, family, caste and class, including the assumption that women should be natural carers (Ghai, 2009).

A more ambivalent approach to these contradictions would acknowledge the substantial problems associated with contemporary psychiatry and mental health services, not least their tendency to over-medicalize experiences of mental distress, over-prescribe medication and rely on coercive treatments. It would also recognize that there are many positive aspects of indigenous cultures and healing practices that have been suppressed and lost, and that a 'global mental health movement' imposes at least questionable practices on other countries. However, it would also problematize and question the tendency of some activists to demonize all aspects of 'Western' mental health care and romanticize pre-colonial family structures and indigenous systems of healing. Oversimplified characterizations of the 'Global North' versus the 'Global South' and 'Eastern' healing practices versus 'Western' psychiatry have created a polarized discourse that often fails to consider the complexity of the circumstances and needs of the people with psychosocial disabilities themselves.

An ambivalent politics tries to move away from binary, polarized, for/against thinking, toward what psychosocial theorists refer to as a 'third position' thinking (Britton, 2003) or what postcolonial theorists refer to as Third Space Theory (Bhabha, 2004). In this way of thinking, rather than being insufficiently critical, refusing to take a binary position is seen as an important source of critical knowledge for imagining counter-hegemonic alternatives. For example, 'by affirming and creatively combining complex, contradictory, paradoxical truths, it is possible to identify complex, higher order, synergistic solutions' (Cloke, 2013). By offering concurrent, and even contradictory positions, third space thinking transcends false dichotomies and oppositional dualisms and subverts either/or ways of being and understanding. This helps to reveal and express overlooked concerns and under-represented voices and perspectives. Arguably, we have been trying to offer a 'third space' for ambivalent mental health politics through our involvement in *Asylum* magazine.

Asylum magazine as a 'third space'

Asylum magazine was founded in 1986 in England as 'the magazine for democratic psychiatry'. Influenced by the democratic psychiatric movement in Italy, as well as the anti-psychiatry and psychiatric survivors' movement, it aimed to give psychiatric survivors an 'equal place at the table' to discuss what a progressive politics of mental health might look like (Spandler, 2020). Although it now goes by the sub-title '*The Radical Mental Health Magazine*', it has retained its '*Asylum*' title.

The term 'asylum' (ἄσυλον) has its origins in Ancient Greece. It means a space that cannot/should not be violated, a sacred space. Temples in Ancient Greece were such spaces and if offenders sought refuge in those spaces, they were safe from law enforcement. In the mental health context, the idea of 'asylum' is more complex. In a psychiatric context, while asylum may have originally meant a place of refuge or safety it increasingly evokes something harmful, dangerous and outdated (in terms of containing dangerous patients or inflicting violence onto patients, and often both). Therefore, in the mental health context, 'asylum' itself signifies ambivalence – or at least our ambivalence toward the idea of 'asylum'; given that it evokes *both* our discomfort at the violence of the asylum (psychiatric setting) *and* our individual and collective yearning for its original Ancient Greek meaning of refuge/sacred space. It also allows us to make wider political links and alliances, for example, between the plight of mental health system survivors and refugees and asylum seekers.

The underlying rationale behind the magazine is to provide 'asylum' (refuge) for marginalized radical ideas in the mental health field, where they can be read, discussed and debated. This is not necessarily a safe space, but it might be brave in the sense that it is associated with challenge, uncertainty, risk and discomfort (Winks, 2018). One of the reasons we still publish an in-print magazine is precisely to avoid instant knee-jerk reactions and *ad hominem* attacks on individuals that are common in social media debates when difficult and uncomfortable questions are discussed.

Anzaldúa (1987) uses the metaphor of the 'borderlands' to conceptualize spaces where different debates can coexist and create hybrid culture(s). In a similar vein, *Asylum* might represent a 'paradoxical space' where political differences, conflict and contradiction can be safely contained, without necessarily arriving at a single solution or strategy (Mantas, 2010). In this way, *Asylum* has sought to constantly question both psychiatric and psychological perspectives, as well as anti-psychiatric and anti-psychological perspectives.

In the *Asylum* editorial group, we all have our individual views on highly contested issues in mental health. However, as an editorial group, we are committed to publishing diverse and often conflicting and polarized viewpoints, including those that at least some of us do not necessarily subscribe to. For example, we might individually endorse anti-psychiatry or psychiatric abolition, but as an editorial group we are neither pro- nor anti-psychiatry and we have published articles that both defend and critique psychiatry, diagnosis and medication. In this way, we embrace what Robert Chapman has referred to as 'ambi-psychiatry', that is, an ambivalent position about both psychiatry and anti-psychiatry. In this way, *Asylum* might be seen as an example of 'non-aligned' mental health activism (Aftab, 2022).

Most importantly, in *Asylum*, we try to embrace ambivalence toward madness itself. In other words, we seek to refrain from romanticizing madness by acknowledging its often-catastrophic consequences for people's lives, while at the same time striving to avoid demonizing madness as an inevitably negative state of mind. We do this, for example, by engaging with the – profoundly ambivalent – idea developed by the US activist group, the Icarus Project,[4] of madness being 'a dangerous gift' (Icarus Project, 2004).

By publishing a wide range of critical and radical experiences, perspectives and voices in *Asylum*, and adopting a position of epistemic humility, we try not to assume we know what is the 'right' or 'best' alternative or strategy. Instead of having predefined goals, agendas and formulas, we strive to create an inclusive and radically democratic space that prioritizes survivor agency and solidarity. However, it is important to state that we do not always succeed, and that this mission is often more aspirational. Maintaining ambivalence, especially during times of heightened political polarization, is certainly not an easy way out. It is a continual struggle, with political and emotional consequences, involving considerable emotional labour on our part. It requires us to be sufficiently open to being challenged and the possibility that we might be complicit in reproducing harmful binaries and practices, while still trying to imagine otherwise.

The pitfalls and possibilities of ambivalence

An ambivalent activist stance is often viewed as not being radical enough, 'sitting on the fence', not 'taking sides', and lacking commitment, courage and conviction. Such criticisms often arise from the common conception that ambivalence is the antithesis of activism. For example, rather than being a useful and productive resource, it has been suggested that ambivalence signifies a state of confusion or indecisiveness, a privilege or luxury, that clouds our judgement such that we can no longer clearly see how power operates in mental health systems. We have been accused of political paralysis and suspended agency; abandoning the possibility of wider social change; and justifying and maintaining the status quo. Moreover, ambivalence itself can be seen as a position that we adopt and defend against a non-ambivalent position, thereby creating another unhelpful binary.

There is some truth to these concerns, and by no means do we regard ambivalent activism as a panacea that could resolve all our political dilemmas. One requires sufficient agency, space and support to be able to maintain ambivalence, and this is often denied to people at the sharp end of abuse or neglect, especially within mental health systems. In some situations, ambivalence cannot be sustained or is unhelpful and we need to relinquish ambivalence, choose a side and take action. For example, ambivalence in the context of recent polarized debates about trans rights – that is, whether trans people are psychologically damaged (rather than trans) and require therapy (rather than gender affirmative care) – is probably unhelpful in the context of widespread transphobia.

While all these complications make ambivalent mental health activism more fraught and unsettling, this is not necessarily negative. Rather than resulting in inertia, a more ambivalent approach might lead to more creative, contextualized and democratic activism. There may be some truth and validity on what is often portrayed as two opposing 'sides', and therefore it is necessary to create spaces for the possibility of what might turn out to be higher order 'paradoxical truths'. For instance, a more ambivalent approach to psychiatric medication might result in efforts to support people being able to refuse, reduce or come off psychiatric drugs, and supporting people's right to access substances that they might find helpful, as well as developing various alternatives. Similarly, a more ambivalent approach to diagnosis might result in supporting campaigns to abolish certain diagnoses, while also supporting people's rights to reclaim and legitimate their experiences through diagnoses, and forge political alliances based on them.

A recent article in the *Boston Review* makes a plea that social action needs to be discomforting to be effective (Hayes and Kaba, 2023). The authors argue that political transformation is not about creating new sets of orthodoxies to replace the ones we oppose, but about co-creating strategies, in context, and recognizing that we too are on our own messy journeys, and our own transformations will continue as we grow. It is our ability to constructively engage with other people, even those with whom we might not agree, that is ultimately necessary for progressive social change. Applying their plea to the mental health context, activists often grapple with questions like, 'Am I anti-psychiatry?', when the more pressing question might be 'Am I willing to listen, even when it's hard?'. To paraphrase Hayes and Kaba (2023), perhaps we need to nurture our willingness to tolerate discomfort and respect its importance in all the ways that society, and mental health services, do not.

Contrary to the idea that ambivalent mental health politics is insufficiently 'radical', perhaps the very radicality of these third spaces lies in their potential to recontextualize mental health politics beyond entrenched ideological debates. Hopefully, we have shown that it is possible to remain committed to radical social change while also maintaining sufficient ambivalence about contested issues, positions or strategies. Recent books in the field, such as *Mad World* (Frazer-Carroll, 2023), *Left Alone* (Joffre-Eichhorn and Anderson, 2023) and *Burnout* (Proctor, 2024) suggest this is possible. They all express a certain ambivalence about various key issues in mental health, yet still take a strong stance toward individual and collective liberation. Indeed, we believe that ambivalent activism, rather than being an oxymoron, can make mental health activism more democratic and rooted in the needs of those most affected by the issues at stake.

Conclusion

In writing this chapter we have realized how hard ambivalence is to define. It is more like a sensibility or orientation toward key areas of contention in mental health politics. We have given three examples that illustrate the need for this sensibility (psychiatric diagnosis, medication and global mental health politics) and explained how we put this into practice in our work with *Asylum* magazine. In so doing, we have identified many key qualities that effectively constitute our collective definition of ambivalence. They include: embracing complexity and nuance; engaging deeply with contradictions and paradoxes; valuing polyphony and diversity of perspectives, including perspectives that are unpopular; listening to and valuing views that are seldom heard; tolerating the uncertainty, ambiguity and discomfort of not knowing; avoiding binary thinking and adopting 'third position' thinking; practising epistemic humility and avoiding being over-invested in particular concepts and theories; and being emotionally open and not resorting to defensiveness when our views are challenged. We realize adopting all these qualities is a tall order and is therefore aspirational. We recognize there are times when we fail to practise ambivalence, as well as times when ambivalence fails us.

Notes

1. Psychophobia refers to the fear of madness and mad people, and sanism is the systematic oppression of people diagnosed as mentally ill within wider society and in mental health systems.
2. We could have used lots of examples of mental health activism, but we use *Asylum* as it is something we are actively involved in, and we hope it illustrates our attempts at putting ambivalent activism into practice.
3. There is no agreed terminology in mental health activism to refer to people who have been diagnosed with mental illness or mental disorder and have used or survived mental health services. 'Psychosocial Disabilities' is the term used in the UN Convention of the Rights of People with Disabilities to ensure their inclusion. Some activists prefer 'Mad' or 'distressed'.
4. The Icarus Project has now re-emerged as the Fireweed Collective, https://fireweedcollective.org

References

Anon (2018) 'Prescription abolition and the politics of Mad Pride', *Asylum: The Radical Mental Health Magazine*, 25(4): 5–6.

Aftab, A. (2022) 'Psychiatric Psychodrama'. Available at: www.psychiatrymargins.com/p/psychiatric-psychodrama

Aftab, A. (2023) 'A psychopharmacology fit for mad liberation?', *Asylum: The Radical Mental Health Magazine*, 30(1): 19–20.

Anzaldúa, G. (1987) *Borderlands/La Frontera: The New Mestiza*, Aunt Lute Books.

Atterbury, K. and Jones, N. (2022) 'Overcoming factionalism in serious mental illness policy making: a counter-perspective', *Psychiatric Services*, 73(5): 574–576.

Aves, W. (2022) '"Trauma-Informed Care" Left Me More Traumatised than Ever', Psychiatry is Driving Me Mad.com, 12 July. Available at: www.psychiatryisdrivingmemad.co.uk//post/trauma-informed-care-left-me-more-traumatised-than-ever

Beresford, P. and Russo, J. (2021) *The Routledge International Handbook of Mad Studies: Critical International Perspectives on Doing Mad Studies*, Routledge.

Bhabha, Homi K. (2004) *The Location of Culture*, Routledge.

Breslow, J. (2021) 'Q and A with Dr Jacob Breslow on Ambivalent Childhoods: Speculative Futures and the Psychic Life of the Child', *LSE Review of Books*, 5 October. Available at: https://blogs.lse.ac.uk/lsereviewofbooks/2021/10/05/q-and-a-with-dr-jacob-breslow-on-ambivalent-childhoods-speculative-futures-and-the-psychic-life-of-the-child/

Breslow, J. (2022) 'Gender as Ambivalent Politics of Belonging: Trans Childhood in an Era of Gender Critical Activisms', paper presented to the Ambivalent Activism online seminar series, 1 July 2022, University of Edinburgh and University of Warwick.

Britton, R. (2003) *Belief and Imagination: Explorations in Psychoanalysis*, Routledge.

Bruce, L.M.J. (2021) *How to Go Mad Without Losing Your Mind: Madness and Black Radical Creativity*, Duke University Press.

Callard, F. (2014) '"The indispensability of ambivalence" in psychiatric diagnosis debates', *Journal of Medical Ethics*, 40(8): 526–530.

Chapman, R. (2021) 'Neurodiversity and the Biopolitics of Diagnosis: Can Psychological Formulation Save Us?' *Psychology Today*, 24 March. Available at: www.psychologytoday.com/gb/blog/neurodiverse-age/202103/neurodiversity-and-the-biopolitics-of-diagnosis?msockid=17e2f3d652916e02070de696530e6f08

Clare, E. (2017) *Brilliant Imperfection: Grappling with Cure*. Duke University Press.

Cloke, K. (2013) 'Conflict and Movements for Social Change: The Politics of Mediation and the Mediation of Politics', mediate.com, 7 July. Available at: https://mediate.com/conflict-and-movements-for-social-change-the-politics-of-mediation-and-the-mediation-of-politics/

Chapman, R. (2023) *Empire of Normality: Neurodiversity and Capitalism*, Pluto Press.

Davies, J., Read, J., Kruger, D., Crisp, N., Lamb, N., Dixon, M. and Marshall-Andrews, L. (2023) 'Politicians, experts, and patient representatives call for the UK government to reverse the rate of antidepressant prescribing', *BMJ*, 383: 2730.

Finch, S.D. (2018) 5 Ways Your Critiques of Psychiatry Might Be Ableist, Everyday Feminism Blog, 12 November 2018. Available at: https://everydayfeminism.com/2018/11/5-ways-your-critiques-of-psychiatry-might-be-ableist/ (last accessed 18 April 2025).

Frazer-Carroll, M. (2023) *Mad World: The Politics of Mental Health*, Pluto Press.

Frances, A. (2013) *Saving Normal: An Insider's Revolt Against Out-of-Control Psychiatric Diagnosis, DSM-5, Big Pharma, and the Medicalization of Ordinary Life*, Mariner Books.

Fricker, M. (2007) *Epistemic Injustice: Power and the Ethics of Knowing*, Oxford University Press.

Ghai, A. (2009) 'Disability and the millennium development goals: a missing link', *Journal of Health Management*, 11(2): 279–295.

Hart, A. (2018) 'Pursuing choice, not truth: debates around diagnosis in mental health', *Asylum: The Radical Mental Health Magazine*, 25(3): 19–20.

Ho, A. (2011) 'Trusting experts and epistemic humility in disability', *The International Journal of Feminist Approaches to Bioethics*, 4(2): 102–123.

Hayes, K. and Kaba, M. (2023) 'How much discomfort is the whole world worth?' *Boston Review*, 6 September. Available at: www.bostonreview.net/articles/how-much-discomfort-is-the-whole-world-worth/

Icarus Project (2004) *Navigating the Space Between Brilliance and Madness: A Reader and Roadmap of Bipolar Worlds*, Icarus Project.

Jacob, J.D. and Holmes, D. (2011) 'Working under threat: fear and nurse–patient interactions in a forensic psychiatric setting', *Journal of Forensic Nursing*, 7: 68–77.

Joffre-Eichhorn, H.J. and Anderson, P. (2023) *Left Alone: On Solitude and Loneliness amid Collective Struggle*, Daraja Press.

Johnson, M.L. (2021) 'Neuroqueer feminism: turning with tenderness toward Borderline Personality Disorder', *Signs: Journal of Women in Culture and Society*, 46(3): 635–662.

LeBlanc, S. and Kinsella, E.A. (2016) 'Toward epistemic justice: a critically reflexive examination of "sanism" and implications for knowledge generation', *Studies in Social Justice*, 10(1): 59–78.

Mantas, N. (2010) 'Review of G. Rose's Book: "Feminism and Geography: the Limits of Geographical Knowledge"', Queen Mary, University of London.

Mills, C. (2013) *Decolonizing Global Mental Health: The Psychiatrization of the Majority World*, Routledge.

Moncrieff, J., Cooper, R.E., Stockmann, T., Amendola, S., Hengartner, M.P. and Horowitz, M.A. (2023) 'The serotonin theory of depression: a systematic umbrella review of the evidence', *Molecular Psychiatry*, 28: 3243–3256.

Poursanidou, D. (2013) 'A journey through madness and back: how I became involved with *Asylum* magazine and what this has meant for me', *Asylum: The Radical Mental Health Magazine*, 20(3): 22–23.

Proctor, H. (2024) *Burnout: The Emotional Experience of Political Defeat*, Verso Press.

Raekstad, P. and Gradin, S.S. (2020) *Prefigurative Politics: Building Tomorrow Today*, Cambridge Policy Press.

Recovery in the Bin, Edwards, B.M., Burgess, R. and Thomas, E. (2019) 'Neorecovery: A Survivor Led Conceptualisation and Critique'. 25th International Mental Health Nursing Research Conference, The Royal College of Nursing, London, UK.

Roberts, T. (2023) 'Trench warfare in mental health', *Asylum: The Radical Mental Health Magazine*, 30(4): 12–14.

Soans, S. (2022) 'A critique of the romanticisation of pre-psychiatric systems of care in the Global South', *Asylum: The Radical Mental Health Magazine*, 29(1): 30–31.

Spandler, H. (2016) 'From psychiatric abuse to psychiatric neglect?' *Asylum: The Radical Mental Health Magazine*, 23(2): 7–8.

Spandler, H. (2018) 'Uncomfortable Relations: Reflections on Learning From Psychiatric Survivors', *Mad in America*, 22 August. Available at: www.madinamerica.com/2018/08/uncomfortable-relations-reflections-on-learning-from-psychiatric-survivors/

Spandler, H. (2020) '*Asylum*: a Magazine for Democratic Psychiatry in England'. In T. Burns and J. Foot (eds) *Basaglia's International Legacy: From Asylum to Community*, Oxford University Press, pp 205–226.

Spandler, H. (2023) 'Chemical imbalances or problems in living? You don't decide!', *Asylum: The Radical Mental Health Magazine*, 29(3): 17–19.

Spandler, H. and Allen, M. (2018) 'Contesting the psychiatric framing of ME/CFS', *Social Theory and Health*, 16(2): 127–141.

Stephen, C., Kumar, J.S. and Soans, S. (2021) 'Erwadi: a tragedy and its aftermath', *Asylum: The Radical Mental Health Magazine*, 28(3): 4–5.

Widdowson, A. (2023) 'Embracing schizoaffectivity through the neurodiversity paradigm', *Asylum: The Radical Mental Health Magazine*, 30(3): 4–5.

Winks, L. (2018) 'Discomfort, Challenge and Brave Spaces in Higher Education'. In W. Leal Filho (ed) *Implementing Sustainability in the Curriculum of Universities: Approaches, Methods and Projects*, Springer, pp 99–111.

8

Ambivalence and Veganism: Rethinking Sentiment in Moral Choices

Jordan McKenzie and Zoei Sutton

Introduction

This chapter offers a discussion of ambivalence and sentiment in moral choices specifically pertaining to non-human animal justice and veganism. Ambivalence is understood sociologically in two key ways in this chapter: first, it captures the emotional experience of being pulled in opposing directions by contrarian circumstances (Merton, 1976), and second, it is the recognition that modernity itself functions through a range of contradictions that individuals must navigate, balance and selectively ignore, in order to participate in society (Bauman, 1991). By bringing together an understanding of ambivalence as a potentially positive way of navigating complex moral issues (Kołakowski, 1968; McKenzie, 2018) with a sentiment-based theory of moral judgements (Greenspan, 1995; Prinz, 2006; McKenzie, 2019), this chapter will unpack the roles of emotion and rationality in moral decision making. In this context, sentiment refers to feelings that contain an element of personal reflection, and philosophers from Hume to Smith have employed the concept to consider the role of feeling in moral decision making. The area of animal justice serves as a useful place for this kind of analysis given that (a) intensely emotional responses to animal cruelty are common and relatable, and (b) ambivalence is a common response to the problem of animal cruelty for both vegans and non-vegans. This speaks to both forms of sociological ambivalence we have just described, as the norms that frame human interactions with animals are loaded with contradictions and inconsistencies. Ambivalence can serve to maintain veganism in a non-vegan world and, in another way, it can validate the position that individual actions will not lead to significant change. While it is generally agreeable across social demographics that animal suffering should be avoided or minimized, most people contribute to it in some way on a daily basis. For this reason, calls to eradicate animal cruelty are presented as extreme or unrealistic, and animal justice activists (including vegans) are seen as out of touch with the mainstream (Cole and Morgan, 2011; Buttny and Kinefuchi, 2020; Oliver, 2021). Those who claim to care about animals but continue to eat them are therefore positioned within an uncomfortable contradiction that can take a variety of different forms including cognitive dissonance, speciesism and ambivalence. There is a variety of other social and cultural factors that shape views about the consumption of animal products, including cultural traditions, masculinity, class, religion and structural inequality (Asher and Cherry, 2015; Gambert and Linné, 2018; Aavik, 2019). Finally, this chapter aims to demonstrate that functional ambivalence is a necessary component of a lasting commitment to veganism.

We use a sociology of emotions approach to unpack the process of navigating these moral contradictions with ambivalence and sentiment. Ambivalence can be a healthy response to contradiction and can even be a place from which meaningful changes are made, but it can also be a form of stalling or avoiding the seriousness of an issue. Sentiment and ambivalence are contrasted here precisely because the former involves a singular and penetrating emotive reaction, whereas ambivalence often involves balancing conflicting feelings and delaying immediate gut reactions. While ambivalence can be read as a failure of either/or decision making, it more accurately represents a form of emotional withdrawal endorsed by a preference for calm and unemotional moral choices (Rees et al, 2013). It can be understood as a kind of background emotion (Barbalet, 2011), a part of what Georg Simmel described as the 'Blasé attitude' (Simmel, 1903), or an example of unemotional feeling states (Roberts, 2023).

Case study: the Cube of Truth

In January 2017, animal justice protesters led a demonstration known as the 'Cube of Truth' in Sydney's bustling Pitt Street mall. The demonstration is made up of an outward facing group of protesters in Guy Fawkes masks holding screens that play a mini documentary called 'Thousand Eyes'. The intention is to disrupt shoppers and passersby with confronting footage of extreme animal cruelty from current agricultural practices. This protest is not a one-off, there have been countless demonstrations around the world that adopt this tactic of making people confront what they presumably would prefer to ignore. The strategy relies on the assumption that witnessing violent and shocking content will disrupt the status quo and lead to changes in behaviour. But does it work? While it is difficult to see these images without feeling disgust, guilt, shame or anger, the sustained motivation to change behaviour is doubtful. In many cases these demonstrations have an inverse effect by channelling the anger of bystanders toward the activists rather than the animal cruelty. When interviewed, one of the activists noted, 'One guy, he walked past and made a passing comment like, "These fucking idiots. There's kids starving overseas and you want to worry about fucking animals"' (McCasker, 2017). While these demonstrations certainly have impact, the majority of the passersby will ultimately decide not to make changes to their lifestyle. These decisions are heavily supported by a pervasive social order that values and treats animals in accordance with their perceived dis/utility to humans (Cole and Stewart, 2014).

Footage from slaughterhouses, mega farms and live animal export ships are difficult to un-see, and they are arguably more visible now than ever. This visibility has impacted the growth and popularity of vegetarian and vegan diets, as well as public opinion on animal circuses, racing and hunting. For many vegan activists, such 'politics of sight' activism drove their decision to become vegan or get involved in animal activism (Fernández, 2021). Jennifer Barker (2011) has written about the use of disgust in the film *Food Inc*, and Tiplady, Walsh and Phillips (2012) have investigated the emotional reactions to an Australian *Four Corners* documentary on live animal exports. In each case, negative emotional responses including shame, anger, pity and disgust were intertwined with both action and inaction from the viewers and the general public. The clear evidence of abject cruelty in the live animal export industry led to the temporary ban of the practice in 2011 with considerable support from the Australian public. However, as Pendergrast's (2015) frame analysis of media responses to the *Four Corners* documentary demonstrates, any initial outrage to animal cruelty can be quickly confined by a hegemonic 'welfarist' frame adopted by the mainstream media, animal industry and mainstream animal activist organizations. This means that instead of presenting an 'animal rights' frame to the public that problematizes the objectification and slaughter of animals, the discourse is framed by a focus on 'implementing improvements in the treatment of animals' through measures such as improved uptake of stunning before slaughter, or proposals to export carcasses of already killed animals rather than live bodies (Pendergrast, 2015). As the topic faded from the news the ban was lifted and the live animal export industry continues today. Responses to animal cruelty are also influenced by economistic logics focused on the economy and workers within it, with a 2018 study of public opinion on live export revealing that while negative feelings about the trade prevailed, those in favour of continuing live export cited economic rationales and support for farmers as driving their response (Sinclair et al, 2018). Furthermore, a group of cattle farmers successfully sued the Australian government to the tune of 600 million dollars for lost revenue during the ban. Media reporting on the 'failed' ban described it as 'irrational' and fuelled by emotion rather than reason (Dole, 2017). This response reflects a broader trend in which animal justice messages are positioned as less legitimate than the ostensibly pragmatic messaging of welfarist animal organizations, animal industry and mainstream media (Francione, 1996; Freeman, 2013; Pendergrast, 2015).

Sentiment

Sentiment-based theories of morality offer a unique opportunity to understand ethics as a sociologically grounded process of thinking, feeling and interacting (Barbalet, 2005). Rather than beginning with rationality as the highest form of moral decision making, we recognize feeling as the motivation behind moral action. These feelings are complex, contextual and interactional. Sentiment theories, from Adam Smith to Jesse Prinz, bring the discussion of emotion and lived experience into moral choices. An immediate consequence of this shift is the introduction of a third party into moral actions; there is not only the actor and the recipient of the actor's choices, but also an audience who witness these moral choices within a social and cultural context. Traditional moral and ethical theory begins with the assumption that the individual is self-interested and prone to amoral behaviour. The development of an ethical theory is, therefore, a kind of rational moral intervention that is needed in order to guide the individual to make decisions informed by empathy, compassion or recognition. But in the work of Adam Smith, sentiment is the starting point that acknowledges the socially embedded nature of selfhood in such a way that caring for others is a default (though not necessarily universal) position (Smith, 2010: 116). In the first section of the *Theory of Moral Sentiments* on 'Sympathy', Smith argues that through the ability to imagine the experiences of others, humans are unable to disassociate subjective feeling from the experiences of others. Put simply, to witness the suffering of others causes an unpleasant or even painful response in ourselves. When witnessing violence, harassment or cruelty, it is natural to feel shame, disgust, repulsion and grief. These emotional reactions are branded as irrational and misleading in the rationalist ethical traditions of Kant or Mills. For example, the utilitarian tradition actively encourages the moral chooser to not be swayed by feeling and instead to base choices on a mathematical calculation of suffering, even when the immediate consequences feel unnerving. But for Smith, sentiments (and emotions in general) can be understood as a source of motivation for moral action and, for this reason, we should listen to them as a source of information in making moral choices. Rational choice alone is, therefore, insufficient to motivate actions without some kind of motivational driver. In any moral quagmire, there is the option to do the right thing or the wrong thing, but there is also an option to do nothing or, at least, to claim that the choice is not a moral choice at all and to ignore the issue altogether.

Jesse Prinz modernizes key elements of Smith's ideas using findings from neuroscience and psychology, and shows that 'it is emotionally taxing to violate social and moral rules' (Prinz, 2006: 29). Prinz effectively demonstrates that emotions are not only essential for moral decisions, but that they are the driving force. Rationality is, perhaps, more of an ad hoc sense-making process that follows the immediacy of what Prinz calls 'gut reactions'. Moreover, Prinz is able to show how central social connectedness is to moral choice. To feel guilt or shame as a result of causing harm is one thing, but to do this in the presence of others intensifies these feelings. This can be the case even when external judgements are imagined or hypothetical through a kind of generalized other. Prinz is careful to explain that moral judgements are not only emotions, but that emotion is a necessary component in moral choice.

Meanwhile, Patricia Greenspan's work *Practical Guilt* (1995) makes the important distinction between guilt as a response to a situation and guilt in anticipation of future wrongdoing. Guilt as a response can easily act as a substitute for moral action and this is, perhaps, what we have seen in the example of the vegan demonstration described above. Guilt about senseless cruelty realized after the event may be experienced or rationalized as a sufficient response to the wrongdoing, with no need for further action. Guilt in anticipation is entirely different in that there is still time to assuage anticipated negative feelings, and this places individuals into a scenario with more agency with regard to feeling and action. In either case, acting on guilt or trying to dismiss it will result in lingering feelings of discomfort as neither option offers a clean resolution to the problem. To the vegan who acts on the moral impulse, there is always more that could be done and mass suffering continues to occur. For the non-vegan who feels conflicted about the suffering of animals, it is common to feel as though there is no completely moral response to cruelty, resulting in an immobilizing form of ambivalence about all possible moral pathways. This kind of ambivalence disrupts and undermines the good intentions of individuals wanting to act morally. Navigating this enduringly problematic situation – without individuals emotionally closing off entirely – requires a degree of functional ambivalence. In this application, ambivalence is not functional in contrast to 'dysfunctional' ambivalence, as all forms of ambivalence can be understood as having functional consequences. Rather, it is functional in that it is useful in serving a purpose when trying to achieve a specific goal.

Ambivalence

Ambivalence is not reducible to disinterest, apathy or indifference. Robert Merton rightly established that ambivalence, for the sociologist, is the result of conflicting structural conditions that place individuals in discordant positions (Merton, 1976). It is a feeling of being split between two or more beliefs that are either incompatible or comparably dissatisfying (*ambi* = both, *valence* = feeling). While it is often understood as a form of stalling in a decision-making process, its cause is not dependent on a lack of desire to make a decision. Rather, ambivalence results from the grey area between right and wrong, good and bad, and so on. Adorno famously captured this feeling in *Minima Moralia* with the claim that '[w]rong life cannot be lived rightly' (Adorno, 2005: 39). In this passage, Adorno is describing the tension of witnessing and rejecting the problem of homelessness from the standpoint of having safe housing. The middle-class individual has the fortune of safe housing, but the problem of homelessness is not the direct consequence of their privilege. Ultimately, the guilt felt by those with privilege does not help the homeless, because this problem is structural. There is no 'right' way for the privileged person to act or feel that would solve the problem. In the context of animal justice, the claim that 'it doesn't make any difference if I eat meat or not' is ambivalent about the real-world impacts of moral choices, but it cannot be fully understood in terms of apathy about animal suffering. Similarly, the vegan perspective requires a delicate balance of idealistic change with an acknowledgement that the problem is bigger than the contents of a dinner plate. In Judith Butler's analysis of Adorno's claim, she asks 'whose lives are already considered not lives, or only partially living, or already dead and gone, prior to any explicit destruction or abandonment?' (Butler, 2012: 10). If we are to consider animals lives as 'lives that matter' then Adorno's claim reveals the incredible scale of systematic violence that cannot be undone through individual ethical action. But Butler reminds us that Adorno is not giving up on morality in this statement, rather he is offering a space from which people can act morally without the weight of the world extinguishing their desire for justice.

Ambivalent perspectives *can*, therefore, serve as a productive middle space between two uncompromising ethical or political positions. In Patricia Greenspan's analysis of ambivalence and emotion, she argues that ambivalence allows a person to simultaneously hold contradicting views without being irrational (Greenspan, 1980: 223). Vegans are aware that by existing in the world, they are still contributing to instances of animal suffering despite their best efforts to avoid it, for instance through the use of commodified bees for pollination or animal-derived products in growing agricultural crops. In fact, it can be argued that committing to veganism depends on a degree of ambivalence, and for Greenspan (1980) this allows for actions to be based on judgements that do not always have to be perfectly logical. Ambivalence can be cultivated, deploying emotional management tactics so that activists can carry out their work of documenting the cruelty of animal treatment while leaving those same animals behind to continue their suffering (Bernatchez,

2024). For many humans who work with animals in ways that challenge otherwise held moral commitments, such as animal shelter workers who make decisions to euthanize those in their care, or lab technicians who perform tests on animals, ambivalence must be socially cultivated to facilitate their work (Arluke and Sanders, 1996). In contrast, sustained and long-term veganism relies on the individual's acknowledgement that moral choice is messy rather than clean, contradictory rather than black and white. Veganism in a meat-obsessed world is possible precisely because of ambivalence.

In Bauman's work on *Modernity and Ambivalence* (1991), the project of 20th-century mmodernization has relied on rigid forms of rationality and order to further the European Enlightenment project. But for Bauman, every effort to neatly order and categorize the world is met with exceptions that fall outside of rational systems. Modernity has no use for the unclassifiable, and yet it is unable to rid itself of the chaotic, the contradictory and the incompatible. Furthermore, apparently rational systems have permitted abject suffering from genocides and war, to environmental destruction and global economic exploitation. There is an overarching awareness of the failure of rational mastery in modernity, and the emotional consequence for individuals is a deeply held ambivalence about what modernity was supposed to be and what it is (Bauman, 1991: 231). Since, arguably, this is a problem that cannot be resolved with additional rationality, Bauman argues that the modern individual, taught to find comfort in order and consistency, struggles to process messy or contradictory circumstances such as those just described (1991: 233). In response to contingency, ambivalence is a sensible response to the realization that not every question has an answer and that not every choice is classifiable as right or wrong. As Giesen (2015: 63) notes: '[A]mbivalences, disturbances, paradoxes, misunderstandings, and exceptions are not critical risks to social order but rather indispensable elements of this order. That is, stability of social order relies not only on neat oppositions but also on the acceptance of the unclassifiable, of surprises and coincidences, ambiguity and fuzziness.'

Ambivalence permits the individual to grapple with chaos without resigning to nihilism or the denial of any form of truth whatsoever.

Empathy and the anti-animal status quo

This complex emotional landscape creates a challenging situation for those who would like to see animals recognized as subjects rather than consumable goods. While some scholars have posited a focus on humans' entangled webs of empathic interactions with other animals as key to moving toward these ends (for example, Gruen, 2015), we argue that a focus on emotion as the motivation of moral action is not sufficient to understand or challenge the current environment that legitimates the use of animals for human gain.

This is particularly so given the extent of ambivalent social actors passively consuming anti-animal messaging and animal products, as well as the placement of sites through which humans might interact and build empathy with other animals, as sanctuaries are often located in regional/rural areas where sufficient land is available.

All emotions can function as moral motivations. However, morality is also socially constructed and moral action is driven by external social factors as well as the emotional drivers mentioned earlier. Current Western society subscribes to an anti-animal status quo or, as Dinesh Wadiwel (2015) puts it, a 'war against animals'. This consists of social, political and economic systems that rely upon and perpetuate the objectification and use of other animals in accordance with human preferences and socialize humans into this ideology from birth (Cudworth, 2011; Cole and Stewart, 2014; Wadiwel, 2015). There is an argument to be made that this 'war' will not be won through individual empathetic connection alone, but also requires the normalization of non-animal use through a multitude of channels. These include community building to create more spaces and collectives that reject the (ab)use of animals for human gain and visibilize different ways of relating to other beings (Cudworth and Hobden, 2017), as well as increased availability of non-animal-based products and depoliticization of their use so that consumers can make more ethical choices without social consequence. While visual media are influential in many vegans' decision to pursue this lifestyle change, respondents in Fernández' (2021) study also cited personal relationships and experiences with veg*ns/activists and non-human animals, access to information, the influence of music and musicians and leaving their family home or city. This indicates that a politics of sight activism is not the only avenue through which veganism might be encouraged and sustained (though we are certainly not arguing for its cessation).

Research on ambivalence and meat eating echoes the importance of social connectedness and structural norms in maintaining behaviours that might otherwise be viewed as immoral or challenging to mainstream acceptable practices (Merton, 1976; Prinz, 2004, 2006; Bastian and Loughnan, 2017; Camilleri et al, 2020). Bastian and Loughnan (2017) argue that, in theory, people will experience dissonance and cease immoral actions when made aware that their meat-eating behaviours cause harm to others. However, this course of action is interrupted by 'passive dissonance avoidance strategies' which embed immoral behaviours in the imaginations of individuals and entire cultures (Bastian and Loughnan, 2017: 280). These strategies are the development of habitual behaviour, social norms, and ritualization and institutionalization, all of which serve to move meat eating from minded action to unquestioned 'natural, normal, and necessary' occurrence (Bastian and Loughnan, 2017: 280). Work in this area further supports an argument for ambivalence as a useful site through which veganism and pro-animal ideology might be perpetuated. For instance, actors who have committed to a stance (such as meat eating) are highly likely to align more strongly with the problematized practice when non-animal products or veganism are made visible or accessible, indicating that an undecided position is more amenable to pro-animal moral decision making (Bastian and Loughnan, 2017; Camilleri et al, 2020). Furthermore, where social actors appear ambivalent about veganism rather than staunchly committed to meat consumption there is perhaps more scope for activists to work on the normalization and structural change required to make veganism a habitual choice and facilitate lasting change. Of course, a focus on the normalization of plant-based eating and availability of products runs the risk of perpetuating a capitalist veganism that is excised from intersectional, justice-motivated social change (Giraud, 2021). This poses a particular dilemma for animal activists working from a foundational belief of total liberation – that is the understanding that systems of oppression reinforce each other and thus animal liberation depends on the overturning of other oppressive systems such as capitalism, racism and settler colonialism. From this perspective, leaning into capitalist 'solutions' to reduce animal suffering is by no means an effective way to achieve animal liberation. However, for those employing ambivalence as a response to facilitate the consumption of animals despite sentiment and moral inclinations to do otherwise, this form of almost-depoliticized veganism may provide a safe pathway to moral action that they otherwise would not take.

Conclusion

Emotion is an unavoidable feature of moral judgements. It is, perhaps, the fuel that propels the car forward, not the steering wheel that controls the direction. Therefore, embodied and interactional emotional experiences are essential to understanding moral judgements and moral actions. Reason can be employed to guide decisions and subject them to tests of logical consistency, but the act of making a moral judgement occurs through the experience of moral sentiments. The positioning of animals as objects for use is depoliticized, normalized and heavily supported by industries, discourses and social interactions that continuously supply messages endorsing the consumption of animals (Cudworth, 2011; Cole and Stewart, 2014; Wadiwel, 2015). Despite the widespread increase in veganism in recent years, 'meat culture' remains hegemonic. For the majority of non-vegans, the decision to eat meat is not reducible to a desire to hurt animals. Instead, the decision to eat animals is perhaps better understood as a habit, tradition or right. Eating meat, therefore, is more indicative of a lack of a moral judgement, based on a deep-seated ambivalence about moral choice and social change, rather than evidence of a 'pro-meat' moral judgement. There are examples of 'pro-meat' narratives that are more extreme, such as in links between carnist diets and toxic masculinity (Adams, 2025), or dairy consumption and white supremacy (Gambert and Linné, 2018). And while veganism can be understood as a rejection of dominant norms, animal consumption remains the default position, involving the lack of a decision rather than a conscious choice. However, the claim that a choice is 'not about ethics' does not simply make it so. Ambivalence functions here as a way to avoid confronting information that most of us would prefer not to think about, much like the 'Cube of Truth' demonstration discussed earlier.

We can think about some of these ideas as attempting to establish a distinction between what ethics are and what they do. The social bonds that are reaffirmed by shared ethical positions are not based on the truth of what ethics are in an objective or ontological context. We can determine that emotion is a motivation for moral judgements in the first place, but it is not reducible to this role. Emotions also guide moral judgements in one direction or another. There is useful information about morality to be found in our emotional experiences and our gut reactions (Prinz, 2004), but this does not equate to the claim that there is moral truth in emotion that somehow trumps our reason. The intense feelings that arise in response to witnessing a violent crime or a slaughterhouse killing floor ought to be recognized by processes of moral judgements, but it does not follow that all emotions are evidence of moral truth. Rather, these sentiments are framed by experiences such as ambivalence, which have an ongoing influence on emotions and morality.

In the course of this discussion, it is important to remember that these choices and sentiments are unavoidably human-centric. Existing amid these human debates are around 204 billion farmed animals who simply do not want to die (Mood et al, 2023); animals whose lives are manipulated at every stage from conception to death. So, the role of ambivalence in this instance needs to be constantly evolving rather than stagnant or fixed. It must adapt with cultural norms and developing agricultural practices. Ambivalence is a useful way to navigate complex and overwhelming ethical issues, but it must be a part of a process rather than an endpoint.

References

Aavik, K. (2019) 'The Rise of Veganism in Post-socialist Europe: Making Sense of Emergent Vegan Practices and Identities in Estonia'. In L. Wright (ed) *Through a Vegan Studies Lens: Textual Ethics and Lived Activism*, University of Nevada Press, pp 146–164.

Adams, C. (2025) *The Sexual Politics of Meat – 35th Anniversary Edition: A Feminist-Vegan Critical Theory*, Bloomsbury Publishing.

Adorno, T. (2005) *Minima Moralia: Reflections on a Damaged Life*, Verso.

Arluke, A. and Sanders, C. (1996) *Regarding Animals*, Temple University Press.

Asher, K. and Cherry, E. (2015) 'Home is where the food is: barriers to vegetarianism and veganism in the domestic sphere', *Journal for Critical Animal Studies*, 13(1): 66–91.

Barbalet, J. (2005) 'Smith's *Sentiments* (1759) and Wright's *Passions* (1601): the beginnings of sociology', *The British Journal of Sociology*, 56(2): 171–189.

Barbalet, J. (2011) 'Emotions beyond regulation: backgrounded emotions in science and trust', *Emotion Review*, 3(1): 36–43. https://doi.org/10.1177/1754073910380968

Barker, J. (2011) 'Chew on This: Disgust, Delay, and the Documentary Image in Food, Inc.', *Film-Philosophy*, 15(2): 70–89. https://doi.org/10.3366/film.2011.0026

Bastian, B. and Loughnan, S. (2017) 'Resolving the meat-paradox: a motivational account of morally troublesome behavior and its maintenance', *Personality and Social Psychology Review*, 21(3): 278–299.

Bauman, Z. (1991) *Modernity and Ambivalence*, Cornell University Press.

Bernatchez, A. (2024) 'Emotional reflexivity in the animal justice politics of sight: embodied moral shock and limit of the emotional repertoire', *Emotions and Society*, 6(1): 60–75.

Butler, J. (2012) 'Can one lead a good life in a bad life? Adorno Prize Lecture', *Radical Philosophy*, 176(September): 9–18.

Buttny, R. and Kinefuchi, E. (2020) 'Vegans' problem stories: negotiating vegan identity in dealing with omnivores', *Discourse & Society*, 31(6): 565–583.

Camilleri, L., Gill, P.R. and Jago, A. (2020) 'The role of moral disengagement and animal empathy in the meat paradox', *Personality and Individual Differences*, 164: 110103.

Cole, M. and Morgan, K. (2011) 'Vegaphobia: derogatory discourses of veganism and the reproduction of speciesism in UK national newspapers', *The British Journal of Sociology*, 62(1): 135–153.

Cole, M. and Stewart, K. (2014) *Our Children and Other Animals: The Cultural Construction of Human-Animal Relations in Childhood*, Routledge.

Cudworth, E. (2011) *Social Lives with Other Animals: Tales of Sex, Death and Love*, Springer.

Cudworth, E. and Hobden, S. (2017) *The Emancipatory Project of Posthumanism*, Routledge.

Dole, N. (2017) 'Australian Government's ban on live exports to Indonesia "irrational", cattle farmers tell court', ABC News, 19 July 2017. https://www.abc.net.au/news/2017-07-19/cattle-export-class-action-against-federal-government/8723046

Fernández, L. (2021) 'Images that liberate: moral shock and strategic visual communication in animal liberation activism', *Journal of Communication Inquiry*, 45(2): 138–158.

Francione, G. (1996) *Rain without Thunder: The Ideology of the Animal Rights Movement*, Temple University Press.

Freeman, C.P. (2013) 'Stepping Up to the Veggie Plate: Framing Veganism as Living Your Values'. In E. Plec (ed) *Perspectives on Human-Animal Communication: International Communication*, Taylor and Francis, pp 93–112.

Gambert, I. and Linné, T. (2018) 'From rice eaters to soy boys: race, gender, and tropes of "plant food masculinity"', *Animal Studies Journal*, 7(2): 129–179.

Giesen, B. (2015) 'Inbetweenness and Ambivalence'. In A. Horvath, B. Thomassen and H. Wydra (eds) *Breaking Boundaries: Varieties of Liminality*, Berghahn Books, pp 61 –71.

Giraud, E. (2021) *Veganism: Politics, Practice and Theory*, Bloomsbury Academic.

Greenspan, P. (1980) 'A Case of Mixed Feelings: Ambivalence and the Logic of Emotion'. In A. Rorty (ed) *Explaining Emotions*, University of California Press, pp 223–250.

Greenspan, P. (1995) *Practical Guilt: Moral Dilemmas, Emotions, and Social Norms*, Oxford University Press.

Gruen, L. (2015) *Entangled Empathy: An Alternative Ethic for our Relationships with Animals*, Lantern Books.

Kołakowski, L. (1968) *Toward a Marxist Humanism* (translated by J. Zielonko), Grove Press.

McCasker, T. (2017) '"Cube of Truth": Anonymous Hit Streets with Violent Footage of Animal Farming', *The Guardian (Australia)*, 31 January. Available at: www.theguardian.com/world/2017/jan/31/cube-of-truth-anonymous-hit-streets-with-violent-footage-of-animal-farming

McKenzie, J. (2018) 'Political ambivalence as praxis: the limits of consensus in Habermas's Theory of the Public Sphere', *Critical Horizons*, 19(1): 35–48.

McKenzie, J. (2019) 'Emotion and Morality: A Sociological Reading of the Philosophy of Emotion'. In R. Patulny, A. Bellocchi, R. Olson, S. Khorana, J. McKenzie and M. Peterie (eds) *Emotions in Late Modernity*, Routledge, pp 56–68.

Merton, R. (1976) *Sociological Ambivalence and other Essays*, Free Press.

Mood, A., Lara, E., Boyland, N.K. and Brooke, P. (2023) 'Estimating global numbers of farmed fishes killed for food annually from 1990 to 2019', *Animal Welfare*, 32: e12. https://doi.org/10.1017/awf.2023.4

Oliver, C. (2021) *Veganism, Archives, and Animals: Geographies of a Multispecies World*, Routledge.

Pendergrast, N. (2015) 'Live animal export, humane slaughter and media hegemony', *Animal Studies Journal*, 4(1): 99–125.

Prinz, J. (2004) *Gut Reactions: A Perceptual Theory of Emotion*, Oxford University Press.

Prinz, J. (2006) 'The emotional basis of moral judgments', *Philosophical Explorations*, 9(1): 29–43.

Rees, L., Rothman, N., Lehavy, R. and Sanchez-Burks, J. (2013) 'The ambivalent mind can be a wise mind: emotional ambivalence increases judgment accuracy', *Journal of Experimental Social Psychology*, 49: 360–367.

Roberts, T. (2023) 'Unemotionality—absence, emptiness, and affective insensitivity'. In M.H. Jacobsen (ed) *Exploring Emotions in Social Life*, Taylor & Francis, pp 226–240.

Simmel, G. (1903) 'The Metropolis and Mental Life'. In G. Bridge and S. Watson (eds) (2002) *The Blackwell City Reader*, Wiley-Blackwell, pp 11–19.

Sinclair, M., Derkley, T., Fryer, C. and Phillips, C.J. (2018) 'Australian public opinions regarding the live export trade before and after an animal welfare media expose', *Animals*, 8(7): 106.

Smith, A. (2010) [1759] *The Theory of Moral Sentiments*. Penguin Classics.

Tiplady, C.M., Walsh, D.A.B. and Phillips, C.J.C. (2012) 'Public response to media coverage of animal cruelty', *Journal of Agricultural and Environmental Ethics*, 26: 869–885. https://doi.org/10.1007/s10806-012-9412-0

Wadiwel, D. (2015) *The War Against Animals*, Brill.

9

The Embroidery Collective: Embroidering and Reimagining Community in Times of Struggle

Cristina Florescu

Introduction

The Embroidery Collective was a mutual aid project started in Ireland by activists from migrant and minority ethnic backgrounds as a way of connecting when the COVID-19 pandemic made connection more difficult than ever. It was formed of women and marginalized genders who used to organize together on housing, reproductive justice, anti-racism and anti-fascism before the start of the pandemic and found themselves alone in the face of loss, grief and anxiety during lockdown. The Collective became a political space of shared experiences and now, in a 'post-pandemic world',[1] there are some valuable lessons to be drawn from the Collective about reimagining community and political organizing in spite of and alongside the ambivalence we experience as community organizers in a world of growing anxieties.

During the pandemic, the Collective challenged those of us involved in community organizing to rethink what a political space and political organizing meant for us. Was it just putting your body out in the street? Leading marches and protests? Managing social media accounts? Projecting our resources outwards? Or could a more quiet, internal and self-reflective form of organizing be as valuable and perhaps more sustainable during the pandemic? The Collective showed the importance of care and hope in political organizing. Building on these questions, and with the perspective of the last few years where disasters, wars and genocides dominate our everyday news, I learned that it is important for community organizers to consider the central roles of hope and care, because, if we want to preserve our communities, we need to make sure these two concepts are central to our organizing.

Political organizing is ambivalent in many ways, but one of the main ones is that it stems from people's desire to find hope when they are painfully aware of the hopelessness in the world. Hope, as I am sure many organizers would agree, has been particularly hard to find in a 'post-pandemic' world where our emotional and physical capacity has been decimated by this collective trauma. Centring care is, perhaps, one of the sustainable ways in which we can move forward in a political landscape where one disaster follows another. Looking inward, rather than projecting outward, is a way to avoid the burn-out and numbness that a lot of us are experiencing more and more. This kind of community organizing makes sure that radical politics continue to exist in a world where burn-out, hopelessness and fatigue distract us and stop us from working toward the world we want to see.

Care and hope were central aspects of the Collective, as members gathered together trying to find some hope in the desolate landscape of the COVID-19 pandemic. It also became a space where we offered care through small acts, such as checking in on WhatsApp, sharing embroidery tips and even food recipes. In doing so, the Collective created a space for finding connection in a world where physical connection was impossible.

The Collective was also a space where art, creativity and politics met, and where identities were explored through our emotions. As community organizers, we tend to intellectualize, debate and discuss the issues that affect us. I believe that the Collective showed us the importance of sitting with our emotions through the act of embroidery, which was more than a physical act: it was a way of channelling whatever feelings we were experiencing at the time, be it grief, frustration or sadness, onto a piece of fabric.

I would like to suggest that the Collective was an important form of political organizing, despite having feminine, undervalued characteristics and despite being unconventional and, at a first glance, apolitical. It is, in fact, because of these feminine, undervalued characteristics that the Collective offers some important learnings about what it means *to be political* or to create *a political space.*

As organizers of marginalized genders, the members of the Collective have always come up against sexism in the spaces where we organized. We talk about invisible work or emotional labour in the home, but the same kind of labour takes place in political organizing. Those who are most valued are those who become the face of the movement, who put their bodies on the street, write papers, attend conferences and give speeches. But there is not much praise for those who make meals so that everyone attending a sit-in is fed, for those who let a community member cry in their living room because of the precarity in their lives, or for those who look after the children so that more bodies can go into the street. This is feminized work that goes undervalued and unsung. The majority of the members of the Collective shared the belief in the importance of feminized work and, in an environment where it was impossible and unsafe to put our bodies on the street, to attend conferences and give speeches, this type of care work became central. The Collective was not just an embroidery group, it was a place where comrades shared recipes, talked about the best protective equipment that would keep us safe or ordered food for people who could not cook for themselves. It is because of its feminized work that I think the Collective can show a model of dealing with the ambivalence that activism brings to the surface: finding the strength to organize against issues that seem larger than life, from climate change to racism; creating community in a society that keeps pushing the narrative of individualism; finding horizontal ways of organization when our tendency is to go to the default top-down organization we see all around us. Through its feminized nature, the Collective presents a model of care as resistance.

Audre Lorde writes about carrying her identity as a Black Lesbian into all aspects of her community work, whether it was supporting 'striking students occupying buildings at City College in 1969' or picketing 'for Welfare Mothers' Rights and against the enforced sterilization of young Black girls' (Lorde, 2017: 19). Similarly, the members of the Collective carried our racialized, queer, migrant identities with us, whether we were organizing during the Irish abortion rights referendum in 2018 or creating an embroidery space two years later during a pandemic. Our very existence as minorities – be it because we belong to marginalized genders or ethnicities – is inherently political. As a result, the Collective, as a space formed of minorities with a political consciousness, looking to build a community in times of struggle, became a political space.

Finally, in this chapter, I also explore the Collective's aftermath and my reflections on sharing this space and activity for a brief period of time, now that things have 'returned to normal'. With the benefit of perspective, I would like to pose two questions: What learnings can we take from a time when we tried our hardest to create shared experiences while sharing a physical space was deemed unsafe? Have we, as a society, learned how to be more inclusive and caring with our communities? I am not sure I have the answer to these questions, and I invite the reader to consider them while engaging with this piece.

Starting The Embroidery Collective

The Embroidery Collective was a mutual aid project created as a way of rethinking community and connection. The Collective's members came from marginalized backgrounds due to their disability, gender or sexual identity, race or ethnicity. It is no surprise that for people who were already marginalized, the pandemic was all the more isolating. In the case of the Collective, our feelings of isolation were exacerbated by being far away from our countries, our families or other traditional support systems. The isolation was exacerbated by being far away from each other – the chosen families, communities and ties we had created through our activism before the pandemic. How do we create connection, when breathing the same air or touching the same objects as other people was deemed unsafe? For us, it started with a piece of fabric.

Led by Emily Waszak, a migrant textile worker and artist, our idea was to circulate a piece of fabric alongside threads and needles in the post. Each person who received it was to embroider something on the piece of fabric to their best abilities before sending it on, therefore creating a sense of community and collective through this shared experience and material. This was during the first wave of COVID-19, at the height of a stringent wave of lockdowns in Ireland that made us feel isolated in our anxiety and grief. Some of us were grieving the loss of a person. Others were grieving different losses, like the loss of our social lives, the loss of our connections and communities, the loss of our lives as we knew them. We were all anxious about the future, our families and the precarity of our own lives that had been heightened by the pandemic.

We embroidered our shared piece as a way of connecting to each other and having a moment of peace. This connection became palpable in its most literal sense: as we passed the piece of fabric from person to person, it not only became rich in embroidery telling the story of our state of mind or our passions, but it also became softer. The fabric got shinier and more malleable under the many hands that touched it.

After a few months, the project developed. We secured funding from the Arts Council of Ireland and invested in materials, an artist fee and mentorship from an external artist named Isabel Lima, who facilitated online workshops for us and shared her own journey with embroidering during the pandemic. We each started working on our own samplers, with the theme of exploring the embroidery history in each of our cultures, as the members identified with countries all over the world: China, Colombia, Honduras, Iran, India, Japan, Malaysia, Pakistan and Romania.

We had virtual meetings where we presented traditional embroideries from our countries, which was a culturally rich experience that allowed all of us to reconnect to lost and often complicated feelings about our roots. With being a migrant comes a certain degree of ambivalence: feeling like we are from two places but no place at the same time, trying to make a new country our home while facing discrimination that reminds us it will never truly be our home, having trauma about certain aspects of our culture while trying to defend it in the face of racism and xenophobia. Through our virtual meetings, we discovered that the embroidery history of all our cultures was rich, and that embroidery was never *just* about textile work. As with the Collective, in each country from China to Romania, embroidery was linked to community, to creating connections, to adding value, culture and tradition to a feminized space. By exploring this, we were able to create a new type of connection to our cultures, in spite of the ambivalences and mixed feelings we experienced as migrants and minorities. The Collective became a way of not only being together and sharing a bit of our backgrounds at a time when we had to stay apart for our own safety, but also a way of experiencing our cultures when we could not go back to our countries and experience them in other ways.

The Collective was based on the idea that emotions are felt collectively. It is through these collective feelings that community work emerges. It was certainly what had driven us toward community work before: collective rage, collective frustration, collective hope. The Collective thus became a way of feeling collectively while being apart. It was a way to build a community and have something to look forward to at a time when communal practices and optimism seemed impossible. It enabled us to remember our beliefs in the power of non-hierarchical organizing at a time when all our organizing felt futile. The Collective became a way of celebrating the feminized, domestic work often undervalued in activism, and a way of doing something for ourselves instead of projecting our work outward.

Many of our members doubted their ability to embroider, but as the project developed, we became more confident. Most of us did not feel hopeful about the future, but meeting up online, embroidering and sharing knowledge and support became something to look forward to. The Collective became a testament to how political organizing can take many forms and exist in an ambivalent, insecure space. After all, what is more ambivalent than engaging in the relaxing, peaceful act of embroidery to deal with feelings of grief, anger and hopelessness?

The Embroidery Collective and ambivalence

When we think of embroidery, most of us in Western culture imagine a Jane Austen-style drawing room and women doing dainty embroidery while chatting or wistfully staring out the window. However, many of us in the Collective discovered embroidery as a way of channelling our anger. As our mentor Isabel Lima put it, 'the punctures of the needle against the resistance of the fabric were therapeutic'. They were a way of channelling our anger and frustrations in a world where the inequalities we had been organizing against were becoming more and more obvious because of the pandemic and we felt impotent in our isolation. The subjects of our embroidery on our initial shared piece of fabric were vastly diverse, and ranged from star motifs to the anarchy sign, showing the variety of feelings we were putting into our embroidery: optimism, hope, revolt, frustration. The material ambivalence of the Collective lay in using embroidering – with its dainty needles, fragile threads and soft fabrics – as the vessel for expressing feelings of frustration, anger, hopelessness, grief, sadness. It was an activity that allowed us to take a break from our day and sit with our feelings. The act of embroidery had both calming and cathartic potential. By making us take a break from our anxieties, it provided a safe and peaceful space. By providing that safe and peaceful space, it allowed strong emotions to bubble to the surface. These two sentiments did not go against each other, but rather, they coexisted for most of us.

The Collective also enabled an ambivalent space by helping us to have a community when communal experiences were unsafe; it helped us connect when connection seemed impossible; it made us look forward to doing something when we felt like we had no sense of purpose; it made us invest time in our creativity in an absurd world where our own future as a society was being put into question.

As time has passed and the threat and trauma of the COVID-19 pandemic have been forgotten, I attempt to return to that space of ambivalence, trying to take something from it. What is our future as a society? How has the pandemic changed us? Who are the *us* and *we* and who remains, or is even more excluded, than before? I find more questions than answers as I struggle to process my own emotions and trauma in a world that has forced me, as many others, to move on, to go back to work, go back to worrying about plans, obligations, bills. I find it hard to connect and go back to myself as I did in those times, and I keep thinking that I could have drawn more from that practice. Perhaps the pandemic was our chance – as community organizers, as those politicized and seeking a different world, but also all of us as the inhabitants of this world, and those who became more aware of inequalities and struggles during the pandemic – to reimagine the world and start over. Perhaps we failed as we have returned to the same system of capitalist oppression that we knew before, as we have moved on, uncaring, and continue to leave people behind. But I do want to hang on to something I learned by being part of the Collective: the notion of care and looking inward as a way of radical activism.

Embroidery and political activism

You might ask, what is so political about embroidering? Exploring a new hobby with your friends might not seem like a radical act of political activism, but – as mentioned before – the existence of the Collective was political in a few different ways. First, the Collective was formed of women and marginalized genders from migrant and minority ethnic backgrounds.

Our existence is inherently political. Moreover, by focusing our embroidery samplers on each of our cultures, the act of embroidery gained another political dimension. Our members used the sampler to reconnect with parts of their identity, with cultures we had been removed from at an early age or had been parted from because of migration; cultures we maybe had a complicated relationship with. We let go of intellectualizing our identities and instead connected with them through embroidery. Second, the members were people who are involved in many types of activism. That meant that we brought our politics into the Collective: politics about non-hierarchical organizing, politics about community care, community work and mutual aid. In the absence of a physical space where we could conduct our meetings as normal, the Collective became a place where we tried to apply those same radical politics.

In addition, embroidery and textile work have historically been a political act. At the time of writing this chapter, Palestine comes to my mind. In this ongoing escalated genocide, we see the presence of the Keffiyeh and its symbolic embroidery as a symbol of resistance that has endured through the decades. My social media feed is being populated by people wearing this embroidered fabric to express their solidarity. In the Palestinian context, embroidery is creating a space of resistance; a space where the histories and identities of the oppressed prevail.

This idea of textile work as politics was also explored within the Collective. In exploring our different cultures, a running thread was that embroidery was always feminized and it was an opportunity for women to gossip,[2] share community updates and talk about their thoughts in a society that did not give much space for that group of people to express themselves. It created a space where community work and community care flowed naturally, where struggles were being shared and solidarity was found. Similarly, the Collective entered the space our activism used to occupy. It became a space where we gathered in online meetings and shared life updates, jokes and care work.

Finally, the most politically radical thing about the Collective was that it opposed the common narratives we saw at the height of this pandemic. A capitalist narrative that encouraged us to 'keep on keeping on', to adapt to the new normal, to find a new hobby, bake that bread, buy those plants, make ourselves feel better through consumerism and denial in this crisis. Despite being a new hobby for most of us, embroidering did not have that capitalist framework. It was not a new skill we wanted to master or a way of enforcing toxic positivity. The act of embroidery was there for everyone to make of it what they wanted. Some turned it into a long-term hobby, others worked on confronting their perfectionism and being okay with being mediocre at something. For some it was a meditative practice, for others something to do absent-mindedly in front of the TV. Some of us are not interested in embroidering again, while for others it has become a steady activity.

So, embroidery can be political in more than one way. It can express solidarity, connection, it can provide a space to share updates, it can be anti-capitalist in its steady rhythm that opposes production and productivity, but most importantly it can help us reimagine community organizing in a world where the burn-out and discouragement we are seeing from people in the face of disaster and persistent systemic inequalities make reimagining community work absolutely necessary.

Conclusion: Ambivalence and care in political organizing

When I wrote the presentation for the Ambivalent Activism webinar series in 2022, I had grouped my learnings into neat bullet points:

- political organizing can take many forms;
- political organizing can turn inward and focus on care instead of being projected outward;
- 'feminized' work should be celebrated in activism; and
- grief and negative feelings need to be acknowledged and allowed to exist in political organizing and community.

Four years after the onset of the COVID-19 pandemic, as I sit down to write this chapter, my learning feels a lot murkier. The Collective's activity slowed down and eventually stopped as its members had to go back to their own lives, deal with personal traumas and face an ever-changing world in the transition period that followed the roll-out of the vaccines and the so-called return to normal. That is not to say that the Collective was futile. I truly believe that it served a great purpose of bringing us together in a time when community seemed impossible. I also believe that it achieved its goals: bringing people together, providing a support system, a space of relaxation or a way of channelling anger, a distraction, a hobby or whatever its members needed at that moment.

When I first sat down to write this chapter, I was excited to see the new perspectives the passing of time would give me, but the truth is that I have more open questions than deep conclusions. As I look back on this moment of reimagining communities and collective care, I wonder: How can I be better now at caring and holding space for the more marginalized members in my community? Would we as a society have been better at processing the trauma if we had been given the time and space instead of being pushed to move forward? Have I been able to use the learnings from the Collective to process my feelings better? How has the COVID-19 pandemic changed political organizing?

I truly believe that we have not processed the COVID-19 trauma as the general response in most, if not all parts of the world, has been to move on and pretend it never existed. Capitalism leaves no time to grieve or process complex feelings, but what I see now are political organizers who are even more prone to burn-out than before, people with a limited capacity to hold space and bear witness to humanitarian disasters such as the ongoing genocides in Palestine, Sudan or the Congo. People are faced with the ambivalence of being aware of their power and at the same time being discouraged about the little impact that their actions have on governments and systemic change, which negatively affects social movements. Perhaps this is a direct consequence of the pandemic, or perhaps it is just something that was a long time coming in late-stage capitalism. What I would like to hold on to from my days in the Collective is the notion of making *care* a central element of political organizing; and I mean real, authentic, collective care, not the individualized self-care that we are sold in the shape of long baths and scented candles. The idea that there is room for creativity and embracing the feminized work in organizing, and the idea that it is okay to have ambivalent or opposing feelings. I would like to normalize looking after each other in political spaces even when we feel lonely and desolate; being comfortable with holding space for each other's anger, hopelessness or grief, while also holding space for hope; putting our bodies in the street, while also appreciating the care work that goes behind keeping those bodies on the street; being realistic about how those who rule us will not liberate us, while also celebrating the victory of any small uprising, riot or encampment. Returning to Audre Lorde's work, I draw on her idea of self-care not as an act of self-indulgence, but as an 'act of political warfare' (Lorde, 2017: 95). This invites us to move beyond self-care and think in terms of community care and the central role it can have in how we reimagine the world and hold space for the ambivalence that makes this reimagining possible.

As community organizers we are used to holding space for ambivalence: we organize in spite of oppression, we march in spite of the threat of violent police retaliation, we wear our marginalized identities proudly in spite of racism or homophobia. In a world where we are organizing against escalating unrest, inequalities and disasters, it is important to embrace this ambivalence and remain radicalized and organized *in spite of* and *because of* them. In the face of these escalating threats, it is also important to reimagine politics, expand our understanding of what a political space is, and centre care. I truly believe that by doing so, we might find a way to resist burn-out and a way to overcome the tendency to run away from ambivalence and the desire to 'move on' at all costs without learning or processing complicated feelings and events. And it is only by learning how to do so that we can efficiently organize in the future.

Notes

[1] I use the term 'post-pandemic world' in quotation marks to acknowledge that the COVID-19 pandemic as well as structural inequalities continue to affect disabled people, grieving people and those most marginalized in our societies.

[2] I use the word 'gossip' here on purpose, to reclaim this term that has also been feminized and devalued. I am using it as a word that refers to sharing news about our community and a lighthearted way of building connection.

Reference

Lorde, A. (2017) *A Burst of Light and Other Essays*, Ixia Press.

10

Ambivalent Emotions Empowering Activism: Learning from Youth Activists in Aotearoa

Carisa R. Showden and Karen Nairn

Introduction

> I'm optimistic but I'm very pessimistic as well, so I'm very critical at the same time which is a weird mix.
>
> Ian, Generation Zero

Ambivalence works. Ambivalence *is work*. Popular narratives about activists, especially youth activists, often suggest they are optimistic to the point of naivety. But in our research with young activists in Aotearoa New Zealand, participants expressed a range of emotions that motivate them and a mix of feelings about the possibilities for success. These ambivalent emotions often sustain individuals, groups and individuals in groups as they combat social injustice in manifold forms. This ambivalence is also work, though. Navigating the sources and effects of ambivalence becomes part of the emotional effort required to keep going when facing apathetic publics or movement setbacks.

This chapter looks at how ambivalence motivated and sustained activism among participants in six youth-led groups in Aotearoa New Zealand. In the literature on emotions in activism, ambivalence is often seen as negative, a contradiction to be overcome in order to reduce tension (Rothman et al, 2017). We build on work looking instead at the many uses of ambivalence (McManus, 2011; Moss and Wilson, 2014; González-Hidalgo, 2021; Emejulu, 2022). We start by situating our analysis in recent literature positing ambivalence as a thinking and emotionally regulatory tool (Breslow, 2022; Mrovlje, 2022; Poursanidou et al, 2022), a hesitance or uncertainty that serves as an important resource for epistemic humility and creativity (McManus,

2011; Moss and Wilson, 2014; Poursanidou et al, 2022), and a critique of the 'feeling rules' that discipline the meaning of 'activist' identities (Emejulu, 2022). We then explain our methods and introduce the groups we worked with before discussing three ways that activists in our study understood ambivalence as central to their social justice work: as part of their motivations, their sense of the (im)possible, and as a moderating mechanism within and effected by groups. We conclude with reflections on the pedagogical import of ambivalence in activism.

The meanings and uses of ambivalence in social movements

To be ambivalent is to have contradictory feelings or ideas about a problem or state of being. It is a liminal state of being on a threshold, neither here nor there but 'precariously balanced between competing ways of feeling' (Emejulu, 2022). Ambivalence is not the same as 'ambiguity' because it cannot be resolved with 'more' or 'better' knowledge. Instead, ambivalence is a 'product of our sociological and ecological embeddedness ... an unavoidable condition of being a social actor' (Carolan, 2010: 320).

Embracing ambivalence is a way of resisting the 'reductive binarisms between the social and the antisocial and between positive and negative affect' (Cvetkovich, 2012: 6). For example, social theorist Ann Cvetkovich (2012: 6) argues that happiness does not require eliminating negative feelings but can emerge through 'finding ways to survive disappointment and to remind ourselves of the persistence of radical visions and ways of living'. She describes The Public Feelings Project, whose key aim is 'to depathologize negative feelings so that they can be seen as a possible resource for political action rather than as its antithesis' in service of a future that does not 'assume that good politics can only emerge from good feelings; feeling bad might, in fact, be the ground for transformation' (2012: 2–3). Similarly, Marien González-Hidalgo (2021: 1300) finds that when activists share emotions such as anger, sorrow and frustration 'in their everyday conversations, and in their meetings and rituals', they turn them into positive resources and collectively develop critical subjectivities and communities.

Complex, multi-generational, intersectional problems like climate change, colonization and sexual violence cannot be reduced to simple causes. To insist on a singular emotional register as *the* motor or effect of action against injustice fails to apprehend this complexity. Yet 'hope' or 'anger' or 'fear' are often centrally, and singularly, figured in narratives of political emotions. When discussing youth activists, 'hope' appears frequently, conceptualized as the counter to 'negative affects' that are 'deemed apolitical or reactive' such as anxiety and fear (McManus, 2011). But hope has no political orientation and is neither singular in meaning nor wholly positive. As political theorist Susan McManus (2011) argues, hope can lead to an affirmation of hegemonic relations and not just motivate resistance projects. This is because, she continues, fear and hope are not opposites, even though fear has been harnessed to justify the security state, 'tough on crime' policies and similar political moves, while hope is routinely associated with 'progress'. Instead 'the last best hope of the hope-project in a fearful age might just be in ... critical exploration of the political polyvalence of the affective register, identifying the ways affects can orient or dispose very different agential possibilities' (McManus, 2011). Thus, ambivalence can be a way of orienting hope toward more radical or social justice ends. For those not currently benefiting from the status quo, ambivalence is warranted, and it indicates a particular kind of critical orientation toward politics and the future, a critical orientation necessary for generating critique and praxis that could bring about the conditions for a more just world.

Hope itself is, thus, complicated by and imbricated with other emotions, often fear, depression or other 'bad feelings' (McManus, 2011; Cvetkovich, 2012). Hope is also goal-directed rather than merely wishful thinking (McGeer, 2004; Milona, 2019; Alberro, 2021; Stockdale, 2021). As such, it is anticipatory, intense and pointing to the uncertainty of the future, which is potentially also full of anguish. In this vein, philosopher Victoria McGeer has written about how hope is cognitive, affective and collectively generated and sustained. This kind of complex, political hope is what McGeer (2004) calls *hoping well*. To *hope well* means that we face our agential limits and imagine creative ways to develop our capacities further. This entails actively and reflexively leaning 'into the hard work of negotiating group dynamics' and structural inequities in the process of catalysing a vision of, and working toward, a more just future (Nairn et al, 2024). As we will see later, for our participants, choosing to be hopeful means they felt ambivalent about hope and what they might achieve, but proceeded anyway.

This resonates with scholarship finding ambivalence to be where hopefulness blooms. Sara Ahmed (2002: 559) links ambivalence to an uncertainty about the outcomes of our actions, arguing that 'anticipating what it is that we might yet become' is hope tinged with both fear and nostalgia. Rather than foreclosing action, this emotive ambivalence 'stresses the possibility of restructuring both feelings and agency' (McManus, 2011). Specifically, as Akwugo Emejulu (2022) writes, ambivalent emotions serve as a form of resistance to the 'feeling rules' of activism. These 'feeling rules' are part of the 'relational flows, fluxes or currents, in between people and places' (Davidson et al, 2016 [2007]: 3). Hochschild (1979) and Emejulu (2022) argue that 'misfeeling' these rules becomes a refusal to perform certain kinds of emotional management; as such, it is a form of resistance and 'an emotional process by which solidarity can be built and sustained' (Emejulu, 2022).

Part of this resistance is slowing down, taking time to be with one's feelings and one's people, refusing the timelines and efficiency injunctions of the contemporary neoliberal order. Thus, Emejulu (2022) argues, ambivalence as misfeeling can be deeply satisfying, as it 'can be understood as a moment of contemplation, of recuperation, a state of critical self-reflection ... before meaningful action can take place'. In this slowing down, ambivalence is also a feature of the necessary patience of doing politics on a long-scale time horizon. It is a necessary, understandable and worthwhile response to the slowness and frustrations inevitable in tackling multi-generational injustices. An affective politics of ambivalent emotions 'is a politics that comes from remaining patient with the moments before and after so-called revolution' (Cvetkovich, 2012: 7).

In short, ambivalence has particular, salutatory, effects in forcing us to pause and reflect, to 'camp out, temporarily, in this liminal space of hesitation' (Emejulu, 2022). This rejection of the feeling rules and seemingly requisite certainties of politics and activism can also promote epistemic humility and heterogeneity (Poursanidou et al, 2022; West, 2022). These dispositions are critical for working with others and for being open to creative problem solving.

Further, ambivalent emotional states can lead to, or enhance, creativity (Cvetkovich, 2012; Moss and Wilson, 2014) when they open up different ways of approaching problems. Because ambivalence can accentuate 'the multidirectionality and malleability of the affective register in ways that can encourage ideological disruption and resignification' (McManus, 2011), new possibilities for action can be imagined. A key lesson of The Public Feelings Project is that ambivalence is important for reframing social and political engagement. When despair or anger is all that remains after encountering injustice, or when such 'negative' intensities are built into the design of the economic and political systems, how we approach each other and build community is paramount. Ambivalence, rather than certitude, might allow hopefulness to bloom in the face of recent histories of decolonization, civil rights, socialism and labour struggles (Cvetkovich, 2012).

In sum, ambivalence is a reasonable response to existing political conditions and, possibly, a form of self-protection. Ambivalence is also experienced temporally: a mix of feelings at the same time or a range of feelings over time. And ambivalence is nearly unavoidable in group contexts given the inevitable affective disparities among the individuals comprising groups; this is the case even as groups generate affects that make agency possible. Groups can palliate the potentially paralysing feelings generated by persistent existential struggles such as gender-based violence or the environmental crisis (Fraser, 1996; Alberro, 2021; González-Hidalgo, 2021). This makes ambivalence its own useful state of being, 'that precarious balance between understanding the forces arrayed against you that cause deep harm and the possibilities, the longings for self-tending and pleasure in community with like-minded others' (Emejulu, 2022). Ambivalence works as a critical feature of collective, creative social action, teaching other ways to feel as we create fresh modes of social relations (Emejulu, 2022).

Methods

Our analysis draws from a three-year study with six youth-led activist groups in Aotearoa New Zealand. We defined 'youth' as roughly aged 18 to early 30s, allowing participants to opt into this category because 'youth' can be understood differently depending on culture and context (Eliason et al, 2015; Opai, 2021).[1] The multi-method study was designed to explore activists' motivations for joining groups to create social change, what sustains groups over time, and each group's vision. With 90 participants, we conducted two in-depth activist history interviews roughly a year apart that focused on activists' experiences growing up, catalysts for joining their group, and what bolstered their activism over time. We also engaged in ethnographic fieldwork, including participant observation at meetings, campaigns and events held both in-person and online. This provided information about group processes over a period of two years and allowed us to observe emotions and group affects in action. Finally, each group was also invited to present their vision for social change as a 'living manifesto', which could take any form the group wished, with funding support from the research grant.[2] We received institutional ethics approval for the research, though we also navigated issues of temporality and power in gaining group consent (Nairn et al, 2020) and attempted to practise research collaboratively rather than extractively as much as possible (Nairn et al, 2022, 2024). Throughout the study, we were reflexively mindful of positionalities that differed between research team members and participants (for example, settler/colonial; straight/queer); and remained cognizant that interviews often raised sensitive topics, and so offered additional support as needs arose.[3]

The groups we worked with are tackling an array of urgent issues, many of them interconnected. Some participants were active across multiple groups, and some groups worked together on specific campaigns. Protect Ihumātao fights to reclaim indigenous land confiscated by the colonial government in 1863, resisting a proposed high-end housing project at Ihumātao. JustSpeak aims to reduce, and ultimately eliminate, incarceration by reimagining justice as 'health not handcuffs'.[4] Thursdays in Black is fighting rape culture and working toward a world without sexual violence.[5] Generation Zero is working toward a zero-carbon future to address climate change.[6] InsideOUT Kōaro is promoting rainbow youth visibility and safety in schools and communities. ActionStation is a people-powered online petition platform addressing diverse social and economic justice issues.

Ambivalence among Aotearoa's youth activists

Participants in our study ranged widely in their reflections on the emotional labour of being an activist and doing activism. Here we discuss three of the themes that emerged repeatedly and across groups in ways that speak to, but also complicate, the literatures noted above. These themes intersect as they shape activists' sense of purpose and their actions.

Motivations: mixed emotions and ambivalent meanings

Our initial research project was titled 'Hope in Action?'. Therefore, hope framed our early interviews, but some participants questioned this framing. Thus, we began asking if 'hope' was the right word or emotion to capture what motivated activism. When Letitia and Annie,[7] both from InsideOut Kōaro, were asked this question, each proffered anger and frustration, but then labelled that a form of hope:

> It's more like frustration or anger that kind of motivates me. But then, I guess that's hope at the same time. I don't really know how to categorize it ... like, the future is hopeful [although I'm angry about the past]. But, I guess, that's, I don't know, how to, I don't know how to articulate that. (Letitia, InsideOut Kōaro)

> Yeah I think hope is a very important one. I wouldn't be doing this work if I didn't think that things would change. Sometimes it can be ... anger at why people aren't doing things ... so yeah, both hope and anger. (Annie, InsideOut Kōaro)

Letitia conveys uncertainty about how to name these mixed emotions, while Annie's anger and action are spurred by others' indifference or hostility rather than stifled by it. Here, Letitia and Annie's strong mix of emotions motivate and sustain their work despite facing apathetic or belligerent others, echoing Kathleen Rodgers' (2010) study on emotion work among Amnesty International activists. Their reflections demonstrate how emotions function in 'relational flows ... between people and places' (Emejulu, 2022), such that the feeling rules of an activist organization can help activists challenge the ideologically dominant codes, particularly about the appropriateness of young people's anger (Hochschild, 1979). Both participants reflect Ahmed's and Cvetkovich's rooting of ambivalence in activists simultaneously looking forward and back, conveying how emotions are moderated by the temporalities of activism and exemplify McGeer's sense of hoping well, choosing to be hopeful while facing injustice and indifference.

The temporalities of ambivalence can also be seen in emotional shifts over the course of doing activism, moving backwards and forwards from anger to hope or from optimism to pessimism or pragmatism. Of course, none of these are absolute states, and the weight of any sensation or emotion ebbs and flows through time:

> I think I've become a day-to-day cynic and an overall optimist. … I'm more likely to think something won't work and to try and lower expectations, and I think I'm a realist and I don't trust easily … but I do think we're going to be able to solve these massive problems [laughs] facing society. (Avery, Generation Zero)

> I would say hope motivates me more than anger, definitely, … I mean I often feel frustrated by people in power but I think I'm totally an idealist and you know, I'm possibly … less naive and a bit more cynical now after five years of doing Gen Zero stuff but I think I still do have hope for humanity and I feel like if I didn't, I just wouldn't be doing this. (Daphne, ActionStation)

Rather than interpreting cynicism and optimism or hopefulness as irreconcilable, we follow Cvetkovich's argument that many feelings are resources for political activism and 'good politics' – anti-oppression, social justice work – does not follow only from 'good feelings'.[8] Instead, as indicated earlier, ambivalence is a way of resisting 'reductive binarisms' that shunt affects into exclusive categories labelled either positive or negative, social or antisocial (Cvetkovich, 2012: 6). Indeed, we found that the experience of emotions as 'positive' or 'negative' is highly contextual.

For example, Emerald from InsideOut Kōaro felt that 'you have to have some level of hope to believe that anything would improve' but this is not enough. Activists need 'the sort of bad feelings, you know, disgust and resentment also are quite important'. This disgust and resentment flow from

> knowing that people are being treated the way that they're being treated, people are being killed, people are being put into prisons and … into prisons of a gender that doesn't fit them leading to rape, that people are still tortured on a daily basis. … These are all things that we need to fix. (Emerald, InsideOut Kōaro)

Similarly, when Avante was asked if hope was their motivation for action, they replied:

> I think, yes, partly. And I think … part of it's, like, spite. I think that racists and homophobes and transphobes think the worst of us, and

they underestimate us, and that we can be so much more than what they think of us. ... Yeah. ... Lots of hope. And then, some spite, some anger, some frustration. (Avante, InsideOut Kōaro)

Here we see ambiguity in two senses. First, there is a mix of complex and contradictory emotions that generate tension or unsettled affective energy that is palpable in Avante's quote. Second, spite, in conjunction with other emotions, produces in Avante a positive sense of self and group belonging, alongside a dogged commitment to working to address sexual and gender-based violence. This is a clear example of Hochschild's (1979) and Emejulu's (2022) 'misfeeling' that is, as McManus (2011) argues, generative, restructuring both feelings and agency. It also suggests that ambivalence fosters useful epistemic humility, allowing activists to see creative new paths forward. Emerald and Avante specifically demonstrate the emotion work of activism as they challenge the shape, degree and quality of emotions expected of activists. If 'emotion management is the type of work it takes to cope with feeling rules' (Hochschild, 1979: 551), Emerald's and Avante's refusal to be shamed by homophobic discourses, for example, is emotional work. Their insistence that a vast range and mix of emotions are appropriate in queer activism demonstrates both how ambivalence *works*, and that ambivalence *is* work.

Finally, Tamatha and Charlotte, both activists with JustSpeak, also illustrate McManus's (2011) argument about the generativity of ambivalence, specifically the usefulness of 'the multidirectionality and malleability of the affective register':

> I definitely feel angry quite a lot ... [but] you have to be hopeful in the sense that you can imagine an alternative reality. Otherwise you're just grasping for, you know, nothing. (Tamatha, JustSpeak)

> Hope ... comes and goes, depending on what is happening. But, yeah, it's absolutely a driver. I think anger, particularly as a Pākehā [non-Māori New Zealander] trying to help fix the criminal justice system, just anger at what our ancestors have done is a big driver. ... I don't know if it's an emotion, but kind of heartbreak, I can't think of a better word for it than that, again, at what our ancestors have done and what many communities are facing as a result of that. ... What else? ... again, I don't think it's an emotion, but a sense of obligation. Particularly with community law, I see it as a professional obligation when, once you're a lawyer, you've got all these tools, it's an obligation to use those, at least in part, for the benefit of the community, without receiving a reward for it. (Charlotte, JustSpeak)

Like many of our participants, Tamatha expresses an intense and anticipatory ambivalence about an uncertain future that motivates a critical politics (McManus, 2011; Cvetkovich, 2012), while Charlotte, like Letitia earlier, struggles with how to describe feelings. For her, as for many in our study, hope is complicated by anger. The ambivalence she feels about her ancestors' actions and her role as an ancestor herself raises difficult questions about how to take responsibility in the present for past and future generations.

Emotional ambivalence is a condition of the (im)possibility of activism

Intersecting with the first theme, this second theme captures the uncertainty undergirding any activist campaign: will we win? What would it mean to win? What are the criteria for success?

Qiane from Protect Ihumātao expresses an uncertainty that conveys the conditions of (im)possibility that indigenous activist groups have to navigate when confronting settler colonial governments. Within this sea of uncertainty, Qiane is anchored by the guidance of *atua* and *tūpuna* (deity and ancestors) across generations and time:

> I just always have to think our *atua* and our *tūpuna* have got some lesson for us to learn. It's taking a little while for them [laughs] to teach it to us and ... I don't know whether we're supposed to win this. ... When I first started, I thought I did. And now I'm like are we supposed to learn something else? ... Sometimes I wonder, is this our lesson into leadership? Like is this our *tūpuna* trying to give us the fastest, hardest way possible for us to realize what a good leader is and how you're supposed to lead and get us ready for that? (Qiane, Protect Ihumātao)

At the time of this interview, Qiane did not know that they would ultimately be successful in halting the private housing development on Māori land. Yet her ambivalence acted as a catalyst for considering what else this political movement she and her cousins led might teach them. Qiane's ambivalence prompted 'a pause, a hesitation' that facilitated her 'critical self-reflection' (Emejulu, 2022) and a wider perspective about what might be achieved, irrespective of the outcome of the campaign.

Other participants, working on climate change and sexual violence, expressed similar types of ambivalence about what the 'right' goal would be, how success should be measured (Ian), or the idea that 'success' may not even be the right metric (Jenna). 'Obviously not everything you do is going to work. But you can learn new skills and you can learn from things that don't work out as well ... which can be hopeful for the future, in what you do next' (Ian, Generation Zero).

In his second interview, Ian elaborated on this point, saying:

> I guess you just kind of roll with the punches because I think being an activist and being volunteers, you don't know what's going to happen. You don't know what's going to be guaranteed because I mean there's no play book ... so you've just got to do it. Yeah, you kind of don't know what you're being measured against, if that makes sense. (Ian, Generation Zero)

Building on this, Jenna grapples with hopelessness at solving the intersectional and intractable problems of systemic injustices while getting excited about small, pragmatic wins, yet also feeling the sense of defeat that nothing will ever be enough:

> It just feels like there are so many problems. ... And it's like, how can we fix one of these, you know, I don't think we can fix sexual violence until we address poverty. And in order to address poverty, we need to ... [gestures] ... it's all so complicated and intertwined with so many other issues. And I think it's really difficult to separate them, and be like, 'oh, when everyone has access to sexual violence counselling, and learns about consent' [we'll have fixed this] but still that's incredible, that would be so great. That would be such a good thing. But it's not going to solve sexual violence. (Jenna, Thursdays in Black)

In their own ways, Jenna, Ian and Qiane are open to not knowing what counts as 'winning' and do not allow this unknowingness to stand in the way of learning and pushing forward. They demonstrate ambivalence rooted in a realistic assessment of the state of politics: what success means, and whether it is possible, are unknown (Mrovlje, 2022). Embracing this orientation toward (im)possibility energizes and sustains a commitment to doing *something* with others (Alberro, 2021). This commitment to collective action leads us to our third theme.

Groups are essential in moderating ambivalence

Across a range of groups, participants talked about how engaging in activism collectively rather than individually facilitated productive ambivalence and lessened the likelihood of burn-out. As an individual's energy ebbs and flows, others in the group can help pick up the slack. The social environments in which emotions are experienced are vital for making sense of the feelings motivating and arising from activism (Rodgers, 2010: 288), and we found that groups provided opportunities to feel together, and to feel less alone. González-Hidalgo (2021: 1295) found that group emotions assuage the potentially paralysing feelings generated by environmental activism, which we also observed in our interviews with Generation Zero participants:

> We all understand that reading scary climate change news too often can be quite detrimental to our mental health. And we're also aware that we need to talk about it, and not just store it, or repress it. But talk about it in a healthy way. ... And it's, I guess, those shared experiences and solidarity and, also, shared emotions, not all emotions are shared, but understanding, which is quite key to keeping us moving forward together. (Olivia, Generation Zero)

This moderating effect of feeling together was not limited to climate change activists. At least a few members of all six groups noted its importance. Significantly, in our view, this was raised frequently by members of the anti-sexual violence group Thursdays in Black. We postulate that collective ambivalence was front-of-mind because of how stigmatizing and isolating sexual violence can be. We also conducted these interviews as important #MeToo cases in New Zealand were making the news nearly every day:

> I definitely feel sometimes like, why am I doing this, we can't make a difference, people are going to keep doing [sexually violent] things, but then having events like the [community panel discussion] makes me realize no, we've got to keep going. (Angela, Thursdays in Black)

> I guess everyone has a level of anger and frustration and sadness about the topics that you deal with or the topics that you are actively working against because it's such an emotional thing anyway, and it's such a horrible thing, and it's so prevalent, and it's such a big deal that you kind of can't help be a bit overwhelmed by the scale of what you have to do to combat it, like you know 24/7 kind of thing. But [Thursdays in Black] gives people direction for their emotions, for their frustration, for their overwhelmedness, kind of gives them a path to go on and to say 'look it is scary and overwhelming and you know, it's a horrible place out there but if you do this, it could get better'. (Rose, Thursdays in Black)

These quotes illustrate that groups could facilitate a productive rather than destabilizing ambivalence by validating, mitigating and reconciling different ways of feeling (Emejulu, 2022). Groups facilitate choosing to be hopeful despite ambivalence, and this is enabled by the affects generated through difficult conversations and the ebb and flow of emotions between people. While not all group interactions are affirming and consensual, our research showed that groups do provide designated spaces for processing contradictory emotions with others who have similar goals and a need to act. Where, earlier, we saw participants such as Ian, Letitia and Tamatha expressing ambivalence that was motivating, here we see how the connection of individuals within groups can affirm ambivalence and modulate emotional intensities.

Conclusion

Our research leads us to agree with scholars arguing that ambivalence is useful in motivating and moderating activism. As a critical orientation that generates critique and praxis, ambivalence can lead to new modes of relating to others and to political problems. For example, disgust, rage and frustration *can*, though they will not necessarily, lead to 'good politics'. Researchers have shown that the expectation to express and manage feelings in line with the feeling rules of organizations and activist issue areas can motivate people but can also lead to burn-out. *Misfeeling*, as a form of ambivalence about the 'correct' emotion for a particular situation or time, is itself a form of emotion work (Hochschild, 1979; Rodgers, 2010), but one that can mitigate against disappointments when others fail to respond constructively and 'success' seems uncertain.

Further, as our participants articulate, ambivalence can ward off hopelessness, and temper disappointment and fatalism. Ambivalence can ground people in a realistic sense of what can be accomplished, that is, hoping well (McGeer, 2004). By affirming the 'unknowingness' of taking action and impelling a reflective pause before acting, ambivalence can lead activists and researchers to the 'what else' questions: what else could we do; how else might we act; who else could help us; what questions have we missed? Ambivalence teaches leadership, humility and patience, thereby broadening the remit of activism and encouraging reflections on obligations and opportunities in particular places and times. Though it requires emotional effort from activists, ambivalence works.

Notes

[1] There were five members of the research team: the authors plus Joanna Kidman, Judith Sligo and Kyle M. Matthews. More details on the study design and findings can be found in Nairn et al (2022).

[2] Five of the groups opted to do a living manifesto. These can be viewed on our project website: https://blogs.otago.ac.nz/youngactivists/living-manifestos/

[3] Ethics approval was granted by the University of Otago Human Ethics Committee, reference code 18/045.

[4] www.justspeak.org.nz/aboutus

[5] Thursdays in Black is an international organization with multiple chapters in Aotearoa. We worked only with the University of Auckland group.

6. Generation Zero is a national organization with many chapters. We worked only with the Auckland-based group.
7. Some participants requested pseudonyms while others preferred us to use their real names. We do not indicate when pseudonyms are used in order to better protect the anonymity of those who requested it.
8. Similarly, Bernice Johnson Reagon's foundational discussion of coalition politics makes the important distinction between nurturing and comfortable 'home' spaces and political coalitional spaces where people should feel 'as if [they are] going to keel over any minute and die' (1983: 343). For Johnson, 'good politics' are unlikely to follow from 'good feelings'.

References

Ahmed, S. (2002) 'This other and other others', *Economy and Society*, 31(4): 558–572.

Alberro, H. (2021) 'In the shadow of death: loss, hope and radical environmental activism in the Anthropocene', *Exchanges: The Interdisciplinary Research Journal*, 8(2): 8–27.

Breslow, J. (2022) 'Gender as Ambivalent Politics of Belonging: Trans Childhood in an Era of Gender Critical Activisms', Presentation at the Ambivalent Activism symposium, 1 July.

Carolan, M. (2010) 'Sociological ambivalence and climate change', *Local Environment: The International Journal of Justice and Sustainability*, 15(4): 309–321.

Cvetkovich, A. (2012) *Depression: A Public Feeling*, Duke University Press.

Davidson, J., Bondi, L. and Smith, M. (2016 [2007]) *Emotional Geographies*, Routledge.

Eliason, S.R., Mortimer, J.T. and Vuolo, M. (2015) 'The transition to adulthood: life course structures and subjective perceptions', *Social Psychology Quarterly*, 78(3): 205–227.

Emejulu, A. (2022) 'Ambivalence as misfeeling, ambivalence as refusal', *Post45*, 27 October. Available at: https://post45.org/2022/10/ambivalence-as-misfeeling-ambivalence-as-refusal/

Fraser, S. (1996) 'Reclaiming Our Power, Using Our Anger: Working in the Field of Sexual Violence'. In R. Thorpe and J. Irwin (eds) *Women and Violence: Working for Change*, Hale & Iremonger, pp 162–172.

González-Hidalgo, M. (2021) 'The ambivalent political work of emotions in the defence of territory, life and the commons', *Nature and Space*, 4(4): 1291–1312.

Hochschild, A.R. (1979) 'Emotion work, feeling rules, and social structure', *American Journal of Sociology*, 85(3): 551–575.

McGeer, V. (2004) 'The art of good hope', *The ANNALS of the American Academy of Political and Social Science*, 592(1): 100–127.

McManus, S. (2011) 'Hope, fear, and the politics of affective agency', *Theory & Event*, 14(4). https://doi.org/10.1353/tae.2011.0060

Milona, M. (2019) 'Finding hope', *Canadian Journal of Philosophy*, 49(5): 710–729.

Moss, S.A. and Wilson, S.G. (2014) 'Ambivalent emotional states: the underlying source of all creativity?', *The International Journal of Creativity & Problem Solving*, 24(2): 75–99.

Mrovlje, M. (2022) 'The Disappointments of Rosa Luxemburg', Presentation at the Ambivalent Activism symposium, 4 March.

Nairn, K., Showden, C.R., Sligo, J., Matthews, K.R. and Kidman, J. (2020) 'Consent requires a relationship: rethinking group consent and its timing in ethnographic research', *International Journal of Social Research Methodology*, 23(6): 719–731.

Nairn, K., Sligo, J., Showden, C.R., Matthews, K.R. and Kidman, J. (2022) *Fierce Hope: Youth Activism in Aotearoa*, Bridget Williams Books.

Nairn, K., Showden, C.R., Matthews, K.R., Kidman, J. and Sligo, J. (2024) 'Scaffolding collective hope and agency in youth activist groups: "I get hope through action"', *The Sociological Review*, 0(0). https://doi.org/10.1177/00380261241245546

Opai, K. (2021) *Tikanga: An Introduction to Te Ao Māori*, Upstart Press.

Poursanidou, K., Spandler, H. and Soans, S. (2022) 'Ambivalent Mental Health Activism: *Asylum, the Radical Mental Health Magazine*', Presentation at the Ambivalent Activism symposium, 6 May.

Reagon, B.J. (1983) 'Coalition Politics: Turning the Century'. In B. Smith (ed) *Home Girls: A Black Feminist Anthology*, Kitchen Table Press.

Rodgers, K. (2010) '"Anger is why we're all here": mobilizing and managing emotions in a professional activist organization', *Social Movement Studies*, 9(3): 273–291.

Rothman, N.B., Pratt, M.G., Rees, L. and Vogus, T.J. (2017) 'Understanding the dual nature of ambivalence: why and when ambivalence leads to good and bad outcomes', *Academy of Management Annals*, 11(1): 33–72.

Stockdale, K. (2021) 'Hope, solidarity, and justice', *Feminist Philosophy Quarterly*, 7(2): 1–22.

West, A. (2022) 'Teaching Philosophy in Prisons', Presentation at the Ambivalent Activism symposium, 1 July.

PART III

Activism and the Ambivalent Academy

11

Working with Discomfort: Contesting Ambivalence through Care and Accountability in the University of Edinburgh's 'Skull Room'

Nicole Anderson

Introduction

An air of celebration fills the room as I watch the minister for Taiwan's Council of Indigenous Peoples express his gratitude that four Taiwanese ancestors will finally be repatriated from the University of Edinburgh's Anatomical Museum. The Taiwanese delegation is dressed in their traditional clothing, bright and beaded, to mark the ceremonial exchange after almost two years of negotiation. They take turns signing the papers, and I feel privileged to be able to witness this moment, knowing the amount of labour it took to get here.

There are about a hundred witnesses packed into St Cecilia's Hall in Edinburgh – Taiwanese diplomats and political actors, university officials, curators from the National Museum, students and press officers, all gathered to celebrate the 'handover' ceremony of four Paiwan warriors from the Mudan township. These people's cranial remains were stolen by US navy officers, eventually becoming part of the university's collections in 1907 where they have been sitting ever since. A jubilant feeling marks the end of their displacement and arrangements have been made for them to return home the next day. Camera flashes punctuate the air and journalists swarm the top table, where university administrators shake hands and pose with the Taiwanese descendants.

The press releases that follow in the upcoming weeks emphasize the university's commitment to addressing its contentious colonial legacy and underscore its long and positive history of repatriation. I notice that these accounts do not acknowledge the amount of work undertaken to make the return possible, and that this return happened on the back of a collective effort by various researchers, curators and Indigenous peoples. The press releases do not state that a doctoral researcher in Taiwan was first to learn about these warriors, enabling her to follow an archival paper trail that led her to curators in Edinburgh. They do not mention the lengthy process of provenance research that was needed to confirm these people's identities, and the months of discussion about the logistics of the return. Instead, the process presented seemed simple and seamless. Most pertinently, I note that they fail also to acknowledge the scale of the University of Edinburgh's 'uncomfortable' colonial collection. Aside from the four Taiwanese ancestors that have returned home, there are still nearly 1,700 ancestors awaiting their release.

Hidden relatively out of sight (for the protection and privacy of the ancestral remains and their descendants), the University of Edinburgh's Anatomical Museum contains a high-density display of human crania, held at a site known as the 'Skull Room'. The remains of these people were stolen during the 19th and 20th centuries by various collectors, naturalists, anatomists and curators. They were often 'donated' by former anatomy students working in the British colonies, sending back skulls to the anatomy professor Sir William Turner. Turner, who became principal of the university in 1903, was building a comparative anatomical collection of people's skulls, amassing ancestral remains from 55 countries across the world. Many of these people are from racialized or Indigenous backgrounds. His collection also contains people from western Europe and Scotland, namely executed criminals. The people in this room are displayed here without their consent, often removed from graves, burial grounds, ossuaries and cemeteries without the knowledge of their families.

The press release holds true that the university does have a positive history of repatriation, managing to facilitate the return of 200–300 ancestors to Australia (the exact number is unknown) in the early 2000s, and nine Wanniyalaeto 'Vedda' ancestors to Sri Lanka in 2019. There is a clear willingness by staff to understand the histories of their collections and to work with communities who pursue claims on their own terms as much as possible. Custodians at the museum say '[descendent kin] are pushing an open door' when it comes to pursuing future repatriation claims. However, despite this enthusiasm and goodwill, the Anatomical Museum has so far only had capacity to operate on a reactive (and not proactive) case-by-case basis to facilitate these returns. As no online catalogue currently exists, a paradox is created in that repatriation cannot happen if descendants do not know their ancestors are in Edinburgh. This problem is further compounded when the biographies and the identities of some of these people are unknown or incomplete, due to fragmented archival provenance. Having a reactive process relies on descendants having prior knowledge of this collection, having the time and finances to conduct provenance research, and the capacity to approach the university themselves to pursue a claim. There is currently no legally binding legislation in the United Kingdom that forces institutions to operate proactively, meaning many people risk being stuck in the 'Skull Room', waiting patiently to be encountered, to be moved or move others, to be identified, or to be given back.

Through my doctoral work, I have attempted to examine and disrupt this repatriation paradox. As such, this chapter examines the ambivalence, discomfort and uncertainty within this process. I reflect on the hesitancies and tensions in proactively seeking justice for First Nations and Inuit ancestors held at the university. My project aimed to get the museum's 'house in order' (Bell, 2021) and collate provenance: information that ascertains how these people came to Edinburgh and where they are originally from. Recovering their biographies is the first step to affiliate them with contemporary descendants, who have the authority to determine what a just future would look like for their ancestors. Reparative justice may mean returning ancestors to their own land and Nation and/or a change in culturally specific care practices for them in Edinburgh. This chapter reflects on the ambivalent experiences in charting new anti-colonial processes regarding the care and keeping of ancestral remains at the university. This ambivalence is not necessarily related to whether or not these remains should be retained by the university, but rather are to do with how to establish a sensitive, careful and respectful approach in seeking proactive redress.

This tension also involves considering what it means to do 'activist' academic work within the constraints of a neocolonial institution, where our position as university staff and students afforded us access, insight and (some) influence in these decision-making processes, yet still meant we had to cede control to senior university actors, and operate within their comfort zone. Mixed feelings therefore arise from the desire to do meaningful work and also balance the anxieties of the institution that is navigating proactive repair work for the first time. As a result, ambivalent feelings arise from making decisions on how to balance the needs of both senior university decision makers, community members, and our own emotional investments and political motivations. As such, the chapter discusses various tensions experienced in navigating these uncertain conditions to establish what 'good' anti-colonial work would look like in this context, particularly in the stages before rightful custodians are identified, considering these various asymmetric power dynamics in play.

Examining our positionalities also produced ambivalent or conflicting feelings concerning our authority to be leading such a project. I am not Indigenous, and neither are any of the other researchers who were involved in this project. I could not speak for these ancestors or their descendants, nor ascertain what was best for these people. Yet, I am still implicated as a student of the university and also an ethnographer who is accountable to anthropology's racist and colonial legacies. I am an 'outsider' who has 'insider' institutional access to archival records, archivists, curatorial staff and funding to bring visibility to this collection. I was getting involved with pain that was not mine, but also in situations that I am implicated in by being witness to this violence.

As mentioned, another difficulty that produced some hesitancy or mixed feelings toward decision making was the fact that proactive outreach work has never been attempted at the museum. Through my doctoral work, I was hoping to establish a process and precedent to proactively affiliate the other ancestors. Considering there are only two permanent members of staff at the museum, who are short on time and resources to fulfil proactive repatriations, busy already with the reactive ones, charting a proactive process meant taking on this labour. To successfully facilitate this work, the project team grew to encompass several other anthropologists and curators across Edinburgh and Toronto who were invested in repatriation to fulfil these goals. As institutional actors, who are operating somewhat adjacently to the museum, we were operating with limited institutional power to formally coordinate repatriation with ancestors. As a project team, we were university actors but were not employed by the museum and therefore had no authority to make decisions in this space. Understandably, navigating this experience often brought up moments of uncertainty, challenge and hesitancy that meant we had to reckon with our privileged, yet in some ways powerless institutional positions.

In this chapter, I argue that these ambivalent and uncomfortable feelings are not only intuitive, but necessary in ensuring one treads carefully within contentious spaces and situations. Considering the historical context of the 'Skull Room', and the fact that the provenance for these people is often fragmented, inconsistent or missing, especial sensitivity is required to not cause further harm, particularly when seeking to share potentially upsetting knowledge with descendant communities. This chapter reflects on this process of knowledge sharing and examines the instances in which these complex, and sometimes contradictory emotions arise, that remind the researchers of the stakes and their impact on the process. Instead of understanding these feelings as counterproductive or harmful, I suggest that these emotional states are rational and politically effectual, creating transformative pedagogical conditions that challenge hegemonic norms within institutions, and disrupt the status quo. I ask what it is about these certain emotions that inspire individuals to seek action and take up commitments to seek social justice, particularly in examining the pedagogical value of discomfort produced through ambivalence.

Political emotions matter

The emotional realities of researchers have long existed as sites of sociopolitical control and arise from a long history of gendering and prioritizing certain feelings (Boler and Zembylas, 2016: 1). Historically, the power of emotions with research was dismissed, and in the past emotions were often theorized in opposition to reason and rationality, and as a hindrance within the research process (Chubbuck and Zembylas, 2008: 277). Since the 1980s, feminist scholars have been disrupting the binary of emotion/reason that has underpinned positivist approaches (Jaggar, 2001; Ahmed, 2004). Feminist scholars have continued to show that emotions have pedagogical value and are significant in their ability to 'establish, assert, challenge, or reinforce power or status differences' should we pay attention to them (Abu-Lughod and Lutz, cited in Chubbuck and Zembylas, 2008: 279). Affect studies have further legitimized these approaches, understanding affective moments as 'non-conscious experiences of intensity … a moment of unformed and unstructured potential' which may allow affected actors to 'move' in certain ways in the world (Shouse, 2000: 5). As Ann Cvetkovich remarks, affect 'includes impulses, desires, and feelings that get historically constructed in a range of ways' and so is not separate from emotional and bodily responses (Cvetkovich, cited in Zembylas, 2014: 398). Therefore, scholars such as Sara Ahmed (2004) continue to question the need to split emotion/reason, the mind/body, or even emotion/affect, as these seemingly dichotomous states happen simultaneously and correspond with each other. Therefore, emotions – as expressly political forces – should be a site of concern as they elucidate embodied and sensory forms of knowledge within social research (Boler and Davis, 2018).

Affect, and the emotional responses it produces, can reproduce or maintain social relations or orders, and may work to subvert and transform them to produce new ways of knowing and being. Rochelle Chadwick further theorizes affects and emotions as 'lively actants' that have the power to 'mobilize actions, representations, decisions, meanings, and interpretations' (2021: 557). For this reason, I am interested in the presence and tensions of emotions in social justice work, and particularly in how they affect and construct methodologies of discomfort within research. In this understanding, affects and emotions are not obstacles to overcome or irrational inconveniences, but are epistemologically and theoretically significant in that they chart new directions and processes for one to follow, and provide new grounds to think with (Chadwick, 2021).

Political emotions have the capacity to transform subjectivities. Discomfort – or the sense that something is not quite right – is an important precursor for this change. Often, it begins in that lingering or unsettling sensation; a gut-feeling and a sense of being at odds with something. I felt this sensation the first time I set foot in the 'Skull Room' as an undergraduate. Despite not knowing the extent of reparative and repatriation work ongoing in the 'Skull Room', even at that time in 2017, it was the scale of the room and the violence that it contained that seemed to blow the ground underneath my feet. It changed the way I thought about the institution that presented itself as safe, authoritative and legitimate.

Apart from the shock of seeing dead bodies outside of expected locales of death, the discomfort was more to do with the discrepancy or disjuncture of emotions and dispositions that seemed to circulate within the space. The curator I was interviewing seemed unaffected by the room (and why would he visibly be? He works closely with these people and cares for them every day). As I concluded the interview and walked through campus in a daze, head heavy and full of thoughts, I walked past swathes of disaffected students moving to their next class; unmoved and unaware of the fact that our university contains a room with shelves full of disinterred people.

Clare Hemmings (2012) writes about this feeling of being 'at odds with' as dissonance, and theorizes its importance in constructing affective solidarities that spur social action. Elsewhere, Deborah Gould (2010) describes this need for change beginning with 'an inarticulable sensation that something in the established order is not quite right' (2010: 32). This hard-to-describe feeling of discordance – a sensation that something is wrong or off – I see as an experience of affect, and the beginning of a process of becoming politically moved. Hemmings argues that this discordance creates new subjectivities born out of this affective engagement (2012: 147). Drawing on Elspeth Probyn's (1993) concept of 'feminist reflexivity', she shows how dissonance bridges ontology and epistemology to create a 'reflexive disruption' (Hemmings, 2012: 149) and an awareness of the structural conditions within which one lives. This may spur one to move toward changing these conditions, disrupting previous feelings of indifference. Discomfort through dissonance in this instance is not a negative, but something generative, transformative and perhaps even a universal experience and necessary condition for those involved in social justice work.

Ambivalent emotions within proactive repatriation

Political feelings thus counter indifference and push people to be aware of their participation within hegemonic systems. Within contentious situations, holding space for multiple conflicting feelings can be a radical act in its countering neutrality and feelings of passivity. Roth et al (cited in Emejulu, 2022) define ambivalence as the 'simultaneous experience of positive and negative emotional or cognitive orientations toward a person, situation, object, task, goal, or idea and the feelings of tension and conflict that result'. Akwugo Emejulu (2022) highlights ambivalence as a state of having multiple, conflicting feelings that are often in opposition, but also come together to 'comingle'. Within behavioural science, Iris Schneider and Norbert Schwarz (2017: 40) demonstrate this opposition by showing how 'people experience mixed feelings because they both dislike *and* like something, want to approach *and* avoid it, and are positive and negative at the same time'. This tension exemplifies one's move away from indifference which is defined as '*the lack* of either positive or negative evaluations' (Schneider and Schwarz, 2017: 39). The presence of multiple emotions acts as a political catalyst that agitates the self and prompts one to move toward or away from something. As Hemmings had argued, the presence of strange, tense and even unclear feelings is an essential precondition in seeking social change: 'affective dissonance has to arise if a feminist politics is to emerge' (Hemmings, 2012: 158). Affective experiences within these specific contexts, therefore, have a particular pedagogic potential – they produce new forms of knowledge and solidarities. Such knowledge rises out of our bodily states as 'in order to know differently, we have to feel differently' (Hemmings, 2012: 150).

Ciara Kierans and Kristen Bell (2017: 25) reflect on how ambivalence may seem to be an undesirable ideal, causing decision-paralysis and fence-sitting, and can be accompanied by feelings of distress. They argue that ambivalence can be used as a methodological heuristic within anthropological research, suggesting that it can be employed as 'a strategy to understand what is going on around us' (2017: 23). Within complex situations, it becomes a means to see social circumstances with nuance, rather than immediately taking a fixed position (2017: 37), which prevents researchers from adopting 'oversimplified solutions' (2017: 24) to complex social problems. Methodological ambivalence then allows researchers to question stances, categories and positions when faced with complicated situations in the field. Rather than seeing this approach as justifying fence-sitting, they call for researchers to maintain fluid understandings of social and political problems. Relatedly, Emejulu (2022) shows that rather than seeing ambivalence as an unproductive, or paralysing feeling, it indicates the need for deep thought and contemplation that surrounds a specific issue. Emejulu (2022) argues that it is productive to sit with the feeling, to pause and contemplate these contradictions before proceeding. Hesitation necessitates a 'state of critical self-reflection' which allows for meaningful, appropriate and generative ways forward (Emejulu, 2022).

Rather than this manifesting in a reluctance to take a moral stance, I relate to this ambiguity in the deliberation needed to constitute a careful reparative approach. I can attest to the worthiness of pause and hesitation as I reflect on my changing feelings surrounding activism in this space. Part of this change involves accepting that activist intervention cannot necessarily always be spurred by immediate, gut-feeling responses, but must also come from considering the wider political and institutional contexts within which we act. From rereading my earliest field journals, I note a sense of outrage and urgency in my response. I remember distinctly feeling that these people should all 'be sent back' and that the most ethical iteration of this room would be for it to be completely empty. When engaging in dialogue with members of the public, it is a response I often hear; concerned and well-meaning locals and outraged students wanting to rid this horrible and violent space, to wash their hands and their conscience clean of it.

While I understand where this feeling comes from, I now see this endeavour as violent in itself. Repatriation is a sticky issue, and it is not simply resolved through just return – there is no one-size-fits-all approach here. It is harmful to assume that all descendant communities would consider repatriation as always appropriate. Within my interviews with curators in Canada, they note how each Nation will have culturally specific protocols surrounding death, and the safety of the living. For example, Blackfoot First Nations may not handle disinterred remains and therefore do not always seek repatriation. Others may be willing to have their ancestors return home, but do not have the capacity to receive them. Through conversations with Indigenous folks, I learn that some communities are in the process of building or enlarging mortuary houses, and so would need to wait to secure a safe resting place for their kin. Further, considering the often conflicting, fragmented and uncertain provenance, many of the people in the 'Skull Room' are unaffiliated. Communities want to know there is a high probability that this person is indeed their ancestor before they are reburied. Making a mistake here would cause further spiritual harm, so the stakes are high. Institutions cannot just push remains onto people who may not be able to receive them yet, just because the university finds them too uncomfortable to contain. And then, there are people who do not have any identifying information at all, their provenance revealing only that they were stolen from somewhere in North America. Where will these people go? How can this room ever be emptied?

The complexities of 'solutions' regarding repatriation require one to challenge immediate emotional responses. It is not that one is opposed to repairing the harm caused here, but it requires a sensitive understanding of how to proceed without causing further damage. It also requires one to critically question and be reflexive on the desire to 'fix' things. Discomfort arises in noticing the desire to 'solve' this problem as a way of becoming absolved from it. Being ambivalent and hesitant in thinking about next steps acts a reminder that decolonial work is a process. Decolonial processes must be seen as open-ended, which involves understanding that repatriation is not the only possible future happening. Rather than seeking to fulfil a repatriation 'end goal', ambivalence allows us to consider and look at multiple possibilities for a decolonizing process that is as much about the journey as the destination. It requires close collaboration and dialogue with communities, and an awareness of the uneven structural conditions in which these conversations take place. Reconciliation and restorative justice do not operate on linear trajectories, but rather involve a journey that contains many contours, barriers and multitudes of time-consuming, bureaucratic and/or expensive tasks – some of which our project team proposed to fulfil as 'helpful outsiders'.

Ambivalence, therefore, can be instructive in pinpointing paradoxes and contradictions within certain 'contact zones' of power (Pratt, 1992), giving researchers room to pause to examine the power inequalities in these spaces. Before beginning outreach processes, it was important to question our institutional positions and solidarities. On one hand, as members of the institution that originally dispossessed these remains and continues to hold them, the collection troubled us and pointed to our complicity. We came to the 'Skull Room' and left as witnesses and saw it as a call to action to seek redress. Learning about the current processes that underpinned repatriation, and the paradoxes that existed in prevented returns, it felt disingenuous or wrong to look away, especially when we had the capacity and time to contribute our skills.

On the other hand, despite being part of this institution, we were aware that we were instigating a process that we did not have much control over. None of us had real decision-making power, even the curator who was a collaborator within the project. The capacity to facilitate returns is nestled between several strata of university administrators. This process is neither straightforward nor particularly transparent. The policies read that repatriation requests must come from a suitable representative and should ideally further be supported by a state-level or governmental body (Edinburgh University, 2015: 115). The University Collections Advisory Committee (UCAC), which meets quarterly, deliberates the 'appropriateness' of the representative who is initiating the claim, and debates the cultural significance of the 'item/object' (not person) to the claimant, and to the university. As university collections are deemed to be their legal property – despite being taken by illegal means – the University Court must further approve any transfer of title (Edinburgh University, 2015). As the UCAC meets quarterly, and the University Court meets only twice a year, the process is slow and it often takes years for an ancestor to be returned.

These two feelings were in tension – it did not feel 'right' but it also felt wrong to do nothing at all. We were aware that the process for return is bureaucratic, arduous, and often painful for descendants. By sharing provenance, we were potentially bringing in descendants into these harmful systems with no guarantee of a positive outcome or that they would be treated fairly. We could be potentially construed as making uncertain promises. The repatriation paradox still underpinned this problem, whereby communities had no means of knowing that their ancestors were here. The process is not without its fault, but if no information is shared, no one would be aware that this room exists at all.

On this evaluation, we decided to proceed despite knowing the system was complex and laborious. From working closely with curators, I began to understand that this system is used as a form of due diligence. It is a way to safeguard university actors – and the university would argue, also descendants – to ensure no mistakes are made and a documented process is followed. I learned to see it also as a form of accountability, or a practice of ambivalence, even though it may seem unduly bureaucratic and not particularly hospitable. This is the only way the institution knows how to proceed, and although it could be more flexible and adopt more collaborative systems, we hoped that through our involvement the processes would shift. Our reasoning was also that by supporting provenance work, by corroborating the fragments and doing due diligence ourselves, our research team may be able to expedite the process and make it more transparent for descendants. By understanding how repatriation operated, we could then begin to advocate for descendants from our institutional position.

Assembling the provenance to present to communities also meant examining the power that we hold as a project team. This action was a source of conflict as we became implicated in reproducing the same colonial logics that first displaced the ancestors. The information needed to affiliate ancestors can be found in various catalogues, minute-books and letter correspondence in the university archives. For many of these individuals, their identities are described through racist language, inaccurate community affiliations, misspellings or transliterations. The stories of these people are obstructed by a 'colonial common sense' that attempted to subjugate people through different genres and forms of documentation (Stoler, 2009: 4). Hesitancy and uncertainty here helped us pause and consider our impact on this process. How do we engage proactively with stories that are not our own, and share them with people in light of this blatantly racist language and traumatic knowledge? Who has the right to make these choices, and make this material digitally accessible? Who has the right to even assume that this knowledge is traumatic in the first place? It felt uncomfortable to make these initial decisions ourselves and to deliberate how best to present these stories and archival traces about the deceased. We discussed how to balance sharing the provenance while also ensuring the language and content was not unduly harmful, and how to rewrite these biographies without inserting ourselves too much in narratives and histories that were not our own.

The discomfort that surrounded this process helped me think about how to represent these records with humility, hospitality and care. Instead of presenting descendants with an Excel spreadsheet with catalogue numbers, unhelpful racist categorizations and scores of violent descriptions, care was taken to use correct and contemporary names for their Nation. Numbers that were used to identify the ancestor internally in the museum were removed, so the paragraph referred to 'this individual' or 'this person'. In the biographies, we tried to be clear about what we knew about this person based on the archival record, what information was still missing, and what could potentially be knowable through morphological and physical anthropological analyses, if consent was obtained. Alongside these biographies, we also included digitized and transcribed original copies of the archival records. On the coversheet, a content note warns the reader that some of the material may contain offensive and sensitive language, and offers my contact details for anyone who may need further support.

The intention was to offer a more sensitive representation of the colonial material, but still provide full transparency and access to the original records. This allowed descendants to have an informed choice of whether they wanted to read ahead and encounter this difficult knowledge in more detail. It also ensured that the researcher was not making paternalistic assumptions about what material was traumatic to view or not. I was conscious of how the provenance researcher still occupies a position of power in the control of these records, and in their assessment of the impact of these stories on others. It is important for museum professionals to offer the possibility to encounter material without derogatory or dehumanizing language, but at the same time not to limit or distort the histories of these collections.

Despite the discomfort about terminology, we took these feelings as reminders to approach situations with care and openness about previous and ongoing harm and our responsibility in instigating repair. Being honest about difficult truths is the first step in reconciling these legacies. Unlike the press releases that celebrated the successful outcome, highlighting the extent of uncertainty, hesitancy and ambivalence provides a realistic account of working with contentious collections. It shows that perfect, seamless processes do not exist. Repair here works through a case-by-case basis, and thus each decision needs to be carefully assessed. Mistakes are inevitable as we weighed up different approaches and directions, and there are considerable ethical grey areas that we paused at, but still chose to continue through, perhaps sometimes erroneously. Previous mistakes, and the anxieties that surround them, remind us to tread carefully, and approach situations with caution. These feelings keep us on our toes. Ambivalence and discomfort act as reminders to double- and triple-check things, to keep our information better organized, to seek advice, to be honest and open. It helps orientate ourselves to a project that has no fixed end-point, which also may cause distress. Have we started something that we cannot finish? How do we put systems in place to continue this work when project members graduate and move elsewhere? What other funding can we apply for to ensure this work continues? Political feelings move people to act, but they must also move researchers to commit.

Conclusion

It is clear that this work is not over, and more must be done. Although some provenance has been uncovered and some ancestors have been affiliated, we still often know more about the collectors, than the collected. The museum Excel sheets still use outdated categories and numbering practices, and can be changed to include Indigenous naming practices and terminologies. There is still provenance to be shared for nearly 1,700 other people. Discomfort calls on people to move beyond and through our comfort zone to 'shift' spaces like the 'Skull Room'. Taking ambivalence and other 'political emotions' seriously means acknowledging that emotions – even uncomfortable ones – 'do things' and spur things to happen (Ahmed, 2004). These emotions beckon researchers to be accountable witnesses to ongoing colonial injustice and to continue seeking its resolve. It is a call for us to be actively engaged in these spaces, and not just passive bystanders – whether we are an instigator or recipient of discomfort (and oftentimes we occupy both these positions). Staying with discomfort, and leaning into ambivalence as a methodological approach, allows researchers to question 'cherished beliefs and assumptions' (Boler, 1999: 175) and directs enquiries in ways that undertake our historical responsibilities (Boler, 1999: 184). Decolonial work is a process and relies on understanding that these rooms are not immoveable, but can be reckoned with by learning and unlearning how to do work in this field and approach these situations with humility. Ambivalence and mixed feelings become calls to act less passively and to be moved to resolve them in ways that honour collaboration, dialogue and relational accountability.

References

Ahmed, S. (2004) *The Cultural Politics of Emotion*, University of Edinburgh Press.

Bell, L. (2021) 'Global Conversations: Indigenous Led Initiatives', *Illinois State Museum* [webinar], 20 May 2021. Available at: www.youtube.com/watch?v=mPWr-kS_QDw&ab_channel=IllinoisStateMuseum (accessed 29 January 2024).

Boler, M. (1999) 'The Risks of Empathy'. In M. Boler (ed) *Feeling Power: Emotions and Education*, Routledge, pp 155–174.

Boler, M. and Zembylas, M. (2016) 'Interview with Megan Boler: From "Feminist Politics of Emotions" to the "Affective Turn"'. In M. Zembylas and P.A. Schutz (eds) *Methodological Advances in Research on Emotion and Education*, Springer International Publishing, pp 7–30.

Boler, M. and Davis, E. (2018) 'The affective politics of the "post-truth" era: feeling rules and networked subjectivity', *Emotion, Space and Society*, 27: 75–85.

Chadwick, R. (2021) 'On the politics of discomfort', *Feminist Theory*, 22(4): 556–574.

Chubbuck, S.M. and Zembylas, M. (2008) 'The emotional ambivalence of socially just teaching: a case study of a novice urban schoolteacher', *American Educational Research Journal*, 45(2): 274–318.

Edinburgh University (2015) 'Collections Management Policy', Edinburgh University [online]. Available at: www.ed.ac.uk/files/atoms/files/uc_collections_management_policy_final_approved_22_june_2015-_0.pdf (accessed 29 January 2024).

Emejulu, A. (2022) 'Ambivalence as Misfeeling, Ambivalence as Refusal', *Post45*, 27 October. Available at: https://post45.org/2022/10/ambivalence-as-misfeeling-ambivalence-as-refusal/ (accessed 30 January 2024).

Gould, D. (2010) 'On Affect and Protest'. In J. Staiger, A. Cvetkovich and A. Reynolds (eds) *Political Emotions*, Taylor & Francis Group, pp 18–44.

Hemmings, C. (2012) 'Affective solidarity: feminist reflexivity and political transformation', *Feminist Theory*, 13(2): 147–161. https://doi-org.eux.idm.oclc.org/10.1177/1464700112442643 (original work published 2012).

Jaggar, A.M. (2001) 'Feminist Politics and Epistemology: The Standpoint of Women'. In S.G. Harding (ed) *The Feminist Standpoint Theory Reader: Intellectual and Political Controversies*, Routledge, pp 55–66.

Kierans, C. and Bell, K. (2017) 'Cultivating ambivalence', *HAU: Journal of Ethnographic Theory*, 7(2): 23–44.

Pratt, M.L. (1992) *Imperial Eyes: Travel Writing and Transculturation*, Routledge.

Probyn, E. (1993) *Sexing the Self: Gendered Positions in Cultural Studies*, Routledge.

Schneider, I.K. and Schwarz, N. (2017) 'Mixed feelings: the case of ambivalence', *Current Opinion in Behavioral Sciences*, 15: 39–45.

Shouse, E. (2005) 'Feeling, emotion, affect', *M/C Journal*, 8(6). https://doi.org/10.5204/mcj.2443

Stoler, A. (2009) *Along the Archival Grain: Epistemic Anxieties and Colonial Common Sense*, Princeton University Press.

Zembylas, M. (2014) 'Theorizing "difficult knowledge" in the aftermath of the "affective turn": implications for curriculum and pedagogy in handling traumatic representations', *Curriculum Inquiry*, 44(3): 390–411.

12

The Poetry of Ambivalence: A Nudge toward Tending

Roxani Krystalli

My classrooms are saturated with poetry.[1] I am not a poetry teacher, nor do I teach in a literature department. The label on my office door marks me as belonging in a School of International Relations, my academic background is primarily feminist and anthropological, and my curiosity renders me what Si Transken calls 'a joyful undisciplined discipline-jumper' (Transken, 2002: 1). I teach with – rather than 'about' – poetry because I welcome the questions it brings into the room.

My students welcome the poems with grace and impatience alike. They want to know what this poem is about, they seek reassurance that they got it. They insist on the 'about' question because much of their education has taught them (us!) to orient our curiosity that way: find the point, highlight it, cite it, file it away in the repository of human knowledge. I reinforce this message when I give feedback on student work. 'This essay would benefit from a more readily identifiable argument', I write in the margins. Another generation of 'In this essay, I will …' marches toward its graduation.

I teach with poetry as a counterweight to my own scribbles in the margins. A good poem, I tell my students, does not argue. It does not defend its reasons for existence by having or making a singular point. This does not render the poem pointless, but it does reorient our relationship with it away from seeking to extract a single use. A good poem leaves space for interpretation by making literal room on the page, as well as emotional, interpretive room for the reader's experience to filter between the lines. A good poet tells a story in the poem, *through* the poem, giving the listener whatever she needs to imagine a world, or perhaps enough confidence to trust that she does not need to know everything in order to imagine. A good poem reminds us that we are not just creatures of language, but that we are *embodied* creatures who respond to rhythm and voice, and who are moved by what feels right on the tongue or sounds right to the ear. A good poem does not tell us how to live (and it may even bristle at the question), but it may nonetheless offer ways of living as invitations, like flares in the night. A flare reminds us that other vessels are floating alongside ours, and that noticing them is a matter of urgency.

★★★

When much is hurting in the world, as it often does, it helps to have clarity about one's domain of action. Unions, protests, local councils, community groups, faith-based organizations, volunteering, social media and art all offer possibilities for coming together with others to create change. Though many people are active in several of these domains, it is difficult to be meaningfully and sustainably involved in every mode of activism across the diverse configurations in which change happens. When I feel overwhelmed by the magnitude of work there is to do to address the world's injustices, I reflect on my most meaningful domain of action. This is another way of asking: Which communities am I part of? Who are the people to whom I feel accountable? What are the actions through which I can fulfil the duties that flow from living in relation to those people? What are the spaces and places I care about, and what tethers me to them? How can I best channel my care?

Though these are questions I ask myself, they are outward-looking, beyond the individual self. They bring into view worlds of entanglement. Reflecting on my domain of action and entanglements points me toward the classroom. I teach on the subjects of feminism, peace, nature and place – all of which require and inspire action. It is hardly a surprise that students interested in activism are drawn to these classes, and it is a treat to think alongside them about what meaningful and sustainable activism can look like in theory and practice.

My seminar on peace is called 'Critical Approaches to Peacebuilding'. The title is more inquisitive than declarative. Who is critical of whom or what? The critical approaches that most resonate with me reveal the workings of power, remaining attentive to how power shapes relationships, senses of self, possibilities, and ways of being in the world, as well as curious about how power hides itself. Critique, I tell students, is 'about more than flaw-finding' (Krystalli, 2024: 23). This proposition intrigues them, as it does me, and they want to know more: What is the 'more than'?

Imagining an answer to that question requires making friends with uncertainty (Krystalli et al, 2023), developing a relationship with doubt, and finding comfort in ambivalence. Ambivalence is most generative as a concept when those of us who are moved by it refuse to pin it down, instead remaining attentive to its multiple possibilities and to what ambivalence opens up as an orientation to life. Inspired by Akwugo Emejulu (2022), I think of ambivalence 'as a moment of contemplation, of recuperation, a state of critical self-reflection – a pause, a hesitation – before meaningful action can take place'. Ambivalence is a breath between the singing of notes.

Some critique can feel breathless, manifesting in adjectives articulated between gasps. Gasps are a sign of urgency, and there are many reasons to feel it in the world. Though curiosity about the workings of power is a skill honed through practice over time, critique can look deceptively easy, quick as a judgement: this is 'wrong' or 'unfair' or 'unjust' or 'patriarchal' or 'extractive'. What comes next is the slower, more challenging part: what would fair and just look like? What is the feminist 'political project about what *could be*?' (Olufemi, 2020: 1). What kinds of relations can we imagine that enact less extractive, more mutually nourishing ways of living? 'I think of feminism as a building project', Sara Ahmed suggests (2017: 14). If we take up her invitation as readers, feminists, students, teachers and humans entangled in webs of action and relation, we must not only ask what worlds we are critiquing and deconstructing, but also direct energy and imagination at what worlds we are breathing into being.

★★★

Formal education and academic training have not prepared me well for the making of worlds, or for even considering that kind of imagination part of my duties in the world. Rather than dwelling on this fact, rather than lamenting lack, I choose to direct energy at what sustains life. Where am I learning abundance? Who are my teachers and companions in reciprocity and mutuality? Robin Wall Kimmerer reminds us that 'all flourishing is mutual' (2013: 20). How can we sharpen our attentiveness to what survives and *flourishes*, not as an elusive future state, but as a reminder of what sustains life in the violent, unjust present?

It helps, I find, to treat these questions as material and relational, rather than rhetorical – in other words, to get out of our own heads and to *tend*: to soil and to soup bubbling on the stove, to fellow humans and to light. Students in my class on 'The Politics of Nature and Place' keep care diaries, in which they document the acts and relations of care they experience over a period of time. Some report that this documentation practice makes them more caring, with the exercise being an accountability compass that reminds them to practise care that they can report on. They sow seeds in trays perched on top of radiators in dorm rooms, and they make their flatmates supper. Others say that it makes them more attentive to the care they receive, noticing the way their worlds are not only shaped by precarity, but also anchored by others' acts of attention and care. I encourage students to read their diaries with a curiosity to what they did *not* record. For example, how are other-than-human elements showing up in their accounts? Did they make note of having watered the houseplants, but not of feeling nurtured by January sunlight during a walk on West Sands beach? My questions are offerings, seeking to remind us that we live in a world of relation, and that there are models of care, nourishing and thriving that exist right alongside the injustices we read about in our academic texts every week (Krystalli and Schulz, 2022).

I begin each of my tutorials by asking students what brought them joy that week. They do not have to answer. I would hate for joy to become an obligation, another duty weighing on their shoulders. In the beginning of the semester, they often do not answer, or they say that they are not used to the question, that this question is not one they had prepared for when they were getting ready for our discussions. This question is a compass. More than wanting to teach my students 'critique' or 'feminism', I hope to be a human in their lives who models what Anna Tsing calls the 'arts of noticing' (Tsing, 2015: 132). Attentiveness has tending at the heart. Joy, too, requires tending. It helps, I find, to have another human in your life who will reliably enquire about it. The enquiry anchors a practice of noticing, and sharing what we have noticed can, in turn, slowly become one of the ways we tend to what sustains life.

★★★

It is tempting sometimes to tell ourselves that the sources of joy, care, mutuality and thriving – the relations and practices that sustain life – unfold in a separate domain from our work (or, indeed, our activism). After all, work can be miserable, and activism requires much of the people who engage in it. I worry, however, about the romanticization of life-beyond-work, and about surrendering to a care-less, joy-less relationship to what we spend much of our time on. To address this worry, I think about how to introduce ambivalence into the classroom, and how to build a generous, caring practice toward the work and words we generate within universities.

To contemplate this task, I return once again to poems. Poems are fitting companions *not* because they are always already pure or because they only ever reflect the supposed goodness of the world. I am sceptical of purity, of its attachment to innocence (Ticktin, 2017) and its invulnerable resistance to ambivalence (Ravecca and Dauphinee, 2022). What a limited fate it would be for poems – or for anything in this world – to only ever reflect goodness! Instead, what draws me to poems is that they are exercises in imagining a world and condensing it onto the page, inviting a reader or listener into that world one line and image at a time. The poem is the writer's offering. The best poems are ones that leave room for the reader to make her own offering, resisting closure and declaration, instead allowing air to circulate.

Ambiguity and ambivalence converge in allowing for the possibility of multiplicities (of meanings, feelings and ways of being alike).

It is hard to build a world, in a poem or in the classroom, without multiplicities, without doubt. The pause that ambivalence introduces into this exercise is not one I wish to chase away. If some critique can happen with the illusion of aspirational purity, world-building is mess-making. 'Ambivalence might be a teacher in which we learn other ways to feel', Emejulu (2022) offers, 'and perhaps, we can feel our way to other kinds of social relations and modes of being'.

Ambivalence, then, invites and requires a kind of generosity. In the classroom, this is a generosity toward authors and texts. Generosity in action looks like beginning with the question of what resonates, what is promising, what seeds an author, text or idea sows. It is a generosity toward ideas that are not our own, and a starting point that emphasizes possibility. Generosity does not foreclose disagreement; in fact, it does not foreclose anything. It does, however, reward questions ('what work is this text or idea doing in the world?') before declarations ('it is not a feminist text'). The kind of generosity ambivalence invites also requires patience from readers: patience with uncertainty, with multiple meanings, with sometimes living without rigid definitions and closure. Humility in the face of others' work and words is only possible if we, as readers receiving their offerings, involve ourselves in the messy work of world-building.

Where I see world-building in poems, you, dear reader, might see it in your garden, in music or in dancing, or in the way your daughter says your name. My intention here is not to get everyone to become a poetry lover, but to invite us to collectively notice what tunes our attention to what sustains life. It is these acts of attention – and of embodied, sensory, relational existence – that make it possible for me to build a companionable relationship with ambivalence, and to imagine just worlds beyond critiquing the world as we now know it.

Note
[1] A version of this introduction appeared as part of an essay I wrote for the British International Studies Association on care, conferences and convening (Krystalli, 2023). Many thanks to BISA for the invitation. www.bisa.ac.uk/articles/gathering-vulnerable-times-conferences-care-and-bringing-each-other-along

References
Ahmed, S. (2017) *Living a Feminist Life*, Duke University Press.

Emejulu, A. (2022) 'Ambivalence as Misfeeling, Ambivalence as Refusal', *Post45*, 27 October. Available at: https://post45.org/2022/10/ambivalence-as-misfeeling-ambivalence-as-refusal/ (accessed 25 January 2024).

Kimmerer, R. (2013) *Braiding Sweetgrass: Indigenous Wisdom, Scientific Knowledge, and the Teachings of Plants*, Milkweed Editions.

Krystalli, R. (2023) 'Gathering in Vulnerable Times: Conferences, Care, and Bringing Each Other Along' [online], British International Studies Association. Available at: www.bisa.ac.uk/articles/gathering-vulnerable-times-conferences-care-and-bringing-each-other-along (accessed 4 July 2024).

Krystalli, R. (2024) *Good Victims: The Political as a Feminist Question*, Oxford University Press.

Krystalli, R. and Schulz, P. (2022) 'Taking love and care seriously: an emergent research agenda for remaking worlds in the wake of violence', *International Studies Review*, 24(1): 1–25.

Krystalli, R., Tripathi, S. and Hunfeld, K. (2023) 'Making friends with uncertainty: hopeful futurities in telling stories about global politics'. In M. Matejova and A. Shesterinina (eds) *Uncertainty in Global Politics*, Routledge, pp 252–269.

Olufemi, L. (2020) *Feminism Interrupted*, Pluto Press.

Ravecca, P. and Dauphinee, E. (2022) 'What is left for critique? On the perils of innocence in neoliberal times', *Las Torres de Lucca: revista internacional de filosofía política*, 11(1): 37–49.

Ticktin, M. (2017) 'A world without innocence', *American Ethnologist*, 44(4): 557–590.

Transken, S. (2002) 'Poetically teaching/doing the profession of social work as a joyful undisciplined discipline-jumper and genre-jumper', *Critical Social Work*, 3(1). https://ojs.uwindsor.ca/index.php/csw/article/view/5646

Tsing, A. (2015) *The Mushroom at the End of the World: On the Possibility of Life in Capitalist Ruins*, Princeton University Press.

13

The Role of 'Stuckedness': Ambivalence in Scholar-Activism

Aylwyn Walsh and Paul Routledge

It is October 2022, raining heavily, it is cold and only one third of those that signed up have turned up. We are expecting a diverse group of multiple ages at a workshop introducing arts activist approaches specifically related to climate justice. 'Disruption, Disobedience and Creativity: Arts activism in climate justice' aimed to set out some principles from our collaborative toolkit (Walsh et al, 2022) and generate capacity in local organizers in Leeds for adopting more creative approaches in their movements. We find ourselves mid-workshop feeling thwarted by bringing together individuals rather than a collective – our potential feels limited by the short time we have together. Engaging activities can open up imaginative responses, but a single workshop is not going to enable us to achieve our aims to embed arts activism into the various groups or initiatives across greater Leeds, particularly as routinely, the established climate justice organizers do not take up our offers to develop interventions. We feel ambivalent, wondering why we continue to offer workshops and trainings, waiting, it seems for the 'serious' organizers to allow some space for creativity and play in their movements. We feel stuck in what Akwugo Emejulu calls 'misfeeling' (2022a): we ought to be celebrating our successful, if damp, arts activist workshop. Instead, we are judging our limited progress bringing playful, embodied praxis to our local climate justice movements in Leeds. Our sense of failure and ambivalence results in a lack of energy to keep proposing, mobilizing and activating our networks. We feel stuck.

Opening on this scene of ambivalence thrusts us into the 'both-and' formulation of ambivalence in activism – at once circling on a feeling of frustration and riven with hope for the potential activity. Ambivalence plays out as a sense of incompleteness; structural, interpersonal and emotional. It is not, however, a site between two equal oppositional forces, but a mode of negotiating complexity. Ambivalence is explored as a relational affect and mood that seeks resolution but does not necessarily achieve it. Having experienced this sense of struggle, loss of momentum and doubt in our collaborative work, we began exploring how ambivalence, and indeed the sense of being 'stuck' could provide some leverage for scholar-activism. In the chapter, we have aimed to work across diverse examples, locales and issues to bring the focus to the scholar-activist (rather than issues inherent to the movements, organizing tactics and outcomes as such). To set this up, we explore Ghassan Hage's concept of 'stuckedness' (2009, 2015), and thereafter we introduce the entrenched hierarchies and power inequalities that we have experienced across a range of movements. What we aim to draw attention to in ambivalence is the contours of 'stuckedness', a form of 'hesitation' (Emejulu, 2022b: 74), a sense of in-betweenness, experienced as 'refusal' (Emejulu, 2022a) that emerges in specific conditions within movements. We are also interested in how this (negatively coded) affect can also forge a mode of reflexivity that can engender new directions for the movement, or indeed, for the scholar-activist.

'Stuckedness' as scholar-activist condition

The grammatically challenging term put forward by anthropologist Ghassan Hage is defined as 'the sentiment and the state of being of experiencing oneself as essentially "stuck"' (2015: 3). It is not only 'being stuck', but the reflexivity of the experience; a looping of self-consciousness, temporality and affect. Becoming stuck has a sense of being 'done to' those experiencing it, and so 'to be stuck' becomes 'stuckedness'; a condition of 'crisis' as understood by Hage as an everyday temporality. He refers to 'waiting it out' (2015: 5) in the sense of enduring a circumstance that is hoped to be temporary, despite all evidence to the contrary. This is understood as decisions based on 'sunk costs' (usually correlating to time and money), that result in keeping people 'in place'. In much of his work, Hage is referring to a political/ juridical 'stuckedness' of migrants unable to move but who exist in an ambivalent existential waiting that is in opposition to the hope of 'imaginary mobility' (2015: 3). But, as he puts it in an earlier work, 'stuckedness' relates to a sense that there are no 'choices or alternatives to the situation one is in and an inability to grab such alternatives even if they present themselves' (2009: 100).

Hage's analysis centres on the migrant condition, though it can be applied as an ontological and epistemological mode to forms of relating that combine identity, activity and community. In our examples, we want to position the work of activists (specifically the often unpaid, coalitional work of scholar-activists) as partaking in this temporal and existential tension. By doing so, we are interested in moving beyond a sense of being 'done to' by authorities and bordering regimes that pervades migrant uncertainty, in order to conceive of how the informing contexts, collaborations, relationships and intentions of scholar-activists are inflected by a form of weighing up of issues, disagreements, power dynamics and outcomes. In that sense, Hage's formulation of being 'done to' finds its tenor in the delicate negotiations of roles, responsibilities and desires taken on by scholar-activists.

Hage finds the 'analytical ramifications of the ambivalence and uncertainty that are at the core of hope' more generative than 'the more general conception of hope as a relation to the future' (Hage, 2016: 465). We could see this as what Lauren Berlant calls 'cruel optimism' (2011). For them, this attachment includes the 'inclination to return to the scene of fantasy that enables you to expect that this time, nearness to this thing will help you or a world to become different in just the right way' (2011: 2). In that sense, 'stuckedness' is a description of material circumstances but also a theorization of the tension between hope and material circumstances. Such 'hope' that is so central to Hage's concept of 'stuckedness' is critical, but also serves to circle the scholar-activist in affects of 'cruel optimism' (Berlant, 2011). Being 'stuck' is not only a description of immobility or stasis, but a temporal/spatial feature of organizing or movement building in the sense of asking both 'where are we moving?' and 'what vision of the future are we organizing towards?' However, our ambivalence as scholar-activists emerges in part because the feeling of being stuck (affectual/emotional) is open to change and challenge as we attempt to negotiate ever-present yet problematic power relations (interpersonal and structural issues).

In the rest of the chapter we consider how this condition can be understood in relation to scholar-activism, as distinct from the organizing/mobilizing itself. A methodological commitment to ambivalence or 'stuckedness' helps to set up the multiple directions and complexity of desires, hopes, disappointments and failures that permeate scholar-activism. In the following sections, we engage more closely with the activity of the scholar-activist drawing from our own praxis; in particular, considering how these interrelate in the context of funded research as distinct from long-term affiliation with movements. We produce a three-part model identifying registers of an ambivalent scholar-activism: 'dissonant intimacies' (Roy, 2023), 'language in common' (Lyons and Jones, 2020) and 'radical vulnerability' (Nagar, 2019). These three registers are mutually constitutive, forging the conditions for 'stuckedness'.

Dissonant intimacies and the politics of knowledge

Our first register emerges from the South African context, which is where Walsh grew up. Srila Roy's account of an ambitious South–South partnership on feminist collaborative research reveals what she calls 'dissonant intimacies' (see also Macharia, 2016). These are grounded in ambivalence resulting from what was presumed to be shared ground (feminist, activist aligned) in her South Africa–India–Uganda partnership, but which were inevitably structured by the 'coloniality of knowledge and power in higher education', resulting in 'complex, uneven relationships' (Roy, 2023: 1237). Her reflection engenders the distinction between hopes or intentions and how they can rub up uncomfortably against the mechanistic, often logistical, sensibility of global funding in research.

'Dissonant intimacies' requires recognition of the forces, resources and structures that keep power dynamics in place, or that entrench the positions of, for example, those with permanent academic roles as distinct from collaborators who are working multiple jobs to survive. The concept is helpful, too, in scholar-activism that inevitably includes the intractable power differentials of North–South (Minority World–Majority World) collaborations. It requires reflexivity and openness to how the dynamics of relationships can reproduce and reinforce 'stuckedness'.

In ImaginingOtherwise, a project on youth arts activism in South Africa that we both worked on with Tshisimani Centre for Activist Education, we faced several scenarios, all of which were characterized by the temporality of waiting, forged in the 'dissonant intimacies' of navigating ongoing relationships. We were delayed dispensing the funding for the project because our university was unable to muster a contract to initiate our project. We attempted emails, phone calls and eventually threats, in our attempt to get unstuck, and to get the project partners paid so that we could proceed. Our comradeship was strained by the stickiness of the funding. Eventually, the funding was received and the project started in March 2020. Because of the COVID pandemic, our planned visit to South Africa was curtailed (see Walsh et al, 2020). That meant that, in practice, our forging of solidarities and mutual ways of working were mediated by Zoom, WhatsApp and periods of waiting.

We, as the scholar-activists based in the North, were mired in 'stuckedness'. For instance, we needed to recognize that the pace of UK funding schemes did not match the trail of contracting, recruiting and managing projects on the ground in a Southern (Majority World) context. The relentlessness of project milestones and tranche reporting carried on, and sat alongside the disproportionate power that accrued to 'Northern' activists who controlled the funding and had easy access to institutional resources. These powers 'stuck' to us in certain ways in our attempts to practise solidarity with South African partners, and impacted the relational side of the project (see also Walsh and Burnett, 2021).

We refused to start activity while 'contract delays' would have meant partners in South Africa would need to subsidize the project. We were alert to asymmetries: projects inevitably roll out differently for local organizers than for distant scholar-activists, and our temporal (and on the ground) distance from daily dynamics lent itself to misunderstanding what we could expect. Once things finally opened up in South Africa, we remained unable to travel, though we continued to try to be present for online arts activism workshops, which was less satisfying than the 'real' conviviality of workshop spaces. In terms of tensions that exert pressures in different directions, as the distant partners not working on the ground, we had less access to the impacts and daily rhythms of the project in action. The rewards and affective flows of scholar-activism were mediated and distanced.

We waited far too long for the final design of our arts activism toolkit because the graphic designer that was hired was not accustomed to complex projects (Walsh et al, 2022). As a result, we became ambivalent about imposing rigour or nit-picking once proofs were in place (resulting in the repetition of a bell hooks quote). We experienced the 'dissonant intimacy' of collaborating with South African comrades and the positionality of holding Minority World/North institutional power alongside the timelines of urgency that are often attributed to 'cultures' of 'white supremacy' (cf Okun, nd). This engendered a mode of waiting precisely because we did not want to exert pressure on our partners, for fear of taking on the logics of our institutions. Such hesitancy enabled the toolkit production to emerge, later than hoped, without imposing urgency. Although a frustrating experience, imbued with self-critical judgement (Sealey-Huggins, 2016), ambivalence in this example enabled us to maintain the relational aspects of the partnership. However, there was a sense that unavoidable power dynamics were held (or stuck) 'in place'.

Language in common

Our second register concerns what Lyons and Jones (2020) term a 'language in common': modes of communication that produce and are produced by activist collectives and mediate between the material and the symbolic. The language in common refers to the construction and repetition of images, songs, dances, rituals and performances that help to construct and express collective power. Such a language draws upon and incorporates lessons and practices from earlier struggles (Estes, 2019), and in so doing enables us to see 'how social movements communicate across space and time, and how our shared images, rituals, and signs both produce and make visible our collectivity' (Lyons and Jones, 2020).

This language in common also encodes at least three grammars: (1) a 'claim to represent' as material bodies – intimately connected through bonds of trust, radical vulnerability and struggle – create a common political syntax; (2) a 'right to appear' in relation to power, presence and visuality as public space is claimed by bodily collectives as a staging ground for political legitimacy and contestation (see Butler, 2015; Rancière, 2010); and (3) a claim to legitimate political identity and belonging that is otherwise to forms of political, economic and cultural domination (Rai and Reinelt, 2015). All three processes inform and fashion processes of embodied political action. Such a language in common must attempt to deploy grammatical idioms that are different from the performance of dominant powers, so that they are not so easily regulated or recuperated by those powers (Nield, 2006).

The language in common emerges from the collective power of those who use and transform it, and by which the world is understood and related to. Actions, slogans, images, stories and symbols give shape to an emergent 'we', whereby symbolic and material actions reinforce one another as narratives of social transformation are developed. Further, as such images and rituals are shared between activists and between social movements, so the possibility arises that common repertoires and traditions develop that can contribute to the development of continuity between struggles, and to shared worldviews that are counter-hegemonic.

For example, between 1998 and 2006, Routledge was a participant in People's Global Action (PGA) – an international network for communication and coordination between diverse social movements resisting neoliberal capitalist development. PGA attempted to fashion solidarity between peasant farmers, trade unions, autonomist groups and other activists in Asia, Latin America, Europe and North America (Routledge, 2017).

PGA's 'language in common' consisted of three dimensions. First, it encoded a political syntax representative of all participant movements. This included (1) a rejection of all forms and systems of domination and discrimination including capitalism, patriarchy and racism; (2) a call to direct action and civil disobedience against neoliberal globalization, and the construction of local alternatives; and (3) an organizational philosophy based on decentralization and autonomy. Second, it practised a right to appear through multi-scalar political action effected during conferences, activist caravans and global days of protest action (GDAs) against international organizations such as the World Bank and International Monetary Fund. Third, PGA claimed political legitimacy through its coordination of social movements from around the world in opposition to the architects of neoliberal globalization (Routledge, 2017). Routledge worked in the Asian part of the PGA network, PGA Asia. Much of PGA Asia's organizational work – preparing, organizing and participating in discussions, meetings, conferences and GDAs – was conducted by key European activists (of whom Routledge was one) and key movement contacts (usually movement leaders or general secretaries), who helped to organize conferences, mobilize resources (for example, funds), and facilitate communication and information flows between movements and between movement offices and grassroots communities. Possessing English-language skills (the lingua franca of PGA Asia), and computer literacy, these folk constituted the 'imagineers' of the network. They conducted ideational labour, attempting to 'ground' the concept or imaginary of the network (what it was, how it worked, what it was attempting to achieve) within the grassroots communities who comprised the membership of the participant movements (Routledge, 2017).

For Routledge, feelings of ambivalence were generated because the imagineers' resource access and communication skills, as well as their experience in activism and meeting facilitation, enabled them to wield disproportionate power and influence within the network. Frequently mobile (both in that they had the time and resources to travel outside of their home countries and through their access to distance-shrinking technologies), they performed much of the routine work that sustained the network. Meanwhile, grassroots movement activists remained firmly stuck in their communities (Routledge, 2017).

Routledge's scholar-activist role as an imagineer in PGA Asia meant that he embodied a 'stuckedness' in how the language in common was articulated. First, he had a disproportionate power to represent the network in international forums such as PGA conferences and in the functioning of the PGA Asia network itself. Because the imagineers possessed the cultural capital of (usually) higher education, and the social capital inherent in their transnational connections and access to resources and knowledge, they not only routed more than their 'fair share' of informational traffic, but often determined the 'content' of that traffic. They did not necessarily constitute themselves out of a malicious will-to-power: rather, relational power defaulted to them through the characteristics noted earlier and personal qualities such as energy, commitment and charisma, and the ability to synthesize politically important social moments into identifiable ideas and forms (Routledge, 2008). This was accentuated further because structurally, PGA Asia's organizing language in common was English – a language that the majority of peasant farmers were unable to speak. While the network attempted to use interpretation clusters for Hindi, Bengali and Nepali speakers, the quality of interpretation was uneven.

Second, as a scholar-activist employed in a UK university and conducting research on PGA Asia, Routledge had the resources and the time to participate in many GDAs and other network events and actions. As an imagineer, he embodied a disproportionately greater 'right to appear' and 'right to represent' than most peasant farmers who constituted the 'rank and file' of the PGA Asia participant movements. For example, in a PGA Asia conference held in Dhaka, Bangladesh in 2004, Routledge was asked by movement leaders to suggest an action plan to put before the conference attendees. Routledge's suggestion of a GDA and an activist caravan (see next section) was placed before the conference and immediately passed unanimously. This created a deep sense of ambivalence in Routledge concerning whose vision was shaping the network's activities, and the disproportionate reliance of participant movements on PGA's structure and organizational processes, not least concerning the representational power of certain imagineers.

Such 'stuckedness' of the imagineers created ambivalent effects: on the one hand they enabled PGA Asia to communicate and act; on the other, they embodied a disproportionate power that vitiated against the ideals of horizontal, networked coordination.

Radical vulnerability

Our third register is defined by Richa Nagar, who argues that solidarity between those engaged in struggles for sociopolitical, economic and environmental justice invariably involve complex and unequal relationships. Further, she posits that the very meanings of 'justice' (as well as 'ethics' and 'politics') are shaped by the place and time specifics of particular struggles, as well as the specificities of 'particular convergences of subjectivities and articulations' (2019: 20). She comes to this concept through an account of 'hungry translation' and this alerts us to the necessity of how struggles are circumscribed by language and the politics of mutual understanding across difference. The politics of alliance also necessitates the acknowledgement of our raced, classed and gendered differences – both bodily and within our movements. The material, intellectual and embodied differences between collaborators inform the possibilities and challenges of creating such collectives (Nagar and Shirazi, 2019).

The concept of 'radical vulnerability' (Nagar, 2019; Nagar and Shirazi, 2019) provides an ethical basis for constructing solidarities, that actively engages with the persistent yet uneven risks and possibilities of generating shared dreams, practices and strategies within collective action. It implies an active engagement with these very differences and divergences – in positionality, in aspiration – that ground the everyday work of creating such solidarities.

Radical vulnerability, then, means opening ourselves to the inequalities and inequities within and between members of the collective: our differences of experience, our mistakes, our memories. Through practices of trust and critical reflexivity we open ourselves to be questioned and evaluated by those we work with as an integral part of forging a collective-in-struggle.

For example, Routledge participated in the Climate Change, Gender and Food Sovereignty Caravan (hereafter, 'Climate Caravan') that travelled through Bangladesh in November 2011, and that was organized by the Bangladesh *Krishok* (farmer) Federation (BKF), the Bangladesh *Kishani Sabha* (Women Farmers' Association, BKS) and the international farmers' network to which they both belong, *La Via Campesina* (Routledge, 2015). The purpose of the Climate Caravan was to educate and mobilize vulnerable peasant communities engaged in land occupations about the interrelated issues of food sovereignty, gender inequality and the effects of climate change. In addition, it aimed to facilitate networking connections in the form of movement-to-movement communication, sharing of experiences and strategies, and in so doing deepen and extend solidarity networks of grassroots movements in South Asia. However, the politics of affinity that was generated through such activities necessitated a recognition of the complexity and inequality of the relationships formed and this generated a deep emotional ambivalence and discomfort in Routledge. The political, economic and cultural legacies of British colonialism fed into contemporary contexts, and intersected with political opportunities, processes and relations that operated across space: as an academic from a British university, Routledge could often obtain an entry visa to an Asian country without problems (unlike Bangladeshi activists who might wish to visit the UK), and English was frequently the lingua franca among Asian activists, and so on (see Routledge, 2008).

Further, Routledge was involved in helping to devise, raise funds for, document and participate in the Caravan. He spoke at, and led many of the workshops and seminars that were held, as well as interviewing Caravan participants. He wrote, in English, the handbook given to the Caravan participants, which only a few activists with English-language skills could read.

Scholar-activism requires a recognition of Routledge's privileged positionality as a white, male, able, Western academic in such a context, and as a disproportionately empowered participant in the Caravan. There were critical inequalities between him and most of those with whom he worked – in physical mobility across space, access to resources such as money and technology, ability to leave Bangladesh when he chose to do so, and so on. Further, gendered inequalities between peasant farmers involved in Caravan activities, could not be adequately addressed (see Routledge, 2015).

Practising radical vulnerability enabled a recognition that these inequalities necessarily resulted in solidarity-building that was contested and unstable, imbued with ambivalences, ambiguities and contradictions. Routledge's scholar-activism occupied an 'in-between positionality' (Stephens and Bagelman, 2023) that, while generative of movement-to-movement communication and mobilization through Climate Caravan activities, was also 'stuck in place' given the power inequalities that existed between him and Bangladeshi farmers. Even though an unwelcome affect, 'stuckedness' revealed what was unhelpful, uncomfortable and perpetuated by his positionality as a white, British male scholar-activist.

Conclusion: The generative potential of 'stuckedness'

In work on activist Rosa Luxemburg, Clare Hemmings (2018: 17) proposes that: 'A sustained focus on ambivalence helps us to engage past politics and theory as complex or contradictory, and to foreground the importance of current complexity, despite our desire to have resolved both past and present paradoxes.' What we have emphasized here is that there is value in a capacity to endure the lack of resolution as a site of learning and of prompting continued efforts. In another mode, Emejulu puts forward some of the generative conceptions of ambivalence, calling it 'a kind of temporal politics in which, if attuned to it, we are forced to slow down, to wait, to pause, to hesitate' (Emejulu, 2022a). If we reflect back through the main examples explored in the chapter, the temporal dimension is important – not becoming mired in judgement of 'failures', nor giving up on future change. This pause is a relational one: a condition that invites attentiveness to the ongoing, iterative labour of solidarity, not least because of sedimented social conditions.

This returns us to Ghassan Hage's concept of 'stuckedness', which emphasizes enduring the present in pursuit of change. Such waiting 'involves both a subjection to the elements or to certain social conditions and at the same time a braving of these conditions. It is this ambivalence which allows it to take heroic forms' (Hage, 2009: 102). Hage signals ambivalence as a site of 'heroism' because any action undertaken in a state of such waiting 'lies in this ability to snatch agency in the very midst of its lack' (2009: 100). His characterization is partially a critique of post-hoc ontological meaning-making. We depart from Hage's description of 'stuckedness' as being 'done to' – from a temporal perspective there are structural issues such as academic year cycles, funding cycles and obligations that may inform the conditions of 'stuckedness'. There are also the global circuits and flows of knowledge that seem inevitably to flow away from Majority world contexts, but in our hopes for a more equitable praxis of scholar-activism we contend that meaning-making is not at all the sole domain of privileged scholars. Hage suggests in the ontological conditions of 'stuckedness', such meaning-making tends to grasp any mode of 'heroism' or agency in the face of being 'stuck'. We acknowledge this as a significant criticism of scholarship about social movements as opposed to scholar-activism. The heroic narrative is also inflected with hegemonic meanings (patriarchal, imperial, supremacist) that inevitably become attached to such gestures.

What we have aimed to do by introducing the diverse set of examples is attend to how the figure of the scholar-activist is afforded the route through complexity (Hemmings, 2018) via reflexivity (Sealey-Huggins, 2016). Unlike, perhaps, our organizing comrades, whose movements and campaigns for change necessitate momentum, the capacity to hold onto ambivalence, a temporal pause or indeed, 'stuckedness', is part of the scholar-activist's repertoire. That is, a relational reflexive mode that manifests differently from movement organizers' experiences while 'in the mix'. Scholar-activism does more than inform the terms of any struggle: it emerges in and through social movements, themselves defined by entrenched hierarchies and power inequalities. As such, scholar-activists are invested in the always incomplete work of solidarity-building which, at times, benefits from 'stuckedness'. That is, solidarity is never fully achieved, resolved or completed; rather it must keep emerging. This chimes with Emejulu's reminder that ambivalence can be recast 'as a space for experiments in becoming' (2022b: 49), which could be either an interpersonal and/or affective dimension.

Our three registers of 'stuckedness' that underpin the practice of solidarity in different contexts are helpful here. First, a recognition of 'dissonant intimacies' alerts us to the ambivalence that results from what was presumed to be shared ground between collaborators, but that requires recognition of the forces, resources and structures that keep power dynamics in place within collectives. Second, attending to the 'language in common' that underpins solidarity enables a questioning of its 'claim to represent', its 'right to appear' and its 'claim to legitimate political identity and belonging'. Finally, this requires practising 'radical vulnerability' concerning the differences, inequalities and inequities within and between members of a collective. Scholar-activist praxis, therefore, not eschewing ambivalence but dwelling or waiting, allows for the negotiation of power and proportionality and the requirement to reflect. Together, these three registers provide the necessary prerequisites for the generative work of transforming the ambivalences that are inherent in the practice of scholar-activism.

References

Berlant, L. (2011) 'Cruel optimism'. In M. Gregg and G.J. Seigworth (eds) *The Affect Theory Reader*, Duke University Press, pp 93–117.

Butler, J. (2015) *Notes on a Performative Theory of Assembly*, Harvard University Press.

Emejulu, A. (2022a) 'Ambivalence as Misfeeling, Ambivalence as Refusal', *Post45*, 27 October. Available at: https://post45.org/2022/10/ambivalence-as-misfeeling-ambivalence-as-refusal/

Emejulu, A. (2022b) *Fugitive Feminism*, Silver Press.

Estes, N. (2019) *Our History Is the Future: Standing Rock versus the Dakota Access Pipeline, and the Long Tradition of Indigenous Resistance*, Verso.

Hage, G. (2009) 'Waiting out the crisis: on stuckedness and governmentality'. In G. Hage (ed) *Waiting*, Melbourne University Press, pp 97–106.

Hage, G. (2015) *Alter-politics: Critical Anthropology and the Radical Imagination*, Melbourne University Press.

Hage, G. (2016) 'Questions concerning a future-politics', *History and Anthropology*, 27(4): 465–467.

Hemmings, C. (2018) *Considering Emma Goldman: Feminist Political Ambivalence and the Imaginative Archive*, Duke University Press.

Lyons, S. and Jones, J. (2020) 'The Language in Common', *E-Flux* #113. Available at: www.e-flux.com/journal/113/359927/the-language-in-common/

Macharia, K. (2016) 'On being area-studied: a litany of complaint', *GLQ*, 22(2): 183–189.

Nagar, R. (2019) 'Hungry translations: the world through radical vulnerability: the 2017 *Antipode* RGS-IBG Lecture', *Antipode*, 51(1): 3–24.

Nagar, R. and Shirazi, R. (2019) 'Radical vulnerability'. In *Antipode* Editorial Collective (ed) *Keywords in Radical Geography: Antipode at 50* (1st edition), John Wiley & Sons Ltd, pp 236–242.

Nield, S. (2006) 'There is another world: space, theatre and global anti-capitalism', *Contemporary Theatre Review*, 16(1): 51–61.

Okun, T. (nd) 'White Supremacy Culture'. Website. Available at: www.whitesupremacyculture.info/characteristics.html

Rai, S.M. and Reinelt, J. (2015) *The Grammar of Politics and Performance*, Routledge.

Rancière, J. (2010) *Dissensus: On Politics and Aesthetics*, Continuum.

Routledge, P. (2008) 'Acting in the Network: ANT and the politics of generating associations', *Environment and Planning D: Society and Space*, 26(2): 199–217.

Routledge, P. (2015) 'Engendering Gramsci: gender, the philosophy of praxis and spaces of encounter in the Climate Caravan, Bangladesh', *Antipode*, 47(5): 1321–1345.

Routledge, P. (2017) *Space Invaders: Radical Geographies of Protest*, Pluto Press.

Roy, S. (2023) 'Dissonant intimacies: coloniality and the failures of South–South collaboration', *The Sociological Review*, 71(6): 1237–1257.

Sealey-Huggins, L. (2016) 'Depoliticised activism? Ambivalence and pragmatism at the COP16', *The International Journal of Sociology and Social Policy*, 36(9): 695–710.

Stephens, A.C. and Bagelman, J. (2023) 'Towards scholar-activism: transversal relations, dissent, and creative acts', *Citizenship Studies*, 27(3): 329–346. doi: 10.1080/13621025.2023.2171251.

Walsh, A. and Burnett, S. (2021) 'Voicing ambiguities in the *Ilizwi Lenyaniso Lomhlaba* co-creator collective', *Research in Drama Education: The Journal of Applied Theatre and Performance*, 26(4): 605–620.

Walsh, A., Sutherland, A., Visagie, A. and Routledge, P. (2020) 'ImaginingOtherwise: a glossary of arts education practice on the Cape Flats', *ArtsPraxis*, 7(2b). Available at: https://sites.google.com/nyu.edu/artspraxis/2020/volume-7-issue-2b/walsh-sutherland-visagie-routledge-imaginingotherwise

Walsh, A., Sutherland, A. and Routledge, P. (2022) *Arts Activism Toolkit: Disruption, Disobedience & Creativity*. Available at: www.tshisimani.org.za/wp-content/uploads/IMAGININGOTHERWISE_WEB-toolkit-final.pdf

Conclusion: Thinking with Pessimism

Akwugo Emejulu, Marlies Kustatscher and Callum McGregor

This is a book about space-time. In this edited collection, activists, practitioners and scholars from across the globe have analysed how the past, present and future interact with the social spaces of activism to elicit complicated emotional and somatic responses from a range of different kinds of activists. Authors have written passionately about living with and seeking to reconcile past injustices while also trying to interrupt these harms to marginalized groups in the present and future. This struggle, of trying to think and work with different timescapes, while also attempting to remain curious, reflexive and efficacious, is just one of the many challenges activists must confront in their work. Juggling community building, solidarity work, direct action and a healthy private life is almost an impossible task, and yet, as our authors have so brilliantly argued, it is the acknowledgement and embrace of difficult and ugly emotions that makes activist work possible in the short and long term.

We, as editors, took a gamble on whether an idea of ambivalence would resonate in the present moment. Certainly, in our separate work on climate justice, children's rights, migrants' rights, anti-racist and anti-fascist activism, we encountered activists taking their complex emotions very seriously, particularly in terms of how it impacted the social relations within their groups and networks and how those emotions both positively and negatively shaped their identities and relations outside of their respective activist milieux. Indeed, given our observations and empirical work, we thought we could press further and explore an unpopular, unlikely and non-heroic emotion that is not often associated with activism: ambivalence. To our delight, this focus on ambivalence struck a chord. Certainly, there is something rather liberating about working with ambivalence. Being freed from unconditional positivity, a belief in the arc of history inevitably bending toward justice and/or the clarity and assurance in the righteousness of one's cause, allowed authors a space for critical reflection.

Because ambivalence demands nuance and no easy answers, it offers a portal to a kind of radical honesty about both the problems and possibilities of activism. Some authors highlighted how they did not like their comrades very much or how their comrades' dogmatic commitments to abstracted radical ideals led to the destruction of their organizations. Other authors demonstrated how ambivalence created vulnerability and allowed for the creation of new spaces to think again about the legacies of colonialism, enclosures and captivity. Another group of authors use ambivalence as an opportunity to consider the different ways in which activists might care for themselves and others – ambivalence shapeshifts into a new strategy for practising solidarity. Across 13 chapters, authors demonstrated how ambivalence speaks across and collapses different space-times, as past, present and future are understood through the complex emotional responses of activists feeling their way to solidarity and justice. How authors in this volume have conceptualized ambivalence complements each other in many ways. Yet, the variety of ambivalent feelings and experiences also speaks to the difficulties – and perhaps futility – of seeking to resolve the emotional and intellectual tensions surrounding it. Working with ambivalence is so powerful because it allows space for, and honours, the unflattering emotions that make us human.

Thinking about the difficulty of the human condition and putting this in the context of past, present and future catastrophes, we can see how ambivalence offers us a framework for understanding what might be possible through activism for social change and yet what also gives us pause for thought, makes us hesitate, given the immense challenges that face us.

In this book, we have drawn attention and awareness to the multiplicity of experiences of ambivalence in activism. We do not seek to conclude on an instrumentalized view of ambivalence, as a means to more impactful or more endurable activism. However, in their complexity, the thoughtful accounts of our authors not only legitimize, but also inherently value, ambivalent emotions in activism, especially within the fraught sociopolitical challenges of our time. We are living through a time of multiple, overlapping crises. From the climate emergency to the cost of living crisis to an emboldened far right – what might the future hold? The unpredictability of the moment combines with a deep pessimism about the future to spark a collective sense of foreboding and insecurity. And yet, with a clear-eyed analysis, activists regard this precarious moment and are nevertheless called to action to make change. Here, we would like to introduce what we think is another helpful emotion to activism – pessimism. If ambivalence helps us acknowledge and accept ourselves and others as contradictory and confounding creatures, we argue that pessimism also offers us a space to dwell and see ourselves anew. Pessimism can be nourishing. Sometimes it is important to allow oneself to sink deep, to disappear at the bottom of a well, to welcome the darkness.

Being enveloped and occluded helps us to see the world as it is – it is a deep and ugly place. We must understand that. And yet – our activism must live in that transitory state – the 'and yet' of seeing clearly and not allowing that to paralyse us. We should expect to be disillusioned and demoralized. Those are hard-won emotions born out of deep and committed struggle. We should welcome this darkness because this is a marker of experience, of learning, growing and changing. Pessimism can be both a mirror and shield. It can show us all too clearly what the world is, what it demands and what it takes away from us. And yet, we know, deep in our bones, that this is not the only world that exists – that of darkness and dismay. The world is also full of love, beauty and kindness. Much of that beauty is found in relation with others – friends, family, lovers and comrades. This beauty is so nourishing and precious, precisely because of the darkness that is lurking in our peripheral vision.

Contra Wilderson (2020), pessimism does not need to be the penultimate step to nihilism but can be used, in tandem with ambivalence, to help us understand the daunting challenges that face us, and support us in struggling against them anyway. Pessimism helps us be better ancestors to those who come after us – it helps us fight knowing that we will not likely see the fruits of our labour but we sow these seeds for a different future, regardless. Pessimism need not always be understood as a negative emotion to be accepted or overcome. Rather, in the clichéd quote often attributed to Gramsci, we find meaning in a framework of 'pessimism of the intellect and the optimism of the will'. Indeed, like ambivalence, pessimism helps us think about the space-time of activism. Pessimism offers us a keen and realistic analysis of the past, present and future and gives us a disposition to help us cope with the monumental task before us, that of changing the world. And yet, and yet and yet, we struggle against this dark and disastrous future both so that we can sleep at night and so we do not condemn future generations to having to resolve our mistakes. Pessimism, then, is a useful emotion for sober assessment and playing in the dark. And from that space of disenchantment, we re-emerge refreshed and resolved to build new worlds.

Pessimism is risky, however. We must resist the temptation to *only* see and expect the worst in ourselves, each other and the world. Certainly, that is a reasonable conclusion to draw from the current state of affairs but that outlook must be integrated into a sophisticated reckoning with the world as it is and the world that might be. Taking Alyson Cole's gentle rebuke of Akwugo Emejulu's understanding of ambivalence to heart, we follow her nuanced operationalization of ambivalence and seek to apply it to pessimism. She argues (Cole, 2025: xx, our emphasis):

> Ambivalence is more than a prelude to action. *Ambivalence constitutes a praxis integral to political activism,* though one that straddles agency/

passivity, inoperative/productive dichotomies. By deemphasising the idea of ambivalence as incompatibility or dissonance, we can reconceive of ambivalence the product of the politically fecund effort to hold divergent views and feelings, not something to overcome but instead the basis of our shared condition and an essential aspect of political struggle. *Rather than assuming that ambivalence should or can be settled prior to action, we need instead to understand better how to act with ambivalence.*

Thinking about pessimism as a praxis opens up many productive political possibilities. Rather than fearing disillusionment and despair, we need to think carefully about how to understand – but not resolve – these feelings. Acknowledging feeling hopeless and lost can, counterintuitively, lead to stronger community ties and solidarity. As Emejulu and Bassel (2020: 405) found in their study of women of colour activists and exhaustion:

> 'I'm exhausted' expresses an emotional and psychological state of being. At the same time, it acts as a structure of mutual recognition within precarious collectives. This is an assertion of fear, anxiety, fatigue, disbelief and despair as shared burdens, collective properties that – sometimes – enable reading and recognising the pain of others with whom space is held. This mutual recognition may not 'succeed' according to the conventional understandings of social movements studies, in the sense of achieving specific campaign objectives. Nor do reciprocity and acceptance necessarily follow, especially when other oppressions go unchallenged. But it can become possible to set different terms of solidarity by hailing the equally exhausted. It can be possible to express the desire to build solidarity on terms that resist white supremacy, patriarchy and capitalism.

Articulating pessimism, rather than being a taboo act among activism, can be a path to community. This is because pessimism is an expression of vulnerability. Expecting the worst is another feeling of fear – fear of the future, fear of disappointment, fear of being betrayed. As we know in all of our meaningful relationships, sharing one's anxieties and vulnerability is an act of deep courage that, more often than not, creates a space for others to discuss their difficult and complex feelings too. Pessimism, then, does not need to be resolved but worked with, moulded, cherished even, as a state of being vulnerable and an act of reaching out to others in the darkness, to find comfort and, perhaps, to find the strength needed to continue.

Just like ambivalence, pessimism also bends and twists space-time. Here, our task is to not only live with contradiction, hesitation and doubt but to also acknowledge and integrate the reality of catastrophe in our lives. To not shy or explain away these judgements, but to face them with a steady eye and undertake collective action anyway. Activism fits in that transitory state of 'and yet' – 'and yet' is a space that is really rather capacious because it contains a whole range of feelings including hope, love, fear and despair. In that messy space of feeling all the feelings, we embrace the chaos, find like-minded others and take a step into the unknown.

References

Cole, A. (2025) 'Orchestrating the Furies: Anzaldúa's Evolving Conception of Ambivalent Political Struggle' (Chapter 4, this volume).

Emejulu, A. and Bassel, L. (2020) 'The politics of exhaustion', *City*, 24(1–2): 400–406.

Wilderson, F.B. (2020) *Afropessimism*, Liveright Publishing Corporation.

Index

References to endnotes show both the page number and the note number (231n3).

A

Abd El-Fattah, Alaa 60
ACT UP 25, 26, 30–31
ActionStation 147
activism
  activist spaces 84
  ambivalent academy 7–8
  as ambivalent praxis 5–7
  burn out 77–78, 84, 85
  careerism 95
  dedication 78
  definition 2
  demands of 77
  flexibility 85
  learning 38
  of the in-between 82–84
  political 39, 138–140
  practice of 83–84
  responsibilities and commitment 79
  retention of members 79
  self-care 83
  self-funding 79–80
  small organizations 79–81
  uncertainty 35–38
  see also ambivalent activism; mental health activism; queer activism; scholar-activism
activist academic work 161–162
activist knowingness 30–34
Adorno, Theodor 125
affect 163
Ahmed, Sarah 145, 163, 174
AIDS activists 25–26, 30–31
ambi-psychiatry 113
ambivalence 1
  ambivalent meanings 64–65
  as an anti-capitalist emotion 15
  bad faith 3–4
  complexity 178–179
  contradictory emotions 14
  definitions 1–2, 88, 124–125, 165
  disavowal of 3
  emotional shifts 148–149
  exhaustion and joy 17–18
  generosity 176
  groups 152–154
  hope and 144–145
  inner conflict 99–100
  interpersonal conflict 99, 100
  living with 8
  as misfeeling 14–18, 65, 146, 150, 154
  motivating activism 148–151, 154
  multiple possibilities 173–174
  normative framing of 63
  perspectives 125–126
  pitfalls and possibilities of 114–115
  in political organizing 140–141
  precarity 66, 71
  as recuperation 14–16
  satisfaction and pleasure 14
  slowing down 146
  in social movements 144–147
  temporalities of 148–149, 187
  theorizing 4–5
  as work 143
ambivalent activism 71, 84, 114
  embracing 85
ambivalent mental health activism 105–107, 114
  ambivalent politics 103, 106, 112
Anatomical Museum 160–161
  activist academic work 161–162
  discomfort 166, 168, 169, 170
  proactive outreach work 162
  provenance work 168–169, 170
  repatriation project 160–162, 166–169
  Skull Room 160, 161, 162, 164
Ancient Greece 112–113
anger 16, 18, 30, 103–104, 122, 144, 146, 150, 151
  channelling 137–140
  as motivation 148–149
animal cruelty 120–121, 122, 125–126

195

animal justice 123, 125
  Cube of Truth demonstration 121–123
animal liberation 128
animal rights 122
anti-animal status quo 126–128
anti-diagnosis 107, 109
anti-psychiatry 105, 112, 113
antidepressants 110
Anzaldúa, Gloria 64, 113
  ambiguity 68
  ambivalence 66, 67–68, 70–71, 72
  Borderlands/La Frontera: The New Mestiza 67–68, 70
  conocimiento 69, 72n5
  linguistics 67
  Mestiza 66, 67–68, 69, 70, 71
  Nepantlera 66, 69–71, 71–72
  precarity 66
  Shiva 66, 67
  This Bridge Called My Back: Writings By Radical Women of Color 67, 72n4
  This Bridge We Call Home: Radical Visions for Transformation 69, 70, 72n4
Aotearoa *see* youth activists
Arab Spring (2011) 59
armchair activist knowingness 30–34
arts activism 178
Associated Press 27
asylum 112–113
Asylum: The Radical Mental Health Magazine 104, 112–114
austerity 17, 106
authoritarianism 20, 41, 42
autohistoria-teoria 67

B

bad feelings 149
Bangladesh *Kishani Sabha* (Women Farmers' Association, BKS) 185–186
Bangladesh *Krishok* (farmer) Federation (BKF) 185–186
Barker, Jennifer 122
Bastian, B. and Loughnan, S. 127
Basu, Biplab 84
Bauman, Z. 126
Bellafante, Ginia 27
Berlant, Lauren 64, 88, 91–92, 100, 180
Bernstein, Eduard 56
Beyond Pills initiative 110
Big Pharma 110
Black Lives Matter 23–24, 28, 29, 43–44n12, 43n3
  criticisms by armchair activists 33
Black people
  negative stereotype 15
  see also people of colour; women of colour
Blackfoot First Nations 166
Blake, John 29

Boggs, Carl 51
Bolsheviks 57–58
borderlands 67–68, 113
Borderline Personality Disorder 108
Boston Review 115
Breslow, Jacob 106
British Medical Journal 110
Buffett, Warren 27
Burnett, Erin 28
Burnout (Proctor) 115
Bush, George H.W. 25, 26
Butler, Judith 125

C

Callard, Felicity 109
Campt, Tina 64
capitalism 15, 27–28, 94, 141
  during COVID-19 138, 139–140
  TINA 21–23, 29, 37
capitalist veganism 128
care 133–134, 140–141, 141
care diaries 174–175
Carolan, M. 144
Chadwick, Rochelle 163
Chapman, Robert 113
Choudry, A. and Kapoor, D. 95, 96
Cidam, C. 53
Civil Rights Movement 24, 25, 33
Climate Caravan 185–186
Climate Change, Gender and Food Sovereignty Caravan 185–186
climate justice 178
Clinton, Bill 28
coalition politics 72, 155n8
Cole, Alyson 192–193
collective action 2, 3
collectivization 38
community organizing 133–134
Comrades from Cairo 40–41
conocimiento 69, 72n5
consensus 80, 82
cooperative initiatives 59–60
COVID-19 pandemic 133, 134–135, 136, 137–138, 140–141
creativity 146
critique 173, 174
cruel optimism 180
Cube of Truth demonstration 121–123
Cvetkovich, Ann 144, 149, 163

D

David, Ed 34, 35
Davis, Angela 39
decolonial processes 166–167, 170
depression 110
diagnosis 107–109, 114–115
diagnostic politics 107
discomfort 164, 166, 168, 169, 170

discordance 164
dismissive knowingness 32, 34
dissonant intimacies 180–182, 188
Dixon, Chris 40
domain of action 173
doubt 41–42

E

Egyptian Revolution (2011) 53, 59–60
El-Rifae, Yasmin 59
Elbaum, Max 39–40, 41, 44n19
Embroidery Collective 133–141
  achievements 140
  ambivalence 137–138, 141
  capitalism 138, 139–140
  during COVID-19 133, 134–135, 136, 137–138, 140–141
  embroidery 6, 136, 137–138, 139–140
  expressing emotions 134, 137, 138
  feminized work 134–135
  hope and care 133–134
  origins of 135–137
  political activism 138–140
  as a political space 135
  virtual meetings 136–137
Emejulu, Akwugo 65, 145, 146, 165, 173–174, 178, 187, 188
Emejulu, Akwugo and Bassel, Leah 77–78, 193
emotional ambivalence 151–152
emotional labour 16
emotions 13, 16–17, 123, 124, 127, 129, 170
  in activism 1, 148
  ambivalence *see* ambivalence
  Embroidery Collective 134, 137, 138
  feminist scholarship 163
  multiple 165
  in research 163–164
  see also political emotions
empathy 126–128
epistemic feelings 1–2, 3
epistemic humility 106, 113, 150
epistemic injustice 106
Eschle, C. 93
establishment knowingness 29
ethical theory 123
exhaustion 17, 18–19

F

Facebook 81–82
failure
  changes in consciousness 54
  Egyptian Revolution (2011) 59–60
  embracing 54
  learning from 50–51, 52–54, 59–60
  possibility of alternatives 53–54
  prefigurative responses to 52–54
  sense of 53
  see also Luxemburg, Rosa

fear 145
feeling rules 13–14, 15, 145, 146
feelings 123
feminist reflexivity 164
Fernández, L. 127
Finch, Sam Dylan 103
flat hierarchies 80
Foucault, Michel 99
Four Corners (documentary) 122
Freeman, Jo 80, 82–83
Friedman, Milton 21
functional ambivalence 124

G

Galeano, Eduardo 41–42
Garza, Alicia 38, 40, 41
gender 60, 111, 133–135, 138–139
  gender-based violence 146, 150
  gender differences 185
  inequality 186
  researchers 163
Generation Zero 147, 155n6
German Social Democratic Party (SPD) 55, 57
Giesen, B. 126
Gingrich, Newt 23
Gitlin, Todd 31–32
Giuliani, Rudy 23
Global Mental Health Movement 111
Gonzalez-Hidalgo, Marien 144, 153
good feelings 144, 149
good politics 144, 149, 154
Gould, Deborah 3, 4, 164
Graeber, D. 54
Greenspan, Patricia 124, 125
Gresham, George 32
groups 152–154
guilt 124
gut reactions 124

H

Hage, Ghassan 179
  ambivalence 187
  meaning-making 187
  migrant condition 179–180
  see also stuckedness
Hall, Stuart 29
Harsanyi, David 24
Hart, Akiko 109
Hayes, K. and Kaba, M. 115
Helms, Jesse 26
Hemmings, Clare 164, 165, 186–187
heterotopias 99
Hill, Trevor 21–22
Hochschild, Arlie 13, 145
hope 133–134, 144–145, 148, 149–150
  see also stuckedness
hopelessness 51, 134, 152, 154
hoping well 145

I

Icarus Project 113
ImaginingOtherwise 181
inconvenience 88–89
  embracing 92
  queer activists 91–93
  sources of 93–94
  unresolved tensions 92–93
indifference 165
indigenous healing 111
infrastructure 97–99
InsideOUT Koaro 147
institutionalized precarity 17
institutions 93–94, 97
International AIDS Conference (1990) 25–26

J

Jaggar, Alison 64
Johnson, Merri 109
joy 17–19, 18, 175
JustSpeak 147

K

Khanna, Shyam 38
Kierans, C. and Bell, K. 165
Kimmerer, Robin Wall 174
King Jr., Martin Luther 24–25
Klein, Naomi 36–37
knowingness 4, 42
  activist 30–34
  big knowing what is to be done 21–23, 24–29, 31–33
  characteristics of 22–23, 29, 39
  conservative-to-moderate-to-liberal establishment 23–30
  disparagement of left activism 23–24, 26–29
  status quo 21–23
  TINA 21–23
Krauthammer, Charles 23

L

La Via Campesina 185–186
language in common 182–185, 188
Left Alone (Joffre-Eichhorn and Anderson) 115
left knowingness 39, 40
Lemon, Don 28
Lenin, Vladimir Ilyich 21, 57–58
Life magazine 25
Lima, Isabel 136, 137
Lindsey, U. 59
live animal export industry 122–123
Lorde, Audre 65, 135, 141
Los Angeles Times 28
Luxemburg, Rosa
  acknowledging impact of failure 55
  capacity for self-rule 57–58
  criticisms of Lenin and the Bolsheviks 57–58
  critique of dictatorial rule 57, 58
  disappointment with SPD 55
  learning from failure 50–51, 54–59
  letters to colleagues 55–56
  revolutionary action 56, 58
  revolutionary consciousness 56–57
  solace through nature 55–56
  succeeding by failing 56–57
  unobstructed public life 58–59
Lyons, S. and Jones, J. 182

M

Mad Pride activism 110
Mad Studies perspective 103
Mad World (Frazer-Carroll) 115
madness 113
Mai, Y. 2
March For Our Lives 24
Marom, Yotam 36, 37
Martinez, Elizabeth 'Betita' 39
mass movements 95
McAfee, N. 2
McGeer, Victoria 145
McManus, Susan 145, 150
meat culture 127, 128–129
medicalization 108
medication 109–111
mental health activism 103–105
  diagnosis 107–109, 114–115
  global contradictions 111–112
  medication 109–111
  motivations 103–104
  see also ambivalent mental health activism
mental health systems 103–105
  users and survivors of 105–106
mental illness 105, 106
Merton, Robert 124–125
methodological ambivalence 165
Michaelis, L. 57
misfeeling 14–18, 65, 145, 146, 150, 154, 178
modernity 126
Mohandesi, Salar 37–38
moral action 123, 126, 127
moral choices 123–124, 126
moral judgements 109, 120, 124, 128, 129
moral theory 123
morality, sentiment-based theories of 123
Morris, Aldon 38
Movement for Black Lives 28, 29, 32–33
Munshi, S. and Willse, C. 93

N

Nagar, Richa 185
National Public Radio (NPR) 26
Neilson, Brett and Rossiter, Ned 64–65
New Communist Movement 39–40
New York Post 23–24

INDEX

New York Times 25–26, 27, 28
Ngai, Sianne 16, 65
NGOization 94–96, 98
Nigeria
   NGO activism 95
   poverty 95
   queer activism *see* queer activism
   raves 98
   unemployment 95

O

Obama, Barack 28
Occupy Wall Street 23, 26–28, 38, 40–41, 43n4, 43n11
   criticisms by armchair activists 31–32
   learning from failure 60
   uncertainty 34–35

P

Palestine 139
Parks, Rosa 35
participatory democracy 35
patriarchy 15
Pelosi, Nanci 21–22
Pendergrast, N. 122
people of colour 15
   white supremacy 15
   see also Black people; women of colour
People's Global Action (PGA) 183–185
pessimism 191–194
   articulation of 193
   benefits of 192, 193
   mirror and shield 192
   as a praxis 193
   risks 192
PGA Asia 183–185
pill shaming 110
poems/poetry 172–173
   ambivalence and ambiguity 176
   good poems 172–173, 175
   world-building 176
political activism 39, 138–140
political ambivalence 71
political deliberation 2
political emotions 1, 2, 163–164, 165
political organizing 133–134, 140–141, 141
political participation 64
in-between politics 71–72
   activism of 82–84
politics, doing of 64
politics of certainty 106, 107
politics of exhaustion 78
politics of knowledge 180–182
politics of sight activism 122, 127
post-pandemic world 133, 134, 142n1
power 173–174
precarity 17, 18

ambivalence 66, 71
   living with 64–65
prefigurative politics 50–52, 105
   definition 51–52
   open to challenge 107
   positive examples and practices 54
   responses to failure 52–54
   see also Luxemburg, Rosa
Prescription Abolition 110
Prinz, Jesse 124
Probyn, Elspeth 164
Protect Ihumatao 147
psychiatric diagnosis 107–108, 109
psychiatric drugs 109, 110
psychiatric medication 109–110, 114
psychiatry 111
   Asylum magazine 112–114
psychophobia 104, 116n1
psychosocial disabilities 104, 112, 116n3
psychotherapy 110

Q

queer activism 87–90
   ambivalence 87–88
   case study methodology 90–91
   classist politics 96
   coalitions 97–98, 100–101
   competition over collaboration 97
   conflicts and tensions 98, 100
   Criminal Code Act 89
   discrimination and violence 89–90
   funding of NGOs 94–95
   heterotopias 99
   inconvenience 88–89, 91–93
   individuality 100
   infrastructure 97–99
   institutions 93–94, 97
   NGOization 94–96, 98
   Penal Code 89
   Pride celebrations 97
   Same Sex Marriage Prohibition Act (SSMPA, 2014) 89–90, 98
   self-interested activists 96–97
   Sharia Penal Code 89
   strategic alignment 97–98

R

racism 17, 128, 133, 136–137, 141, 149–150, 162, 168–169, 183
radical vulnerability 185–186, 188
rational choice 123, 124
Reagon (née Johnson), Bernice 155n8
Recovery in the Bin 106
recovery movement 106
recreational drugs 110
reductive binarisms 144, 149
reflexive disruption 164

reformism 56
repatriation 159–162, 166–169
repatriation paradox 161, 168
resistance 60
  end goals 52
  prefigurative approaches to 52–53, 54
revolutionary consciousness 56–57
revolutionary politics 50–51
Rich, Adrienne 31
Roberts, Tony 107
Rodgers, Kathleen 148
Roth et al 164–165
Rothman et al 1, 88
Routledge, P. 183–185, 185, 186
Roy, Srila 180–181

S

Sande, Mathijs van de 53
Santorum, Rick 24
Schneider, I.K. and Schwarz, N. 165
scholar-activism 180
  dissonant intimacies 180–182
  language in common 182–185
  radical vulnerability 185–186
  solidarity-building 188
Schulman, S. 93
self-care 141
self-rule 57–58
Selma 33
sentiment 120, 121, 123–124
Sharpton, Al 33
Shilts, Randy 30–31
Simmel, Georg 121
Slovo, Joe 40
Smith, Adam 123
social media 80–81
social movements 144–147, 187–188
Social Science Research Council 31
socialism 56–57, 58
solidarity 94–96, 140
  dissonant intimacies 180–182, 188
  language in common 182–185, 188
  queer solidarity 99–100
  radical vulnerability 185–186, 188
Sorkin, Andrew Ross 27
space-time 190–191
St Cecilia's Hall 159
stasis 64
stuckedness 179
  definition 179
  dissonant intimacies 180–182
  generative potential of 186–188
  hope and material circumstances 180
  language in common 182–185
  radical vulnerability 185–186
  as a scholar-activist condition 179–180
  work of activists 179–180

Student Nonviolent Coordinating Committee 38
study groups 38
Sullivan, Dr. 25, 26

T

Tahrir Square 53
Taiwan 159–160
Taylor, Keeanga-Yamahtta 40
Tea Party 23
textile work 139
  see also Embroidery Collective
Thatcher, Margaret 21
The Public Feelings Project 144, 146
third position thinking 112
Third Space Theory 112
Thursdays in Black 147, 153, 154n5
time 38, 98, 149, 151, 185, 190, 191, 192, 193
TINA (there is no alternative) 21–23, 29, 37
Tiplady et al 122
Tufekci, Zeynep 81
Turner, Sir William 160

U

ugly feelings 3, 16
uncertainty 20, 148, 151
  activists 34–40, 41, 151
  ambivalence 145
  see also unknowingness
University Collections Advisory Committee (UCAC) 167
University Court 167
University of Edinburgh
  Anatomical Museum *see* Anatomical Museum
  colonial collection 160–161
  colonial legacy 160
  press releases 160
  provenance issues 160–161
  repatriation handover ceremony 159–160
  repatriation policy 159–161
unknowingness 4, 34–40, 152, 154
  dealing with fear 36, 37–38
  disposition of 42
  learning along the way 38–39
utilitarianism 123

V

veganism 122, 125, 126, 127–128
vegetarianism 122
Virgin America 27

W

Wadiwel, Dinesh 127
Wall Street Journal 23
Waszak, Emily 136

white supremacy 16, 42, 129, 182
  manifestations of 15
Wilderson, Contra 192
Winfrey, Oprah 32–33
Wingfield, Adia 13
women of colour 16–18, 193
  ambivalence 14
  see also Black people; people of colour

Y

Young, Andrew 33
youth activists 144
  ambivalence 148–154
  case study methodology 147–148
  definition 147
  groups 152–154
  Hope in Action project 148